Starting an eBay Business For Canadians For Dummies®

General tips for sellers

- Always check how many other sellers are selling your item a̶n̶d̶ ̶d̶o̶n̶'̶t̶ ̶h̶a̶v̶e̶ your auction close within a few hours of a similar one.
- Answer all e-mail questions from prospective bidders and buyers within 24 hours and check your e-mail hourly before the close of your auctions. (Doing so can pay off in higher last-minute bidding.) Good customer service goes a long way in promoting and building your eBay business.
- Before listing, weigh your item and estimate the shipping cost. Be sure to list shipping and handling costs in your ad, whether you use a flat rate or the shipping calculator (for heavier packages).
- Check the eBay guidelines to be sure that your item is permitted and that your listing doesn't violate any listing policies.
- Get to know the listing patterns of sellers who offer similar merchandise to yours and try to close your auctions at different times or days from theirs.
- To encourage bidding, set the lowest possible starting bid for your item.
- When listing a new item, research it and be sure that you know its current value and the going price.

When taking auction photos

- Be sure that the item is clean, unwrinkled, and lint-free.
- Check that you have enough lighting to show the details of your item.
- Make sure the picture is in focus.
- Take second and third images to show specific details, such as a signature or a detail that better identifies your item.
- Take the photo against a solid, undecorated background.
- Try to keep the total size of *all* your pictures less than 50K for a smooth and swift download.
- Using an image that's more than 72 ppi (pixels per inch) for online purposes is unnecessary. Don't worry about megapixels.

When purchasing merchandise to sell

- Attend estate sales — many a saleable gem is hiding in someone's home.
- If you're the handy fix-it type, find items in need of minor repair and list them for sale as "like new."
- Search for unique items that may be common in your geographic area but hard to find in other places across the country.
- Try to pay the lowest possible price for your item — buy at wholesale prices or less whenever possible.
- Visit closeout stores, liquidators, and auctions regularly.

For Dummies: Bestselling Book Series for Beginners

Starting an eBay Business For Canadians For Dummies®

Web sites of interest

You can't depend on eBay for all the information that you need to run your business profitably. The following are a number of URLs that you'll likely want to visit from time to time:

Auction Help

- www.skipmcgrath.com/auction_sr/99tips.shtml: A great site full of tips for buying and selling
- www.auction-lynx.com: Loads of links and resources
- www.freeauctionscripts.com: Tons of additional resources for auction businesses
- www.auctionbytes.com: One of the best auction new sites on the Web

Financial

- www.xe.com: For exchange rates
- www.paypal.com: eBay's most popular payment form
- www.certapay.com: Fast email money transfers for Canadians only
- www.bankofcanada.ca/en/rates/exchange-look: Historical rates of exchange

Free Translation Services

- babelfish.altavista.com: A great translator from the folks at AltaVista
- www.freetranslation.com: Basic translation service with option for professional translation

Image and HTML Help

- www.irfanview.com/: One of the world's most popular picture viewers
- inkfrog.com: Low-cost image hosting
- cooltext.com: Free — and cool — button generator
- www.bulls2.com/indexb/bobstips2.html: Free photo-taking tutorials
- www.softwarecasa.com/pprod/244202.htm: Budget HTML creator
- www.eobcards.com/tutorial3.htm: Excellent HTML tutorials
- www.cuteftp.com: Free trial for a popular FTP program

Shipping Sites

- www.canadapost.ca/business: Canada Post's main business tools site
- www.usps.com/shipping/trackandconfirm.htm?from=global&page=0035trackandconfirm: United States Parcel Services tracking tools
- www.ups.com/canada/engindex.html: Canada's UPS site
- www.fedex.com/ca_english: The main site for FedEx in Canada

Third Party Auction Management Solutions

- www.marketworks.com: One of the biggest and best solution providers
- www.vendio.com: Widely used by many eBay sellers
- www.auctionwizard2000.com: A very popular and easy-to-navigate site
- www.thepostertoaster.com: An excellent bulk lister

Miscellaneous Sites of Interest

- ebaycounters.com: Free auction hit counters
- www.toolhaus.org: Neat eBay feedback-checking tools
- www.cafepress.com/cp/info/sell/: Sell custom logo merchandise with no upfront costs
- www.auctionsniper.com: Places last-second bids on auctions on your behalf
- www.kijiji.ca: Free online classifieds
- www.liquidation.com: One of the better online places to buy inventory at liquidation prices

For Dummies: Bestselling Book Series for Beginners

Starting an
eBay® Business
For Canadians

FOR
DUMMIES®

Starting an eBay® Business For Canadians

FOR DUMMIES®

by Marsha Collier and Bill Summers

BICENTENNIAL
1807
WILEY
2007
BICENTENNIAL

John Wiley & Sons Canada, Ltd.

Starting an eBay® Business For Canadians For Dummies®

Published by
John Wiley & Sons Canada, Ltd
6045 Freemont Boulevard
Mississauga, Ontario, L5R 4J3
www.wiley.com

Library and Archives Canada Cataloguing in Publication Data
Collier, Marsha
      Starting an eBay business for Canadians for dummies/Marsha Collier
Bill Summers.
Includes index.
ISBN: 978-0-470-83946-1
      1. eBay (Firm)   2. Internet auctions.   3. Electronic commerce — Management.
4.New business enterprises — Computer networks. I. Summers, Bill (Bill P.) II. Title
HF5478.C64 2007   658.8'7   C2006-905937

Printed in Canada

1 2 3 4 5 TRI 11 10 09 08 07

Distributed in Canada by John Wiley & Sons Canada, Ltd.

For general information on John Wiley & Sons Canada, Ltd., including all books published by Wiley Publishing, Inc., please call our warehouse, Tel 1-800-567-4797. For reseller information, including discounts and premium sales, please call our sales department, Tel 416-646-7992. For press review copies, author interviews, or other publicity information, please contact our marketing department, Tel 416-646-4584, Fax 416-236-4448.

For authorization to photocopy items for corporate, personal, or educational use, please contact in writing The Canadian Copyright Licensing Agency (Access Copyright). For an Access Copyright license, visit www.accesscopyright.ca or call toll free, 1-800-893-5777.

WILEY

About the Authors

Marsha Collier spends most of her time on eBay. She loves buying and selling — she's a PowerSeller — as well as meeting eBay users from around the world. As a columnist, the author of four best-selling books on eBay, a television and radio expert, and a lecturer, she shares her knowledge of eBay with millions of online shoppers. Thousands of eBay fans also read her monthly newsletter, *Cool eBay Tools*, to keep up with the changes on the Web site.

Out of college, Marsha worked in fashion advertising for the *Miami Herald* and then as a Special Projects Manager for the *Los Angeles Daily News*. She also founded a home-based advertising and marketing business. Her successful business, the Collier Company Inc., was featured in *Entrepreneur* magazine in 1985; in 1990, Marsha's company received the Small Business of the Year award from her California State Assemblyman and the Northridge Chamber of Commerce.

More than anything, Marsha loves a great deal. That's what drew her to eBay in 1996, and what keeps her busy on the site now. She buys everything from light bulbs to designer dresses to parts for her vintage Corvette on eBay. Marsha knows how to apply her business acumen to eBay, and in this book, she shares that knowledge with you.

Bill Summers has been wrapped up in all things eBay on a full-time basis for more than six years. He currently maintains three eBay IDs — two of which hold PowerSeller status — and is recognized as Canada's leading Education Specialist as trained by eBay. He ardently shares his knowledge of eBay and his passion for smart buying and selling on the site through private training and in his classes held at community centres and community colleges.

In his more than 25 years of diverse experience in the sanitation supplies industry, Bill was exposed to all aspects of business buying and selling operations. Over these years he also developed and ran many corporate and industrial training programs across Canada. After a prolonged period of travelling up to 35 weeks a year, and with a young family at home, Bill decided to leave the nine-to-five business world in favour of his own home-run business on eBay.

Bill is the first to admit that eBay has changed his life dramatically — for the better. eBay has afforded him the opportunity to use his accumulated business savvy in his own small business. Also, working on eBay has allowed him the flexibility to go back to school to work towards a Digital Imaging Certificate. Selling on eBay allows him the freedom and independence to live life at a much more relaxed pace.

Bill and his supportive wife, Susan, have been married for more than 30 years and reside with their daughter, Johanna, in Kitchener, Ontario. Johanna is already showing great promise as an eBay shopper.

Dedication

Marsha: I dedicate this book to the eBay entrepreneurs who have a zest for knowledge and the "stick-to-it-iveness" to follow through on their projects and stare success straight in the eye. I also dedicate this book to those who are convinced that get-rich-quick schemes don't work and believe that, in the long run, hard work and loving what you do are what get the job done and will lead you to financial achievement and contentment.

Good luck in your endeavors. I hope this book will help you along the way.

Bill: I dedicate this book to my exceedingly patient wife, Susan, who has long maintained that I am a work in progress.

Authors' Acknowledgements

Marsha: A book like this is a challenge. Lots of people have helped, but the lion's share of assistance has come from the encouragement that I receive from the eBay community and those I've met when "doing it eBay."

Ron Johnson, thank you for managing to squeeze time into your hectic schedule to take my calls. Thank you also to the following eBay sellers for helping me show the best of eBay to the world: Jillian Cline (Preservation Publishing); Joe Cortese (Noblespirit); Robin Le Vine (Bubblefast); Steve Lindhorst (ListingRover); Bob Miller (BobMill); SallyJo Severance (SallyJo); Marjie Smith (Abovethemall); Jeff Stannard (Melrose_Stamp); Ken Tate (Cardking4); and Jonathan and Ellen White (Magic-By-Mail).

Then, of course, I thank the upper crust at Wiley. My publisher, Andy Cummings, always has a new idea, and Steven Hayes, my acquisitions editor, tries hard to help me in my endeavors (although sometimes I make him crazy).

For this book, I had an amazing editor (who I think is now hooked on eBay): Susan Pink. Thank you for allowing me the leverage to make this book different from the others, and thank you for your quality input to help me make it even better. Once again, thanks to Patti "Louise" Ruby, my technical editor. This is the fourth book of mine that she's worked on as a tech editor; I just can't think of a smarter person to go to for bouncing off ideas.

Bill: Canadianizing and updating any book on eBay presents a unique challenge. The Web site is growing daily and is in a constant state of change, making it difficult for any one person to keep track of its development. My thanks go out to the many eBayers who unknowingly encouraged me to grow and learn within the community.

I'd also like to thank the Canadian sellers in Chapter 18 that gave freely of their time and advice so that others may benefit from their experience: Allan Grusie (cdBasement); Ann Hayes (Zarzuella); John and Glenda Cheramy (Muminlaw); Pamela Denis-Iles (Nightlight1960); Sheri and Ron Walker (BeansAntiques); Sylvain Carrier (Flying_Pat); Monique Egerton (WhosCloset); Marian Munro (PurpleFerret999); and Frederic Flower (Marsu450). Their stories inspire me (and, I hope, will inspire the readers of this book) to follow in their steps.

Finally, a major thanks goes out to the Wiley team: Robert Hickey, the editor for this edition, who patiently guided a "newbie" through the process of adapting Marsha's original book; Lindsay Humphreys and Pamela Vokey, Project Coordinators; and Liz McCurdy, Project Manager.

Publisher's Acknowledgements

We're proud of this book; please send us your comments through our online registration form located at www.dummies.com/register/.

Some of the people who helped bring this book to market include the following:

Acquisitions, Editorial, and Media Development

Project Editor, U.S. Edition: Susan Pink

Acquisitions Editor: Steve Hayes

Editor: Robert Hickey

Copy Editor: Greg Ioannou

Cartoons: Rich Tennant
(www.the5thwave.com)

Wiley Bicentennial Logo: Richard J. Pacifico

Composition

Publishing Services Director: Karen Bryan

Publishing Services Manager: Ian Koo

Project Manager: Elizabeth McCurdy

Project Coordinator: Lindsay Humphreys

Layout and Graphics: Wiley Indianapolis Composition Services

Proofreader: Charles Spencer, Techbooks

Indexer: Belle Wong

John Wiley & Sons Canada, Ltd.

Bill Zerter, Chief Operating Officer

Jennifer Smith, Publisher, Professional and Trade Division

Publishing and Editorial for Technology Dummies

Richard Swadley, Vice President and Executive Group Publisher

Andy Cummings, Vice President and Publisher

Mary Bednarek, Executive Acquisitions Director

Mary C. Corder, Editorial Director

Publishing for Consumer Dummies

Diane Graves Steele, Vice President and Publisher

Joyce Pepple, Acquisitions Director

Composition Services

Gerry Fahey, Vice President of Production Services

Debbie Stailey, Director of Composition Services

Contents at a Glance

Table of Contents

Introduction

. . . . .

*T*hank you for taking a look at the second edition of *Starting an eBay Business For Canadians For Dummies.* We've written this book to serve as a manual to get you organized and get your eBay business off the ground. From handling your selling time on eBay more efficiently to stocking your store to the *real* way to set up your books and daily operations, we give you all the details about running a successful eBay business. From years of experience and numerous interactions with hundreds of eBay sellers, we offer countless time-saving and money-saving tips — and secret eBay hints — along the way.

We've both made a successful living while working out of our homes for years, and we share our personal experiences to show you that you, too, can run a successful home business. Marsha started her own marketing and advertising business so that she could be at home and near her preschool daughter. Similarly, Bill left an established twenty-five-year career in sales and marketing management to allow him to stay closer to home with his young family. Through perseverance and dedication, both of us have developed small homegrown businesses that have allowed us to finance our homes and play a more active role in our children's upbringing. We know that the only limit to any eBay business is time. With the information in this book, and some hard work, you too can expand your eBay business.

One thing that we can't guarantee is how much money you can earn selling on eBay. We've discovered — perhaps the hard way — that it takes a good deal of discipline to run a home business. The time you spend and the amount of devotion you give your business will help you boost your success.

About This Book

Success awaits you! If you've read *eBay For Dummies* by Marsha Collier (Wiley), you know just how fun and profitable eBay can be. You've probably picked up this book because you've heard lots of stories about people making big money online, and you're interested in getting your piece of the pie. If you have a retail business, establishing an eBay Store can be a profitable extension of it.

Is selling on eBay something that you'd like to do more of? Do you have a full-time job, but you'd like to sell on eBay part-time? eBay can easily supplement your income. Perhaps you're looking to make a career change, and jumping into an eBay business with both feet is just what you have in mind. If so, this is the book for you.

We've watched eBay change from a homey community of friendly collectors to a behemoth Web site with tens of thousands of categories of items and more than 200 million registered users. We're guessing that you've been buying and selling with positive results, and you can see the benefits of taking this a bit more seriously. What are you waiting for? There's no time like the present to get started on your new career. Thousands of people across the world are setting up businesses online, and now is your time to take the leap of faith to begin a profitable enterprise. eBay gives you the tools, the customers, and the venue to market your wares. All you need is a bit of direction.

Starting an eBay Business For Canadians For Dummies picks up where *eBay For Dummies* leaves off. The tips we include give you the opportunity to improve your eBay money-making ability, and they just might turn an eBay novice into a professional who runs a booming eBay business. We also show the experienced user how to prudently turn haphazard sales into an organized business. This book has it all! We've combined the finer points of eBay with real business and marketing tools to help you complete the journey from part-time seller to online entrepreneur.

In this book, you can find the answers to some important questions as we take you through the following tracks:

✔ Reviewing what you know and introducing some of the finer points of eBay auctions

✔ Setting up your business in a professional manner

✔ Deciding how to handle inventory (and where to find it)

✔ Sprucing up your auctions to attract more bidders

✔ Dealing with customers

✔ Knowing what you need to have an eBay business . . . for *real*

What You're Not to Read

If you use this book the way you'd use a cookbook, jumping around from recipe to recipe (or chapter to chapter), you'll be able to find the answers to your particular questions all at once. Or, read the book from beginning to end if you'd like, and then keep it handy to look up future questions as they come to you. You don't have to memorize a thing — the information you need is at your fingertips.

Foolish Assumptions

Because you're reading this, we assume you're serious about selling on eBay and want to find out the finer points of just how to do that. Or perhaps you want to know how much is involved in an eBay business so that you can decide whether to give it a go.

If we have you figured out and you've decided that it's time to get serious, here are some other foolish assumptions we've made about you:

- ✔ You have a computer and an Internet connection.
- ✔ You've bought and sold on eBay and are fairly familiar with how it works.
- ✔ You have an existing small business, or you'd like to start one.
- ✔ You like the idea of not having to work set hours.
- ✔ You feel that working from home in jeans and a t-shirt is a great idea.

If you can say yes to these assumptions, you're off and running! Take a few moments to read the following section to get a feel for how we've put together this book.

How This Book Is Organized

This book has five parts. The parts stand on their own, which means that you can read Chapter 12 after reading Chapter 8, and maybe you can skip Chapter 13 altogether. (But we know you won't, because that's where we discuss the money!)

Part 1: Getting Serious about eBay

Reviewing what you know is always a great place to start. Considering the way eBay constantly changes, you'll probably find a little review worthwhile. So in this part, we delve into the finer points of eBay. Perhaps you'll discover a thing or two you didn't know — or had forgotten.

Setting up your eBay store is important, and in this part we show you step by step the best way to do it — and give you tips to figure out when the timing is right for you to open your store.

Part II: Setting Up Shop

You need to decide what type of business you plan to run and what type of inventory you'll sell. Here's where we discuss how to find merchandise and the best way to sell it. We also give you the lowdown on eBay Motors, eBay Real Estate, and some of the other unusual areas where you can sell.

You'll also find out how to research items *before* you buy them to sell so you'll know for how much (or whether) they'll sell on eBay.

We also discuss the importance of your own Web site for online shopping and how to set one up quickly and economically.

Part III: Business Is Business — No Foolin' Around!

We discuss exactly how to use available online and offline tools, how to implement auction management software, how to jazz up your auctions, and how to handle shipping efficiently and effectively. Because working with customers and collecting payments is also important, you'll find that information here, too.

Most important, you also find out in this chapter how and where to buy shipping materials for your business and how to purchase postage and insurance for your packages without standing in line at the post office.

Part IV: Your eBay Back Office

Setting up your company as a real business entity involves some nasty paperwork and red tape. We try to fill in the blanks here and also show you how to set up your bookkeeping. This is the place where you'll find a checklist of the items you'll need to run your online business.

You also need to know how to set up your home business space and how to store your stuff. We cover that here, plus bunches more!

Part V: The Part of Tens

You can't write a For Dummies book without including the traditional Part of Tens. So in an untraditional manner, here are ten real-life stories of successful and happy Canadians selling on eBay. You also find out about ten places to move your merchandise (if you want to sell elsewhere than eBay).

Part VI: Appendixes

We include a random collection of terms in Appendix A. You're probably already familiar with many of these words, but others will be new to you. Refer to this appendix often as you peruse other parts of the book. In Appendix B, we briefly discuss home networking, a perk you'll want to have when your eBay business grows.

Icons Used in This Book

If there's something we need to interject — okay, something we're jumping up and down to tell you, but it won't fit directly into the text — we indicate it by placing this tip icon in front of the paragraph. You'll know the tip to follow will be right on target!

Do you really know people who tie string around their fingers to remember something? Neither do we, but this icon gives us the opportunity to give you a brief reminder. Kind of like a Post-It note.

We like this picture of a petard. Yep, that's what it's called — the round bomb device that Wile E. Coyote slam-dunks in those old cartoons. Don't be "hoisted by your own petard," or made a victim of your own foolishness, by failing to heed the warning indicated by this icon.

Here we share some of the interesting thoughts we've picked up from eBay sellers over the years. Because we believe that learning from the successes and mistakes of others enhances knowledge, we include these little auction factoids so that you might gain some insight from them. After all, if someone else has learned from a unique trick, you can, too.

Where to Go from Here

Time to hunker down and delve into the book. If you have time, just turn the page and start from the beginning. If you're anxious and already have some questions you want answered, check out the handy index at the end of the book to research your query.

Take this information and use it to your advantage. A rewarding eBay business awaits you. We always enjoy hearing eBay success stories, and we hope you become one of them.

Our goal is to help you reach your goals. Feel free to contact us through our Web sites:

```
www.coolebaytools.com
```

```
www.learningebayiseasy.com
```

Please e-mail us with any suggestions, additions, and comments about this book. We want to hear from you and we hope to one day update *Starting an eBay Business For Canadians For Dummies* with your words of wisdom. (Humorous stories are also gratefully accepted!)

Part I
Getting Serious about eBay

The 5th Wave   By Rich Tennant

"I don't understand why no one at eBay is bidding on Junior's old baby clothes."

In this part . . .

*e*Bay continually improves its services, and some of its features are like hidden gold nuggets. In this first part, we delve into the finer points of eBay with you. Perhaps you'll discover a thing or two you didn't know or had forgotten.

Chapter 1

Using eBay to Launch Your Business

In This Chapter

▶ Getting serious about your business

▶ Making decisions about what to sell

▶ Having what it takes to make a living online

▶ Running an efficient auction

. . . .

You've decided to get serious about your sales on eBay, so now you have to step up to the plate and decide how much time you have to devote to your eBay business. This book talks about all kinds of eBay businesses. Even though you're probably not quitting your day job and selling on eBay full-time (yet!), we still think you're serious. A large portion of sellers, even eBay PowerSellers (those who gross more than $1,000 a month in sales), work on eBay only part-time.

eBay sellers come from all walks of life. A good number of stay-at-home moms are out there selling on eBay. So many retirees are finding eBay to be a great place to supplement their income that we wouldn't be surprised if the Canadian Association of Retired Persons (CARP) creates a special division for eBay. If you're pulled out of your normal work routine and faced with a new lifestyle, you can easily make the transition to selling on eBay.

In this chapter, we talk about planning just how much time you'll be able to devote to your eBay business and how to budget that time. We also discuss figuring out what to sell, the technical equipment you need to set up a home business, and how to run an auction most effectively. Your eBay business won't grow overnight, but with dedication and persistence, you may just form your own online empire.

Getting Down to Bidness (er, Business)

Before launching any business, including an eBay business, you need to set your priorities. And to be successful at that business, you must apply some clear level of discipline.

We won't bore you with the now-legendary story of how Pierre Omidyar started eBay to help fulfill his girlfriend's Pez dispenser habit, blah, blah, blah. We *will* tell you that he started AuctionWeb with a laptop, a regular Internet Service Provider (ISP), and an old school desk. He and his buddy Jeff Skoll (a Stanford MBA) ran AuctionWeb all by themselves, twenty-four hours a day, seven days a week. In the early days of the service, if you had questions it was always easy to get prompt, friendly answers to your e-mails. When the site started attracting more traffic, Pierre's ISP began to complain, and raised his monthly fees. To cover the higher costs, Pierre and Jeff began charging twenty-five cents to list an auction. Pierre was so busy running the site that the envelopes full of auction-listing cheques began to pile up, and he didn't even have time to open the mail.

When Pierre and Jeff (who had become partners) incorporated eBay AuctionWeb in 1996, they were each drawing a salary of $25,000. Their first office consisted of one room, and they had one part-time employee to handle the payments. They started small and grew.

Budgeting your time: eBay as a part-time moneymaker

A part-time eBay business can be very profitable. One thing that we stress in this book is that the more time and energy you spend on your eBay business, the more money you can make. That said, we now move on to the lowest possible level of time that you should devote to your business.

Maybe you enjoy finding miscellaneous items to sell on eBay. You can find these items somehow in your day-to-day life. So let's suppose that you can spend at least a few (let's say three) hours a day on eBay. Now you must include the time it takes to write up your auctions. If you're not selling only one type of item, allow about fifteen minutes to write your auction, take your picture or scan your image, and, of course, upload it to eBay or a photo-hosting site.

How much time it takes to perform these tasks varies from person to person and will improve according to your level of expertise. Regardless, every task in your eBay auction business takes time. See the sidebar "Some handy eBay timesaving tips" for pointers on how to budget the time you have available.

Only you can decide how much time you want to spend researching the going rate for items you plan to sell on eBay and deciding which day or time your item will sell for the highest price. Even if you take great photos and write brilliant descriptions, a cashmere sweater won't sell for as much in the heat of summer as it will in the winter. Doing your research can take up a good deal of time when you're selling a variety of items.

Also consider how much time it takes to shop for your merchandise. You may have to travel to dealers, go to auctions, or spend time searching online for new ways to obtain auction inventory. Many sellers set aside a full day each week to seek out new merchandise. Your auction items are what make you money, so don't skimp on the time you spend identifying products. The time you spend finding new inventory comes back to you in higher profits.

Here's a list of various activities that you must perform when doing business on eBay:

- ✔ **Photography:** Take a photo of the item, then clean up and resize the image with a photo-editing program. Upload your images to eBay Picture Services or a third-party hosting service. (This can be done either before listing or when you actually list.)

  Pre-package the item (without sealing the box or envelope) and determine the shipping cost.

- ✔ **Listing:** Choose an auction title with keywords, then write a concise and creative description of your item. List the auction with all of its details (including the shipping cost) on eBay.

- ✔ **Customer Service:** Answer questions from bidders. When the auction is over, notify the winning bidder via e-mail.

- ✔ **Administration:** Carry out banking and perform bookkeeping.

- ✔ **Shipping:** Complete the packaging of your item, then affix a shipping label. You can choose to print your postage online or go to the post office to have it weighed and postage attached.

Some handy eBay timesaving tips

Crunched for time? The following are some features that you're sure to find useful:

✔ **HTML templates:** In Chapter 11, we give you some tips on finding basic HTML format templates for attractive auctions. These HTML templates cut your auction design time to a few minutes. Most experienced eBay sellers use preset templates to speed up the task of listing auctions, and this should be your goal.

✔ **TurboLister program:** When you want to list a bunch of auctions at once, we recommend using the eBay TurboLister program. TurboLister can enable you to put together and upload about ten auctions in fifteen minutes. In Chapter 9, we describe in more detail how to use this very cool tool.

✔ **Relisting (or Sell Similar) feature:** When you sell the same item time after time, you can use either TurboLister (it archives your old listings so you can repeat them) or eBay's handy relisting or Sell Similar features. When your auction ends on eBay, links pop up offering to relist your item or to Sell Similar. If you want to run a different auction with a similar HTML format to the one that just ended, simply select the Sell Similar option and cut and paste the new title and description into the Sell Your Item page of your new listing.

✔ **Auction management software:** See the "Using software" section in this chapter under the heading "Making Your Auctions Run More Smoothly." Also, Chapter 9 describes various programs you can integrate into your eBay business.

Time yourself to see how long it takes to accomplish each group of tasks above. Keep in mind that some of the tasks may take longer if you list multiple items — think of the figures that you come up with when timing as your *baseline,* a minimum number of minutes that you must set aside for each task. Knowing how much time each activity will take can help you decide how many hours per month you need to devote to running your eBay business.

Jumping in with both feet: Making eBay a full-time job

From the step-by-step outline above, you can see that the process of preparing and then finally selling an item on eBay can be time-consuming. But careful planning and scheduling can turn your business into an online empire.

The best way to go full-time on eBay is to first run your business part-time for a while to iron out the wrinkles. After you become comfortable with eBay as a business, you're ready to make the transition to becoming a full-time seller. The minimum gross monthly sales for a Bronze-level PowerSeller is $1,000 USD. If you plan your time efficiently, you can easily attain this goal. Head to Chapter 3 for more information on the PowerSeller program.

Running a full-time business on eBay is the perfect option for working parents who prefer staying at home with their children, retirees looking for something to do, or those who'd just rather be their own boss. Read some real-life profiles of happy full-time sellers in Chapter 18.

See Figure 1-1 for an example of the eBay homepage, the first stop for most buyers on eBay. Note how eBay makes an effort to help market the items you put up for sale.

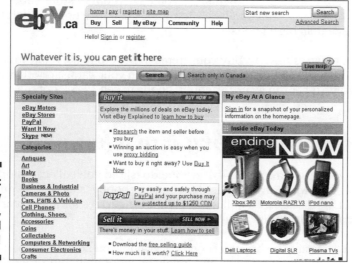

Figure 1-1:
The eBay homepage, where it all starts!

Deciding What to Sell

What should I sell? That's the million-dollar question! In your quest for merchandise, you're bound to hear about soft goods and hard goods. *Soft,* or nondurable, goods are usually textile products such as clothing, fabrics, and bedding. *Hard* goods are computer equipment, housewares, and anything else that's basically nondisposable.

Here are just a few points to consider when you're deciding what to sell:

✔ **Shipping costs:** Some differences exist between shipping hard and soft goods. Soft goods can fold up and be packed in standard box sizes or, better yet, in bubble or Tyvek envelopes. These types of packaging result in much lower shipping costs. Most hard goods come in their own boxes, which may or may not be individually shippable. If the hard goods need to be repackaged, Styrofoam peanuts, bubble cushioning, or double packaging may be required, especially if the item requires an oddly sized box. See Chapter 17 for the lowdown on shipping and packing.

✔ **Other shipping considerations:** Do you want to handle large items and deal with the hassles of shipping them? Also, given that a very large portion of your sales will be exported (largely to the U.S.), are you familiar with any shipping restrictions that might apply? Although the North American Free Trade Act (NAFTA) removed many of the import duties for exports, this only applies to items manufactured within Canada. Items imported into Canada and then exported may not enjoy the same protection from high tariffs. These are factors you may want to consider before investing heavily in inventory.

✔ **Possible storage problems:** Do you have room to store enough merchandise to keep you going? Soft goods can take up considerably less space than hard goods.

You don't always have to buy your items in bulk to make money on eBay. The first things you sell might be items you find in your garage or attic. To find out about some other fun ways to acquire goods to sell, check out the next section.

Turning your hobby into a business

C'mon, you've got a hobby — everyone does! Did you collect stamps or coins as a kid? Play with Barbie dolls? Maybe your hobby is cars. Did you inherit a bunch of antiques? Been collecting Hummel figurines for a few years? eBay has a market for almost anything.

You can't possibly be an expert on everything. You need to keep up-to-date on the market for your items, and following more than four or five basic item groups may divert your attention from selling.

Selling within a particular category or two can be a good idea for repeat business. Should you decide to major in miscellany and sell anything and everything, you may not realize the highest possible prices for your items. This can be okay if you have a source that permits you to buy items at dirt-cheap pricing.

Collectibles: Big business on eBay

Pierre Omidyar started eBay with the idea to trade collectible Pez dispensers. eBay now lists fifty main categories of collectibles (see Figure 1-2), and those categories are divided into thousands of categories subcategories and sub-subcategories. Almost anything that you'd want to collect is here, from advertising memorabilia to Girl Scout pins to Zippo lighters!

If you have a collection of your own, eBay is a great way to find rare items. Because your collection is something dear to your heart — you've likely been collecting for years — you probably know a lot about what it is you covet. Bingo — you're an expert at something! A fun way to get into selling on eBay is to first hone your skills to find the things that you collect at discount prices. (You're liking this more and more, aren't you?) Then, sell them on eBay for a profit. Start small and start with something you know.

Figure 1-2:
The eBay
Collectibles
hub with
links to
categories.

If there's one thing you know, it's fashion!

Are you one of those people who just knows how to put together a great outfit? Do you find your bargains at Goodwill, but people think you've spent hundreds on your garb? Do you know where to get in-season closeouts before anyone else does? Looks like you've found your market (see Figure 1-3).

Figure 1-3:
eBay area
for clothing,
shoes, and
accessories.

y as many of those stylish designer wrap dresses as you can (you-know-
ose at you-know-where) and set them up on the mannequin you've bought
model your fashions for eBay photos. (For more on setting up fashion
photos, check out Chapter 11.) Within a week, you may just be doubling your
money — 'cause sweetie-darling, who knows fashion better than you?

If a ball, a wheel, or competition is involved — it's for you

We don't want to over-generalize, but we think it's pretty safe to say that
most guys like sports. Guys like to watch sports, play sports, and look good
while they're doing it. Could this possibly help you develop a profitable
empire on eBay? We think so. And we don't want to leave out all the women
out there who also love to watch, play, and compete in sports and who love
to show off their sports fashions. They may not be the next Lorie Kane or
Mike Wier on the golf course, but many men and women still make a point to
at least look good when they play, with respectable equipment and a great
outfit.

eBay has an amazing market right now for soccer equipment, and you'd be
amazed at how much football and golf stuff you can also find there — the
last time we checked, there were more than 53,000 listings for golf items
alone! What a bonanza! New stuff, used stuff — it's all selling on eBay
(see Figure 1-4). It's enough to put your local pro shop out of business —
or perhaps put *you* in business.

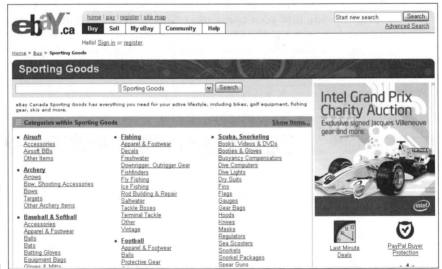

Figure 1-4:
Sporting
goods on
eBay.

Including the whole family in the business

Sometimes just the idea of a part-time business can throw you into a tizzy. After all, don't you have enough to do? School, work, soccer, kids glued to the TV — you might sometimes feel as if you have little quality time with your family. However, the importance of family time is what brings many people to eBay in the first place. Marsha was working long hours at her own business many years ago. At the end of the day, when her daughter Susan wanted to go shopping, perhaps for some Hello Kitty toys or a Barbie doll, she was just too tired. The opportunity to work from home and spend more time with her young family was very attractive to Marsha, as it is to many parents. For those of you who may send your kids to daycare, work long hours, and often find yourself too drained at the end of the day to go shopping or to a ball game with your family (can you relate?), running a small business on eBay can offer some great benefits.

Young children love to contribute and help in any way they can. It can be something as simple as labeling packages or taking a trip to purchase inventory from a local supplier with Mom or Dad. They may love plotting shipping points on a map with pins or helping to restock shelves. Regardless of the task, working with their parents gives many young children a feeling that they're contributing. And we're amazed by what they can learn about the business world from even the simplest of chores.

Here's the point: A family business can succeed, and everyone in the house can enjoy it. Selling on eBay can be a great way for your family to spend time together and is sure to create memories to last a lifetime.

Toys, books, and music — oh MY!

Having children in your home brings you closer to the latest trends than you could ever imagine. Visit any toy store and watch the parents come in with their kids. Often it is the kids that lose interest in the toys and wander off long before the parents.

And what about Star Wars? Star Trek? G.I. Joe? Can you say "action figures"? (If guys have them, they're not dolls — they're action figures.) If you have access to the latest and greatest toys, buy them up and sell them to those who can't find them in their neck of the woods.

If your home is like either of ours, books pile up by the tens! Old educational books that your children have outgrown (even college textbooks) can be turned into a profit. Remember that not every book is a classic that needs to be part of your library forever. Let another family get the pleasure of sharing children's tales!

If anything piles up faster than books, it's CDs or videos. Somehow your old lambada or Macarena music doesn't hold the magic it once did. Or maybe those zany kids' comedies don't mesmerize you the way they used to. You can get rid of your own items and find plenty of stock at garage sales. Buy them cheap and make a couple of dollars.

In fact, Bill's daughter decided, a few years ago, that she needed a whole new school wardrobe. She made a decision that she really didn't want to keep her large collection of VHS Disney movies (after all, VHS was rapidly being replaced by DVD format) that she'd collected since early childhood. With Bill's help she sold all of her movies and had several hundred dollars for the clothes she wanted to buy.

Selling children's clothes

A current check of eBay for the number of infant and toddler clothes listings in progress reveals more than 86,000 — and the bidding is often hot and heavy. For stay-at-home parents, selling infant and children's clothing is a super way to pick up extra income.

If you've had a baby, you know all too well that friends and relatives shower new moms with lots of cute outfits. If you're lucky, your baby gets to wear one or two of these soft, fluffy or frilly gifts (maybe only for a special picture) before outgrowing them. These adorable portrait outfits can earn you a profit on eBay. Many parents with children a few steps behind yours are looking for bargain clothing on eBay — a profitable hand-me-down community. As your children grow up and out of their old clothes, earn some money while helping out another parent.

Bringing your existing business to eBay

Do you already own a brick and mortar business? eBay is more than just a marketplace for unloading slow or out-of-season merchandise. You can also set up your store right on eBay (see Figure 1-5). An eBay store allows you to list a fixed-price item at a reduced fee and keep the item online until it's sold. When you run your regular auctions for special items, they will have a link to your store, thereby drawing in new shoppers to see your store merchandise.

Here are a few ways you can expand your current business with eBay:

> ✔ **Opening a second store on eBay:** How many people run stores that sell every item, every time? If you're a retailer, you've probably made a buying mistake at one time or another. Often, the item that *isn't* selling in

your store *is* selling like hotcakes in another part of the country. eBay gives you the tools to sell those extra items to make room for more of what sells at your home base.

Maybe you just need to raise some cash quickly. eBay has tens of thousands of categories where you can list regular stock or specialty items, allowing you to reach a high volume of potential buyers. For a caveat on which items are *verboten*, check out Chapter 4.

✔ **Selling by mail order:** If you've been selling by mail order, what's been holding you back from selling on eBay? It costs you far less to list your item on eBay than to run an ad in any publication. Plus, on eBay, you get built-in buyers from every walk of life. If your item sells through the mail, it will sell through eBay.

✔ **Selling real estate:** Plenty of land, homes, and condos are being bought and sold on eBay right now. If you are a licensed real estate agent, you can list your properties online and reach a nationwide audience. When you offer listings on the Web, you're bound to get more action. Give it a whirl and read more about selling real estate on eBay in Chapter 2.

You won't find a cheaper landlord than eBay. Jump over to Chapter 5 if you really can't wait for more information about how to set up your eBay store.

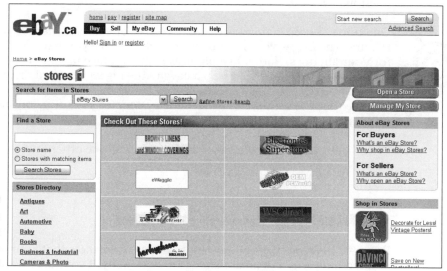

Figure 1-5:
eBay Stores
central.

Getting What It Takes to Sell

We've heard many sellers-to-be say they want to start a business on eBay so that they can relax. Since when is running any business a way to relax? Granted, you don't need a whole lot of money to get started on eBay, and you won't have a boss breathing down your neck. But to run a successful eBay business, you need drive, determination, and your conscience to guide you in addition to a few solid tools, such as a computer and an Internet connection. In this section, we give you the lowdown on the technology you need to start up your eBay business. Also, you find out how to choose an effective user ID, and how to build a strong feedback rating — all the basics you need to get organized and start selling.

Computer hardware

First, you're gonna need a computer. In our basic assumptions about you (see the book's introduction), we figure that you probably already have one and know how to use it. Your computer doesn't have to be the latest, fastest, and best available. It does help if your computer has a good deal of memory to process your Web browsing and image touch-ups. Whether you have an antique Pentium 3 or a new 4.3GHz model, combined with a speedy Internet connection, an older machine is usually quite capable of running most eBay auctions with ease.

One thing to keep in mind is that hard drives are getting cheaper by the minute. The bigger your hard drive, the more space you have to store images for your auctions. (Individual pictures shouldn't take up much space because each should max at 50K.) Here's a caveat: the bigger the hard drive, the more chance you have to make a mess of it by losing files. When you get started, be sure that you set up a sensible filing system for your eBay business using folders and subdirectories.

Check out Chapter 11, where we talk more about the other stuff you might need, such as a scanner and a digital camera.

Connecting to the Internet

If you've been on eBay for any length of time, you know that your Internet connection turns into an appendage of your body. If your connection is down or you can't log on due to a power outage, you can't function — instead, you flounder around, babbling to yourself. We understand because we've been there. Dial-up connections are notoriously slow and will interfere with your ability to use your telephone so if you're selling in earnest, we recommend pulling the plug on your dial-up connection unless you have no choice.

Before investing in any broadband connection, visit `www.broadbandreports.com` (see Figure 1-6) and read the reviews of ISPs in your area. Users from around the country post their experiences with their Internet Service Providers (ISP's) — reading about them can give you a good idea of what's available and reliable, connection-wise, in your neighbourhood. The site also has more testing tools than you can imagine and will test the speed of your (or your friend's) Internet connection at no charge.

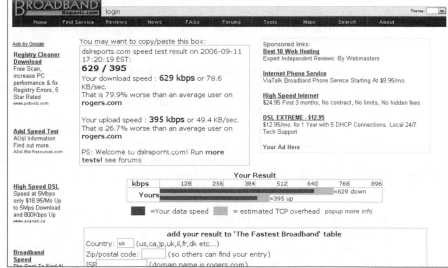

Figure 1-6:
Sample
results of
the free
speed test
for a cable
connection.

Dial-up connections

If you must use a dial-up connection, take advantage of the many free trials that different Internet Service Providers (ISPs) offer to see which one gives your computer the fastest connection. After you find the fastest one, make sure that it's reliable and has at least a 99 percent uptime rate.

Although most of the United States still logs on to the Internet with a dial-up connection, much of Canada is now on broadband. Be warned that a dial-up connection is painfully slow. An auction with lots of images can take minutes to load. The average eBay user wants to browse many auctions and won't wait while your images load; they'll just go to the next auction.

To make the best use of your time when running your auctions and conducting research, you need to blast through the Internet. You need to answer e-mail, load images, and conduct your business without waiting around for snail's-pace connections. Although a modem is supposed to link up at 56K, the best connection speed that most people have realized is 44K (and often quite a bit lower).

DSL

A confusing bunch of Digital Subscriber Line (DSL) flavours (ASDL, IDSL, SDSL, and more) are available these days, ranging from reasonably priced to out of sight. DSL, when it works as advertised, is fast and reliable. A DSL line depends on the reliability of your telephone service: Crackling or unreliable phone lines can be a barrier to using DSL.

The main problem with a DSL connection is that your home or office needs to be no farther than 18,000 feet from your local telephone switching station. Most services cost between $30 and $50 a month, but you may pay even more if you get DSL through a *booster* that boosts the signal to a location farther away than the minimum 18,000-foot border.

Many homes and offices fall out of range for DSL. If you can get it, true DSL service can give you a connection to download as much as 1.5MB per second. (IDSL will only download 144K in the same time.)

Your local telephone company (Telco in DSL-speak) owns your home or office phone lines. Because DSL goes over POTS (plain-old telephone service), your DSL provider has to negotiate connection problems with the folks at your telephone company. As you might guess, one company often blames the other for any problems that may arise.

Some people have tried to simplify things by getting DSL from the local phone company, which sounds great on the surface. Unfortunately, this may not always be the case. Local phone companies often form sister companies to handle high-speed Internet connections. So even though the two companies seem to be one and the same from the consumer's perspective, they will still argue about who's responsible for your problems. Broadband with this much hassle can be too much trouble.

Digital cable

The mother lode of all affordable connections is cable. If you can get cable television, you can probably get a blazingly fast cable Internet connection. Your cable company is probably, even now, completing the replacement of old cable lines with newfangled digital fiber-optic ones. These new lines carry a crisp digital TV signal and an Internet connection as well. (These fancy new lines have plenty of room to carry even more stuff, and I'm sure it won't be long before cable companies have some hot new services to offer us.)

Most digital cable Internet connections are extremely fast and reliable. Performing a speed test on your line can routinely show downloading of data at rates approaching 2500 kilobauds per second and higher. Compare that to the old-fashioned baud rate of dial-up (remember the old 300-baud modems?). Cable Internet service is generally very reliable, and users experience little downtime. For $40 to $50 a month, most consider their cable connection well worth the investment.

You may have heard the myth about more users on the line degrading the speed of your cable connection. The truth is that this type of connection is more than capable of a 10 Mbps transfer. That's already about ten times faster than DSL. It would take a whole lot of degrading to noticeably slow down your connection. (Your computer still has to load the browser.)

Choosing your eBay user ID

"What's in a name?," or so the old quote goes. On eBay, there's a whole lot in your name! When you choose your eBay user ID, it becomes your identity to all those who transact with you online. They don't know who you are; they know you only by the moniker they read in the seller's or bidder's spot.

Ever wonder why you don't see many banks called Joe and Fred's Savings and Loan? Even if Joe is the president and Fred is the chairman of the board, the casual attitude portrayed by their given names doesn't instill much confidence in the stability of the bank. "Joe and Fred" might be a better name for a plumbing supply company — or a great name for guys who sell plumbing tools on eBay! Joe and Fred strike me as the kind of friendly, trustworthy guys who might know something about plumbing.

The lowdown on user IDs

When choosing your user ID, keep the following points in mind:

- Your ID must contain at least two characters.

- You may use letters, numbers, and any symbol except @ and &.

- Your ID will be displayed on eBay in all lower-case letters whether or not you use capitals.

- You can't use a URL or the word *eBay* in your user ID (that privilege is reserved for eBay employees).

- You may not use spaces in your user ID; if you want to use two words, you can separate them using the underscore key (press Shift+hyphen). You may not use consecutive underscores.

- You can change your ID every thirty days if you want to. When you do, you get a special icon next to your name signifying that you've changed to a new ID. Your feedback profile (permanent record) is transferred to your new ID.

- You may want to consider having a second user ID just for buying on eBay. From time to time, you may come across items you want to bid on. Some of your regular customers for your selling ID may take exception to you outbidding them at the last second. A buying ID allows you to make those purchases anonymously and keeps your buying habits secret from your competition.

- You may not use a name that's hateful or obscene (Do I have to tell you this?) eBay (and the community) just won't permit it.

Does your retail business have a name? If you don't have your own business (yet), have you always known what you'd call it if you did? Your opportunity to set up a business can start with a good, solid, respectable-sounding name for your company. If you don't like respectable (too sober), go for trendy, or choose something that describes your services with humour. Who knew what a Fido was? Or a Costco? Or a Bubblefast, the name of one of eBay's largest shipping suppliers.

Are you selling flamingo-themed items? How about pink_flamingos for your selling identity? Be creative; *you* know what best describes your product.

Stay away from negative-sounding names. If you really can't think up a good user ID, using your own name is fine.

You've no doubt seen a bunch of lousy user IDs out there. Here are a few examples of what not to use: iselljunk, trashforsale, or mystuffisgarbage.

eBay protects and doesn't reveal your e-mail address. If another user wants to contact you, he or she can do so by clicking your user ID. eBay's E-mail Forwarding System (EFS) will send you the notice.

If you decide to change your user ID, don't do it too often. Customers recognize you by name, and you may miss some repeat sales by changing it. Besides, the icon that eBay places next to your user ID on the site shows others that you've changed your ID, and it will stick with you for thirty days.

Finding your eBay feedback

The number that eBay lists next to your name is your feedback rating; see Figure 1-7 for an example. Anyone on the Internet can find out how you do business on eBay — and what other eBay users think of you — by clicking on this number. At the top of every user's feedback page is, essentially, a snapshot of your eBay transactions from the past twelve months. For the lowdown on feedback, go to Chapter 3.

Figure 1-7:
An eBay feedback scorecard.

Member Profile: marsha_c (2743 ★) 🏆 **Power Seller** me

| Feedback Score: | **2743** | Recent Ratings: | | |
Positive Feedback:	**100%**		Past Month	Past 6 Months	Past 12 Months
Members who left a positive:	2743	➕ positive	48	384	723
Members who left a negative:	0	◉ neutral	0	0	0
All positive feedback received:	3265	➖ negative	0	0	0
<u>Learn about</u> what these numbers mean.		Bid Retractions (Past 6 months): 0			

If you're really serious about this business thing but your feedback rating isn't as high as you'd like it to be, go online and buy some stuff. Even though eBay now distinguishes between buyer and seller feedback, your numbers will still grow. Feedback should always be posted for both buyers and sellers. Remember to always try to avoid letting your emotions write feedback. Keep your comments brief and factual. Since every positive feedback increases your rating by +1 and each negative decreases it by –1, you'd better be racking up those positives to get a high rating.

Making Your Auctions Run More Smoothly

In this section, we discuss a few more niceties that you'll need to round out your eBay home base. The following tools are helpful, but not for everyone — you must decide which ones you'll use. Some people enjoy a totally automated office, while others prefer to do things the old-fashioned way. One of our favourite eBay PowerSellers works with file folders, a hand-written ledger book, and hand-written labels. If it makes you happy, do it your way. Nonetheless, we're going to suggest a few options that will ease the pain of paperwork.

Using software

These days, software is available to accomplish just about anything. It would seem fitting that an all-encompassing software package exists that can help you with your auction, right? Well, maybe. It depends on how much you want your software to do and how much of your business you want to control. In this section, we describe some types of software that you might find useful.

Auction management

Auction management software can be a very good thing. It can automate tasks that are time-consuming and make your record keeping easy. You can keep track of inventory, launch auctions, and print labels using one program. Unfortunately, most of these programs can be daunting when you first look at them (and even when you take a second look).

You have choices to make when choosing an auction management program: How much do you want to spend? Do you want to keep your inventory and information online? Maintaining your listing information online enables you to run your business from anywhere; you just log on and see your inventory. Online management software is tempting because it simplifies your business and makes it more professional; if these things are important to you, it may be worth your time and money.

A good many sellers prefer to keep their auction information on their own computers. This method is convenient and allows sellers to add a closer, more personal touch to their auctions and correspondence. Some folks say that keeping information local, on their own computer, is more suited to the small-time seller. We think it's largely a matter of preference.

In Chapter 9, we will discuss the wide selection of management software available, including MarketWorks, Auction Wizard 2000, and the eBay-owned Selling Manager and Selling Manager Pro.

HTML software

You may want to try some basic HTML software to practice your ad layouts. We will tell you where to find some templates in Chapter 11, but you'll want to preview your auctions before you launch them.

You can use a full-blown Web page software package, such as FrontPage or Dreamweaver, to check out how your auction will look. Or, you may want to keep it simple. One less expensive and very user-friendly alternative is called CuteHTML, which is about as simple as it can get. Go to the following to download a thirty-day free trial:

```
www.globalscape.com/cutehtml
```

If you like it, you can buy it for only $19.99 USD.

Spreadsheets and bookkeeping

Many sellers keep their information in a spreadsheet program, such as Excel. The program has all the functionality you need to handle inventory management and sales info.

For bookkeeping, we prefer QuickBooks, which is as complete as it gets. It's straightforward, but only if you have a basic knowledge of accounting. Another great thing about QuickBooks is that it integrates with spreadsheets. In Chapter 16, we will discuss QuickBooks in more detail.

Collecting the cash

Credit cards are the way to go for the bulk of your auctions. Often, credit cards make the difference between a sale and a pass. People are getting savvy (and more comfortable) about using their credit cards online because they're becoming better informed about fraud prevention and the security of online transactions. So although you may truly love money orders, taking credit cards as well is in your best interest. In this section, we will discuss another decision you need to make: Do you want your own private merchant account, or would you rather run your credit card sales through an online payment service? For more about these options, read on.

Online payment services

Until you hit the big time, you may want to enlist the help of an online payment service, such as the eBay-owned PayPal. PayPal offers excellent services and their rates are on a sliding scale, according to your monthly dollar volume. Online payment services accept credit cards for you. They charge you a small fee, process the transaction with the credit card company, and deposit the auction payment in an account for you. Unless you sell tens of thousands of dollars worth of merchandise a month, an online payment service can be more economical than your own merchant account. For more about these services and accounts, see Chapter 13.

Your own merchant account

As you may or may not know (depending on the amount of spam in your e-mail), there are thousands of merchant credit card brokers out there offering to set you up to take credit cards yourself. These people are merely middlemen. You will likely wind up having to pay for their services, either in the form of an application fee or as part of a hefty percentage for processing software. Some of these brokers are dependable businesspeople, and others are simple hustlers. If you have decent credit, you don't need these guys: Go straight to your bank!

Your bank knows your financial standing and creditworthiness better than anybody. It's the best place to start if you want to get your own *merchant account,* an account that lets your business accept credit cards directly from your buyers. You pay a small percentage of your revenue to the bank, but it's considerably less than an online payment service charges. Some banks don't offer merchant accounts for Internet transactions because, ultimately, the bank is responsible for the merchandise related to the account if you fail to deliver the goods. Remember that your credit history and time with the bank play a part in whether or not you can get a merchant account.

The costs involved in opening an e-commerce merchant account can vary, but you'll need between $150 and $400 to get started. Here are some of the possible costs you may face:

- ✔ A one-time set-up fee of approximately $99 (Provides a web terminal only — if you're adding credit card processing to your Web site, expect this amount to increase to as much as $350 for the initial setup. The higher rate will include a payment form, online shopping cart, and web terminal.)

- ✔ A transaction charge; usually between 15–30 cents (this is your bank's cut)

- ✔ A monthly gateway fee of approximately $35–$40

r own merchant account is an investment in time and effort.
13, we will get into more detail about merchant accounts and
ctly how all the costs involved are distributed.

base: Your Web site

eBay offers you a free web page — the About Me page — and it's the most important link to your business on eBay. The About Me page is part of your eBay store if you have one, and you can insert a link on the page that takes bidders directly to your auctions. You can also link from the About Me page to your personal Web site. See Chapter 3 for more information about the About Me page and its importance to your success on eBay.

If you don't yet have your own Web site, we recommend that you get one — especially if you're serious about running an eBay business. Check out Chapter 8, where we provide some tips on finding a Web host and putting up your own Web site quickly and easily.

You can keep your complete inventory of items on your Web site and list them as auctions; or you can sell them only in your eBay store as their selling season comes around. Remember that, unlike your eBay store, there's no listing fee (also called an insertion fee) or final value fee when you have repeat customers on your own Web site.

Setting up your shop

Office and storage space are a must if you plan to get big. Many a business was started at the kitchen table — that's how Pierre Omidyar started eBay) — but to be serious about what you're doing, you must draw definite lines between your home life and your online ventures. Concentrating when you have a lot of noise in the background is difficult, so when we say draw a line, we mean a physical line as well as an environmental one.

Your dedicated office

The first step in setting up your work environment is to separate the family from the hub of your business. Many eBay sellers use a spare bedroom as an office; others choose to sacrifice their garage. Depending on the types of items you plan to sell, keep in mind that you may have to move to different parts of the house as time progresses and your business grows. Or you could just turn your two-car garage into a one-car garage, or go the whole way and take over the whole thing instead.

Remember, if you do decide to work out of your garage, without proper heating and insulation, your work environment may be less than hospitable during our cold Canadian winters. Moving your entire business out to the garage means you will have to ensure that you can work there comfortably year round. Here are some more things to consider when deciding whether to work from your garage:

- ✔ Are telephone and internet services available or easily hooked up in the area?

- ✔ Are there sufficient electrical outlets available to run computers, printers, scanners, a fax machine, and your photography lighting?

- ✔ Are furnishings, shelving, and filing cabinets (to keep all the important papers you generate in your business operations for tax purposes) going to fit in the space?

You have many adjustments and decisions to make, as we did, to ensure that you have a working space that is functional and creates minimum distractions.

One PowerSeller that we know moved all the junk out of his basement and set up shop there. He now has three computers and employs his wife and a part-time *lister* (who put his auctions up on eBay) to run the show. His basement office is networked and is as professional as any office.

Your eBay room

If you have a room or two in your home, or you plan to set up shop in your garage, your storage space should be covered for a while. Even though most sellers begin their eBay careers with an eBay closet, for a real business, a closet just won't do. Seclude your stuff from your pets and family by moving it into another room, and don't forget the shelving and other supplies you need to organize things. We'll talk more about this in Chapter 17.

Chapter 2

The Finer Points of eBay Selling

At first glance, eBay is a behemoth Web site that seems way too large for any novice to possibly master. In a superficial way, that's true. eBay is always growing and undergoing facelifts. Under all the cosmetic changes, however, you find the basics. eBay is still the same-old trading site: a community of buyers and sellers who follow the same rules and policies, making eBay a safe place to trade.

When anything gets larger, it must become compartmentalized to stay manageable. The folks at eBay have achieved this organization most handily. The number of categories where you can sell your items has grown from eight very basic choices to several thousand. When a trend begins, the eBay tech gurus evaluate the sales figures and, when necessary, add new categories. As a result, the category breakdown is now clearer and more concise.

All this growth has forced eBay to expand in other ways, too. Aside from the traditional eBay auctions, you'll now find Dutch, private, restricted, and more. All of these types can get confusing! In this chapter, we explain the newest eBay features by reviewing how the site does business. Armed with this knowledge, you can do *your* business more effectively.

The Dilemma: eBay.ca or eBay.com?

At his seminars, new Canadian sellers often ask Bill whether they are better off selling on eBay.ca or eBay.com. Unfortunately, he can't offer a simple answer; the differences are small and largely a matter of preference.

A quick and informal survey of Canadian PowerSellers shows that an overwhelming majority sell exclusively on the U.S. site. Most refer to the reasons we discuss in this section — still, some sell on the U.S. site simply because they always have. Other than increased exposure to the U.S. market, whether you choose eBay.ca or eBay.com is really up to you as an individual.

Nevertheless, in this section, we try to highlight a few of the subtleties on each site so that you can decide which one works best for you.

Currency conversion

Most Canadian sellers recognize that the majority of their sales are shipped to the U.S. They know from experience that many of their American customers have serious issues paying for items with anything other than the U.S. dollar. We Canadians, on the other hand, are less concerned by currency conversion. If it makes no difference to you, selling your items in U.S. dollars might be helpful — and you can do that regardless of which country's site you use.

Provided you specify that you ship to the U.S., eBay.ca listings are displayed on the American site, and you can choose whether you want to sell in Canadian or U.S. dollars. eBay.com automatically assumes you're selling in Uncle Sam's greenbacks. Selling on the U.S. site ensures you never forget to choose the currency of preference.

Search results

The most important reason to consider selling on the U.S. site is that it's favoured by the advanced search engine. This valuable tool allows buyers to find the items they are looking for without weeding through thousands of items in a particular category. One of the default selections in the search parameters is to sort through listings on eBay.com only. Listing on eBay.ca means that your items are not necessarily included in these search results. Selling on eBay.com ensures that your products are visible to the large American market. Simply put, more exposure equals greater sales.

Third-party auction management

If you decide to use a third-party auction management service, you will find that most of them have been designed for use with eBay.com exclusively. Some are now compatible for sales on eBay.ca, but not many. See Chapter 11 for more about auction management services.

Listing promotions

eBay.ca and eBay.com provide virtually equal opportunities when it comes to what listing promotions are available — you needn't worry that you'll miss out if you choose to do business on the Canadian site. Listing promotions are frequent, and we have yet to see a promotion that isn't valid for sellers on either eBay.ca or eBay.com. Reducing all fees for auction and fixed-price format listings to ten dollars regardless of the starting value is a common promotion that sellers on both eBay.ca and eBay.com can benefit from. The only difference we find between access to promotions on the U.S. versus Canadian sites is that eBay.com will reflect a lower listing fee for your items on the day that the promotion runs, whereas eBay.ca prefers to charge the seller full price, then return the difference later as a credit. Regardless, Canadians using eBay.ca are able to enjoy the benefits of promotional campaigns that originate on eBay.com just as easily as those on the Canadian site.

New features

If you enjoy trying out new site features as they are introduced, head to eBay.com; it almost always gets new features before they are launched on eBay.ca. As do most big companies, eBay prefers to introduce major changes to the public in stages so that their techies have a chance to fine-tune new features with limited impact. The Canadian site is often fashionably late to the party.

Finding Where to Sell Your Stuff

The Internet is crowded with auctions, now that many major portals include auctions as part of their site. Still, most bidders and sellers go to eBay. Why? More computers and electronics are sold on eBay than at Buy.ca, more used cars are sold on eBay than at Autotrader.ca, and more toys are probably sold on eBay than at KBKids.com. Even the Canada Post Corporation found a niche on eBay, selling the contents of undeliverable packages and prepaid postage packs.

Whether you're selling auto parts, toys, fine art, or land, you, too, must find your niche on eBay. Sounds easy enough. After all, deciding where to put your stuff for sale is pretty straightforward, right? Not necessarily. The task is complicated by the thousands of categories to choose from on the eBay Category Overview page, shown in Figure 2-1.

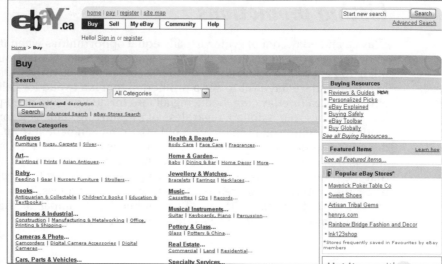

Figure 2-1:
The eBay
Category
Overview
page;
numbers
next to
categories
reflect
active
auctions.

Consider the example of a Harry Potter toy. Harry Potter toys are hugely popular because the story is a continuing saga in both books and movies. The easy choice is to list the item under Toys & Hobbies: TV, Movie Character Toys: Harry Potter. But what about the category Collectibles: Fantasy, Mythical & Magic: Harry Potter? This is the point where you must decide whether you want to list your item in two categories and pay more (see the review of extra charges in Chapter 10) or count on the fact that your beautifully written auction title will draw search engine users directly to your item.

eBay supplies you with a great tool: the Find a Main Category option in the Sell Your Item pages. Type a few keywords for your item and you're presented with a list of categories where items similar to yours are listed, as in Figure 2-2.

So you aren't selling Harry Potter toys? Suppose you're selling a DVD of the movie *The Red Violin*. Would listing it in DVD & Movies: DVD be the right choice? Or would you reach the proper audience of category browsers in Music: Musical Instruments: String: Violin?

Should a book on 1960s fashion be placed in Books: Antiquarian and Collectible? You might also have luck going directly to the fans of '60s fashion in the category Clothing, Shoes & Accessories: Vintage: Women's Clothing: 1965-76 (Mod, Hippie, Disco): Dresses.

The popularity of categories varies from time to time. News stories, the time of year, hot trends, or whether Oprah makes a comment about something can all influence the number of hits a particular category gets. How can you possibly know which category is best for your item? Research your items regularly using our favourite tool: the eBay search engine. (See the tips earlier in this chapter or visit Chapter 7 for more about using the search engine.) After you've found the right category for the item you're listing, give it a try. While choosing a popular category will often bring results, be sure to also try alternatives occasionally.

Even when you've been selling a particular item for a while — and doing well with it — selling your item in a different but related category can boost your sales. A little research now and then into where people are buying can go a long way toward increasing your eBay sales.

Figure 2-2:
eBay's
category
finder
feature.

Automotive? Go eBay Motors

Anything and everything automotive can go in the eBay Motors category (see Figure 2-3), and will sell like giant tires at a monster truck rally. Following are just a few of the car-related items that fit in this category.

Car parts

Got used car parts? eBay has an enormous market for used car parts. One seller we know buys wrecks from police impound sales — just to save some valuable parts that he can resell on eBay.

New car parts are in demand, too. If you catch a sale at your local auto parts store when it's blasting out door handles for a 1967 Corvette (a vehicle for which it's hard to find parts), it wouldn't hurt to pick up a few. Sooner or later, someone's bound to search eBay looking for them. If you're lucky enough to catch the trend, you'll make a healthy profit.

Figure 2-3:
The eBay
Motors
home page.

Cars

Yes, you can sell cars on eBay. In fact, used car sales have skyrocketed online thanks to all the people who trust eBay as a reliable place to buy and sell used vehicles. Check out Figure 2-4 for an example of a used car auction. Selling vehicles on eBay is a natural business for you if you have access to good used cars. Maybe you work as a mechanic; alternatively, you might have a contact at a dealership that lets you sell cars on eBay on consignment or for a commission. (For the ins and outs of consignment selling, check out Chapter 6.)

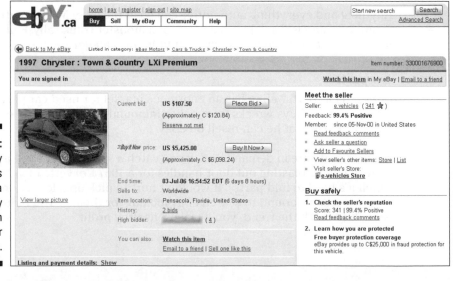

Figure 2-4:
An eBay
Motors
auction for a
previously
owned van
from seller
e.vehicles.

eBay Motors and its partners offer useful tools to complete your sale. eBay Motors features free Passenger Vehicle Purchase Protection up to $20,000 USD or $25,000 CAD, depending on the listing currency. (A $100 USD co-pay exists for every claim.) This program is designed to protect buyers from the potential of fraud. Also, eBay Motors provides one-click access to **AutoCheck Assured Reports**, vehicle shipping quotes from L. Hansen's Forwarding Ltd., and vehicle inspection and escrow services. Access eBay Motors and its services from the eBay homepage, or go directly to `http://cars.ebay.ca/`.

Here are just a few things to keep in mind if you plan to sell cars on eBay:

- Selling a car on eBay Motors is a bit different from selling on regular eBay, mainly in the fees area. Take a look at Table 2-1 for significant differences. In Chapter 10, we include a table of all basic eBay fees for listings, options, and final values.

- To sell a vehicle on eBay Motors, you must enter the Vehicle Identification Number (VIN) on the Sell Your Item page. This way, prospective buyers can always access an **AutoCheck Assured Report** to get an idea of the history of the car.

- Many people who find the vehicle of their dreams on eBay are more than happy to take a one-way flight to the vehicle's location and drive it home. You may not be prepared to do that, and shipping the vehicle is a reasonably priced alternative. You can make arrangements to ship a car quickly and simply. In Table 2-2, we list some sample costs for shipping cars around the country from various sites. Keep in mind that these are sample costs (with fuel surcharges included) that were valid at the time this book was written. They reflect the shipping costs of a current-model family car. Mini-vans, SUVs, or vintage vehicles will be more expensive.

- If your reserve isn't met in an eBay Motors auction, you may still offer the vehicle to the high bidder through the Second Chance option. (We provide more information about that later in this chapter.) You may also reduce your reserve during the auction if you feel you've set your target price too high.

Table 2-1	eBay Motors Vehicle-Specific Fees
Type of Fee	*Fee Amount*
Vehicle insertion (listing) fee	$40.00
Vehicle transaction service fee	$40.00*
Motorcycle insertion (listing) fee	$5.00
Motorcycle transaction service fee	$40.00*
Reserve price in listing (refundable if the vehicle sells)	$6.50

* No Final Value fee exists for selling on eBay Motors. Instead, you pay the transaction service fee when your item gets a bid (or if you've used a reserve, when bidding meets your reserve price).

Table 2-2	Estimated Costs for Shipping a Car	
From Here to There	*Terminal-to-Terminal Cost*	*Door-to-Door Cost*
Halifax to Calgary	$1580	$1710
Edmonton to Montreal	$1125	$1230
Ottawa to Regina	$1140	$1300
Charlottetown to Winnipeg	$1400	$1625
London to Vancouver	$1050	$1200
Toronto to St. John's	$1350	$1500

An item that you list on eBay Motors will appear in any search, whether a potential buyer conducts a regular eBay search or executes a search in eBay Motors.

Live auctions

eBay also holds live auctions, where you'll find rare and unusual items for sale. You can access the live auction area from a link on the home page or by going directly to

```
www.ebayliveauctions.com
```

To sell on eBay Live Auctions (shown in Figure 2-5), you must be a registered, licensed auction house. eBay Live Auctions supplies non-stop, live auction action right on your desktop. Joining a live auction is a great deal of fun. These auctions happen in real time; you can see (and participate in) the bidding action on your screen as it's happening.

Licensed auction houses run the live auctions from where they are located and broadcast them worldwide through eBay. You have to register individually for each auction that you want to participate in, and a buyer's premium is involved. More and more auctioneers are conducting live auctions in this way to expand their base list of customers.

As an eBay community member, you're able to bid on items featured in live auctions. It's a good way to increase your own stock of merchandise to sell.

Figure 2-5:
Non-stop
bidding
action on
eBay Live
Auctions!

Real estate: Not quite an auction

eBay Real Estate isn't quite an auction. Because a wide variety of laws govern the sale of real estate, eBay auctions of real property aren't legally binding offers to buy and sell. Putting your real estate up on eBay is an excellent way to advertise and attract potential buyers. When the auction ends, however, neither party is obligated (as they are in other eBay auctions) to complete the real estate transaction. The buyer and seller must get together to consummate the deal.

Nonetheless, selling real estate on eBay is popular, and the gross sales in this area are growing by leaps and bounds. You don't have to be a professional real estate agent to use the eBay Real Estate category, although it may help when it comes to closing the deal. If you know land and your local real estate laws, eBay gives you the perfect venue to subdivide those 160 acres in the Okanagan that Uncle Regis left you in his will.

For less than the cost of a newspaper ad, you can sell your home, condo, land, or even timeshare on eBay Real Estate (see Figure 2-6) in the auction format.

You can also choose to list your property in an ad format, accepting not bids but inquiries from prospective buyers around the world. On the Sell Your Item form (see Figure 2-7), you must provide specific information about your piece of real estate.

Figure 2-6:
The eBay
Real Estate
home page.

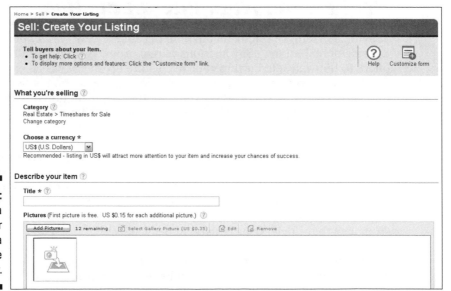

Figure 2-7:
Creating a
listing for
selling a
timeshare
property.

In Tables 2-3 and 2-4, we list some of the fees you can expect to encounter on eBay Real Estate.

Table 2-3	eBay Real Estate Fees
Type of Fee	*Fee Amount*
Insertion (listing) fee for 1-, 3-, 5-, 7-, or 10-day auction	$45.00
Ad format: 30 days	$195.00
Ad format: 90 days	$390.00
Reserve: $300 or more	1% of reserve (maximum $70)
Final Value Fee	None

Fixed-Price Sales on eBay

eBay is branching out (as if you weren't expecting it) into new arenas. To compete with Amazon and Yahoo!, eBay now includes *fixed-price sales* on its site. Fixed-price sales are an extension of the eBay Buy It Now feature. You put an item up for sale at a fixed price, and buyers pay the price that you're asking. Simple as that. Sellers are doing a great job at it, too.

You can also find fixed-price sales at the new eBay Stores. Each eBay store is run by an eBay auction seller. eBay Stores has its own space on eBay — you can access it in the following ways:

- By clicking Browse and then Stores on the navigation bar
- By clicking the eBay Stores link on the eBay home page
- By going straight to www.ebaystores.com from the Web

Potential buyers will be able to access your items from anywhere on the eBay site. The cost of eBay Stores (see Table 2-5) compares favourably to any of the Web's megasite stores, and all eBay Stores are part of the eBay Stores Hub — a giant "shopping centre" that houses all of the stores within.

Table 2-4	eBay Store Fees
Type of Fee	*Fee Amount*
Monthly subscription fee (Basic)	$15.95
Monthly subscription fee (Featured)	$64.95
Monthly subscription fee (Anchor)	$649.95
Listing fee	$0.02
Gallery picture	$0.01
Final Value fees $0.01–$35.00 $35.01–$1,450.00 over $1,450.01	 8% 8% of $35 and 5% of the balance 8% of the first $35, 5% of $35.01–$1,450.00 and 3% of the remainder

For a complete overview of how to set up your own eBay Store, check out Chapter 5.

Types of eBay Auctions

An auction is an auction is an auction, right? Wrong! eBay has five types of auctions for your selling pleasure. Most of the time you'll run traditional auctions, but other auctions have their place, too. After you've been selling on eBay for a while, you may find that one of the other types of auctions better suits your needs. In this section, we review the types of auctions so you can fully understand what they are and when to use them.

Traditional auctions

Traditional auctions are the bread and butter of eBay. You can run a traditional auction for one, three, five, seven, or ten days; when the auction closes, the highest bidder wins. We're sure you've bid on several traditional auctions and won at least a few. You've probably also made money running some auctions of your own.

You begin the auction with an opening bid, and bidders (we hope) will bid up your opening price into a healthy profit for you.

Dutch auctions

When you've purchased an odd lot of 500 sets of kitchen knives or managed (legally, of course) to get your hands on a truckload of televisions that you want to sell as expeditiously as possible, the *Dutch* (multiple item) *auction* is what you'll want to use. In a Dutch auction (see Figure 2-8 for an example), you can list several different items at once, and potential buyers can bid on as many items as they'd like. The final item price is set by the lowest successful bid at the time the auction closes.

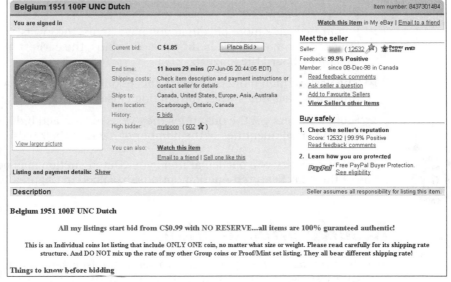

Figure 2-8: A Dutch auction for U.S. proof sets in the U.S. Coins category.

For example, suppose you want to sell five dolls on eBay in a Dutch auction. Your starting bid is $5 each. If five bidders each bid $5 for one doll, they each get a doll for $5. But, if the final bidding reveals that two people bid $5, one person bid $7.50, and another bid $8, all five bidders win the doll for the lowest final bid of $5.

In the following list, we highlight the details of the Dutch auction:

- ✔ The listing fee is based on your opening bid price (just like in a traditional auction), but it's multiplied by the number of items in your auction to a maximum listing fee of $4.80.

- ✔ The Final Value Fees are on the same scale as in a traditional auction, but they're based on the total dollar amount of your completed auctions.

- When potential buyers bid on your Dutch auction, they can bid on one or more items at one bid price. (The bid is multiplied by the number of items.)

- If the bidding gets hot and heavy, rebids must be in a higher total dollar amount than the total of that bidder's past bids.

- Bidders may reduce the quantity of items they're bidding for in your auction, but the dollar amount of the total bid price must be higher.

- All winning bidders pay the same price for their items, no matter how much they bid.

- The lowest successful bid when the auction closes is the final selling price for the items in that auction.

- If your item gets more bids than you have items, the lowest bidders are knocked out one by one. In the case of tie bids, the earliest bidders remain on board the longest.

- The earliest high bidders who are successful ("earliest" by date and time) win their items when the auction closes.

- Higher bidders get the quantities they've asked for, and bidders can refuse partial quantities of the number of items in their bids.

For a large quantity of a particular item, your Dutch auction may benefit from some of the eBay Featured Auction options explained in Chapter 10.

Reserve price auctions

In a *reserve price auction,* you're able to set an undisclosed minimum price that your item will sell for, which gives you a safety net. Figure 2-9 shows an auction in which the reserve has not yet been met. Using a reserve price auction protects the investment you have in an item. If, at the end of the auction, no bidder has met your undisclosed reserve price, neither you nor the highest bidder are obligated to go through with the transaction.

For example, if you have a rare coin to auction, you can start the bidding at a low price to attract bidders. They'll click on your auction and read the infomercial-style description you've written, possibly becoming interested If you start your bidding at too high a price, you might dissuade prospective bidders from even looking at your auction, let alone tempting them to bid. They may feel that the final selling price will be too high for their budgets. (We talk about setting an appropriate first bid later in this chapter.)

Everyone on eBay is looking for either a bargain or an item that is truly rare. If you can combine the mystical force of both of these needs in one auction, you have something special. The reserve price auction enables you to attempt — and perhaps achieve — this feat.

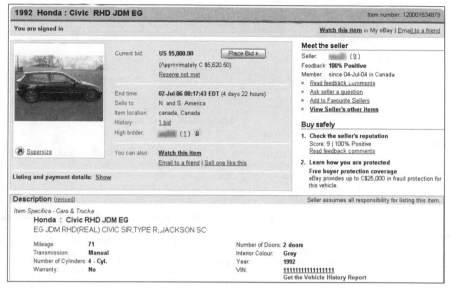

Figure 2-9:
Note that a reserve has been set for this auction.

The fees for a reserve price auction are the same as those for a traditional auction — with one exception. eBay charges between $1.50 and $70 CAD for the privilege of running a reserve price auction. If the reserve price is $300 or more, the reserve price fee is 1 percent of the reserve price (with a maximum of $70). When your item sells, you get that money back.

The reserve price auction is a safety net for the seller, but often an uncomfortable guessing game for the prospective bidder. To alleviate buyer anxiety, many sellers put reserve prices in the item description, allowing bidders to decide whether the item will fit into their bidding budgets.

You can't use the reserve price option in a Dutch auction.

Restricted access auctions

eBay won't allow certain items to be sold in nonrestricted categories, so you must list them in the Adult Only area of eBay. eBay makes it easy for the user to find or avoid auctions of restricted items by limiting access to only users who have registered a password and agree to the terms and conditions of the area.

Items in the Adult Only area are not accessible through the regular eBay title search, nor are they listed in Newly Listed Items.

Anyone who participates in Adult Only auctions on eBay as a bidder or a seller must have a credit card on file to verify that they are at least 18 years old (see Figure 2-10).

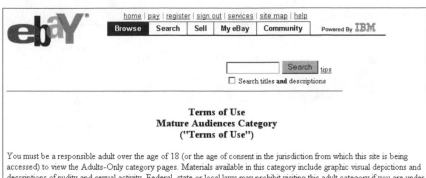

Search | tips

☐ Search titles **and** descriptions

Terms of Use
Mature Audiences Category
("Terms of Use")

Figure 2-10:
You must
agree to the
legalities
before
entering the
Mature
Audiences
category.

You must be a responsible adult over the age of 18 (or the age of consent in the jurisdiction from which this site is being accessed) to view the Adults-Only category pages. Materials available in this category include graphic visual depictions and descriptions of nudity and sexual activity. Federal, state or local laws may prohibit visiting this adult category if you are under 18 years of age. By entering your User ID and Password to access this site, to list an item, or to bid on an item in this category, you are making the following statements:

1. I am a member of the eBay community and I will follow the eBay User Agreement governing my use of the eBay web site.
2. I am willing to provide eBay with my valid credit card number and expiration date, which will be left on file with eBay in order to verify that I am at least 18 years of age.
3. I will not permit any person(s) under 18 years of age to have access to any of the materials contained within this site.
4. I am voluntarily choosing to access this category, because I want to view, read and/or hear the various materials that are available.
5. I understand and agree to abide by the standards and laws of the community in which I live or from which I am

Do not attempt to slip an Adult Only auction into a nonrestricted category. eBay doesn't have a sense of humour when it comes to this violation of policy, and may relocate or end your auction. eBay may even suspend you from its site.

Private auctions

Bidders' names are often kept private when dealing in the world of expensive fine art. Likewise, to protect the innocent, eBay *private auctions* don't place bidders' names on the auction listing. No one needs to know just how much you choose to pay for something, especially if the item is rare and you really want it.

As a seller, you have the option of listing your auction as a private auction at no extra charge.

The eBay search page features an area where you can conduct a bidder search. You — and everyone else, including your family — can find the items you've bid on. For instance, your spouse could tell you that she doesn't want a particular item — something that you may have just bid on — for Christmas. Using the "Search by Bidder" feature on eBay, anyone can easily see what you are buying for the holidays! A private auction can keep your shopping secret.

Not quite adult enough. . . .

We were surprised to see a private auction listed on one of our favourite eBay seller's lists. She usually doesn't advertise items like "Fringe Black BRA 36B SEXY SEXY SEXY," so we checked through this seller's past auctions. What we found was that she didn't get any bids when she listed the bra in the restricted (Adult Only) area of eBay in the category Everything Else: Mature Audiences: Clothing, Accessory. When she put the bra up for private auction under Clothing & Accessories: Women's Clothing: Lingerie: Bras: General, she got five bidders and sold the item. Obviously, the item wasn't sexy enough for the "adult" crowd!

The private auction is a useful tool for sellers who are peddling bulk lots to other sellers. It maintains the privacy of the bidders, so customers can't do a bidder search to find out what sellers are paying for the loot they then plan to re-sell on eBay.

Private auctions are a great option if you are selling items that are a bit racy or you'd like to make a purchase that might reveal something personal about you as the bidder. The private auction can save you the potential embarrassment of being caught buying a girdle or a tie that flips over to reveal a half-nude female.

Although private auctions are a useful tool, they may intimidate the novice user. If most of your customers are experienced eBay users and what you're selling may benefit from being auctioned in secret, you might want to try this option.

Running Your Auction

The basic plan for running an auction is the same for everyone, except when it comes to the timing of the auction and the starting price. If you speak to twenty different eBay sellers, you'll probably get 20 different answers about both effective starting bids and when to end your auction. Until you develop your own philosophy, we'd like to give you the tools to make a sound decision.

You can also successfully promote your auctions online and offline, and now you can legally offer your item to the next highest bidder if the auction winner doesn't come through with payment. We discuss a few of these ideas in this section.

Starting the bidding

The most generally accepted theory about starting bids is that setting the bidding too high scares away new bids. Also, as in the case of the reserve price auction, if the bidding begins too high, novices might be afraid that the bidding will go higher than their limit, and they'll never win the auction.

Some sellers begin the bidding at the price they paid for the item, thereby protecting their investment. This is a good tactic, especially if you bought the item at a price far below eBay's current going rate.

To determine the current auction value of your item, we recommend using the Completed Auctions search function, explained in Chapter 7. If you know that the item is selling on eBay for a certain price and that a demand for the item exists, starting the bidding at a reasonably low level can be a great way to increase bidding and attract prospective bidders to read your listing.

Years of advertising experience can't be wrong. If your item is in demand and people are actively buying, start the bidding low. Retail stores have done this for years with ads that feature prices starting at $9.99 or $14.98. Even television commercials for automobiles quote a low starting price. To get the car with the accessories you need, you may end up paying twice the quoted price.

When sellers know their item will sell, they begin their bidding as low as a dollar or even a penny. Because of the eBay *proxy bidding system* (which maintains your highest bid as secret, increasing it incrementally when you're bid against), it takes more bids (due to the smaller bidding increments) to bring the item up to the final selling price.

The downside of the proxy bidding system is that new bidders who aren't familiar with it may offer only the minimum required increment each time they bid. This can be frustrating, and they may quit bidding when they realize that the current bid to be topped is actually much higher than it appears.

Very few of us know the proxy increments by heart, so as a refresher, we give you the goods in Table 2-5.

Table 2-5	Proxy Bidding Increments
Current High Bid	*Bid Increment*
$0.01–$0.99	$0.05
$1.00–$4.99	$0.25
$5.00–$24.99	$0.50

Current High Bid	Bid Increment
$25.00–$99.99	$1.00
$100.00–$249.99	$2.50
$250.00–$499.99	$5.00

Auction timing

Another debatable philosophy is auction timing. People are always asking how long to run their auctions and which day is best to end them. You have to evaluate your item and decide the best plan. Your options are

- ✔ **One-day auction:** This format can be very successful if you are selling a hot-ticket item that is currently popular on eBay. For instance, Marsha chose a one-day auction to sell some *Friends* TV show memorabilia. The twenty-four-hour auction opened midday before the final show and ended the next day — at a very healthy final price!

  One-day auctions also give you the benefit of pushing your auction to the top of the heap in the listings. Because eBay defaults to show the items ending first at the top of the page (just below the Featured Auctions heading), a one-day listing posts right up there!

- ✔ **Three-day auction:** If, as in the heyday of Beanie Babies, the item's price will shoot up right after you post it, a three-day auction works just fine. And it's great for those last-minute holiday shoppers looking for hard-to-find items.

  With the eBay Buy It Now feature, you can pretty much accomplish the same benefits as a three-day auction. When you list your item for sale, set a price at which you will sell the item; this is your target price. This price can be any amount; if someone is willing to pay it, the item sells.

- ✔ **Five-day auction:** Five days will give you two days more than three and two days less than seven. That's about the size of it. If you just want an extended weekend auction, or if your item is a hot one, use it. Five-day auctions are useful during holiday rushes, when gift buying is the main reason for bidding.

- ✔ **Seven-day auction:** Tried-and-true advertising theory says that the longer you market your item, the more people will see it. On eBay, this means that you have more opportunity for people to bid on it. The seven-day auction is a staple for the bulk of eBay vendors. Seven days is long enough to cover weekend browsers and short enough to keep the auction interesting.

✔ **Ten-day auction:** Many veteran eBay sellers swear by the ten-day auction. Sure, eBay charges you an extra fifty cents for the privilege, but the extra three days of exposure (it can encompass two weekends) can easily net you more than that in profits.

If you're selling an esoteric collectible that doesn't appear on eBay often, run a ten-day auction to give it maximum exposure. Start the auction on a Friday, so it will cover the aforementioned two weekends worth of browsers. In Marsha's book eBay Timesaving Techniques For Dummies (Wiley), an in-depth examination of opinions on how long to run an auction and what day or time to begin it is provided.

Your auction closes exactly one, three, five, seven, or ten days — *to the minute* — after you set it up. Be careful not to begin your auctions when you're up late at night and can't sleep; you don't want your auction to end at two in the morning when no one else is awake to bid on it. If you can't sleep, make your time productive by preparing listings ahead of time with the TurboLister program. You can then upload them for future launching when the world is ready to shop.

The specific day you close your auction can also be important. eBay is full of weekend browsers, so including a weekend in your auction time is a definite plus. Often, auctions that end late Sunday afternoon through Monday close with high bids.

You'll need to do some research to determine the best times to run your auctions and for how long. In Chapter 10, we show you how to combine your research on the eBay search engine with a special kind of statistical counter so you can identify the best closing time for your items. (See Chapter 7 for the details of using the search engine as a valuable research tool.) The best person to figure out the closing information for your auctions is you. Use the tools that eBay provides, and over time you'll develop a pattern that works best for you.

Does a definite time exist *not* to close your auctions? Experience has taught many sellers never to close an auction on a national holiday. Canada Day, Victoria Day, and Boxing Day in Canada and Memorial Day, the Fourth of July, and Veteran's Day in the U.S. may be bonanza sales days for retail shops, but eBay auction items closing on these days go at bargain prices. Most likely everyone is out shopping the brick and mortar stores on those days, away from their computers.

Marketing your auctions

How do you let people know about your auctions? What do you do if all 200 million users on eBay happen to not be on the site the week that your items are up for sale? You advertise.

Pirates of the Caribbean, er, Carribean?

Just before the *Pirates of the Caribbean* movie premiered, Disneyland gave out exclusive movie posters to their visitors. Some savvy eBayers snagged copies to sell on the site. They typically listed, once the movie opened, for a starting bid of $9.99 USD each, and rarely got more than the opening bid.

When we searched eBay for *pirates poster*, we found that the very same posters with a misspelled title, Pirates of the Carriban, in the auction listing were selling for as high as $30 USD each. Some sellers began to change their auctions to have the more popular misspelling (*Carribean*) in the title and quickly saw those dollar signs! Many of the posters listed with the misspelled title sold on the site for between $15 and $27 USD.

Many mailing lists and newsgroups permit self-promotion. Find a group that features your type of items and post a little ad. This works best if you have your own e-commerce Web site. Your site, which is, ideally, the hub for your sales, can give you an identity and level of professionalism that makes your business more official in the eyes of buyers. In Chapter 8, we detail the ins and outs of business sites on the Web.

eBay Merchant Kit

If you have your own personal (non-commercial) Web site — maybe it's a family site — you might wish to spruce it up, pointing to your eBay listings. (You never know, Aunt Patti may just be in the market for your goods!) eBay has a fantastic Merchant Kit that turns your Web page into a mini-eBay, featuring only your listings. In Figure 2-11, you can see the Merchant Kit in action on a family Web site, with active links to eBay sales.

The page in Figure 2-11 is run by eBay's magic API (application program interface), which is far too technical for the likes of us. We're experts at buying and selling — not techie coding! Luckily, you don't need to be a technology whiz to use this tool. It's automatically put on your site after you insert a bit of eBay-supplied HTML code into your Web page. The eBay API updates your listings every ten minutes.

To get your HTML code, go to `http://pages.ebay.com/api/merchant kit.html`, then follow these steps:

1. **On the Marketplace page, click the Get Merchant Kit Now button.**

   You'll be taken to a place where you can select a few options to create an HTML sniplet to insert on your page. As with most eBay tasks, you are required to sign in again and agree to the official license agreement before you can get down to business.

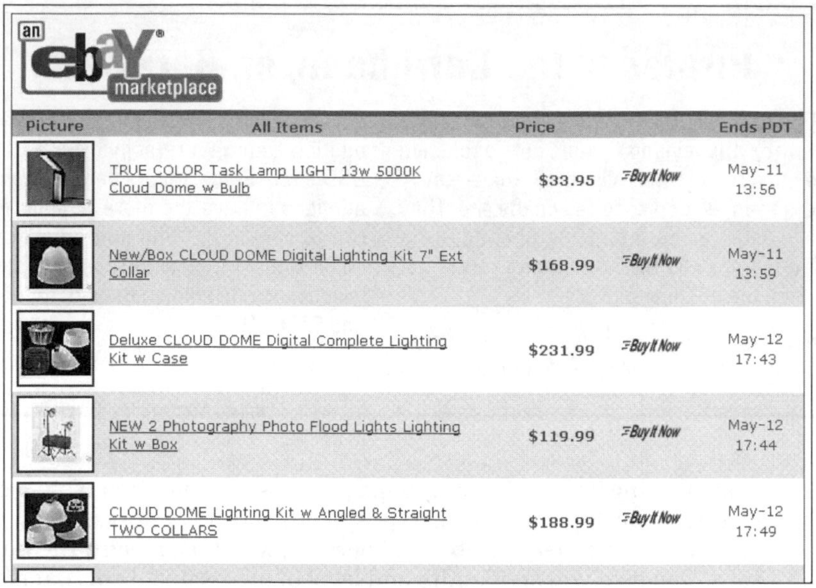

Figure 2-11:
The eBay
Merchant
Kit on a
personal
Web site.

2. **Choose the items that you want to appear.**

   Your choices are All Categories, a selected eBay category number, or (if you have an eBay store) one of your eBay Store categories. If your Web site is devoted to classic VHS tapes, for example, you might want to specify eBay category 309 (DVDs & Movies:VHS) when making your selection.

3. **Choose the number of items you want to show: 25 or 50.**

4. **Choose the way in which you'd like to display your items.**

   You can display your items in order by items ending first, items ending last, highest prices first, or highest prices last.

5. **Choose and indicate whether you'd rather display a different font face than the default, Verdana, and if you'd like to vary the type size.**

   We think Verdana is a perfect font face to use. It was developed for clarity on the Internet. Its default size is two, which fits perfectly on the page — why monkey with it?

6. **Decide whether you want the PayPal icon (if you offer PayPal for your listings) and the highlight feature option (if you use it) to appear on the Marketplace page.**

7. **Click the Preview Sniplet button.**

   You see a representation of how your Marketplace will look and are presented with the proper HTML code to insert on your page.

8. **Copy the HTML code and paste it into your Web page where you want the Marketplace to appear.**

   Voila! A marketplace.

Link Buttons

eBay supplies some nice link buttons (see Figure 2-12) that you can use on your Web site. Visit the following address to add these links to your site's home page:

```
http://pages.ebay.ca/services/buyandsell/link-
            buttons.html
```

Link your site to eBay

If you have your own web page, you can use these buttons to link your visitors to eBay!

With these buttons, you can:

- Promote items that you are selling on eBay, or
- Provide a direct link to the eBay home page at **www.ebay.ca**

Complete the form below to view easy instructions to install eBay buttons on your personal web site.

Select the button(s) you wish to display:

☐ [ebY.CA] Links to the eBay home page

☐ [SHOP ebY.CA WITH ME!] A customised link that goes directly to a list of items you have for sale.

URL of page(s) where you plan to display buttons (required):

Example: www.ebay.ca/thispage.html

[www,]

Figure 2-12: The Shop eBay with Me link buttons.

We're guessing that you already know all about your About Me page, a handy tool when it comes to marketing your auctions. In Chapter 3, we discuss the values of the About Me page. Link to your Web site from your little homepage on eBay.

Here's a great way to market future auctions: When you're sending items after making a sale on eBay, include a list of items that you'll be selling soon — especially ones that may appeal to that customer. (And don't forget to send a thank you note!) When you schedule your auctions, you're given the auction number before the item is listed.

Do not link your auction to your Web site. It's against eBay policy to possibly divert sales away from the auction site. *Do* link to your personal site from your About Me page. See the "Linking from your auctions" section later in this chapter to find out just what you can and cannot link to and from.

A second chance

The new Second Chance feature on eBay helps sellers legitimize something that previously went on behind closed doors and in violation of eBay policy. When a winner doesn't complete a sale, the Second Chance feature allows sellers to offer the item to the next highest bidder.

You must still go through the proper channels and file your non-paying bidder notice with eBay. After doing that, you can send a Second Chance offer to any underbidder, as long as no more than sixty days have passed since the end of the auction. Your Final Value Fee is based on the price you receive when the offer is accepted.

In the Second Chance Offer scenario, the seller can leave two feedback comments: one for the winner (non-paying bidder) and one for the person who bought the item through the Second Chance Offer transaction. The bidder to whom you proffer your Second Chance Offer is covered by the eBay fraud protection program.

This feature does not apply to Dutch auctions.

Listing Violations

eBay does not sell merchandise. eBay is merely a venue where others can put on a giant e-commerce party (in other words, sell stuff). To provide a safe and profitable venue for its sellers, eBay must govern auctions that take place on its site. eBay makes the rules, and all eBayers are expected to follow those rules. We like to think of eBay as being like the place that lets you hold your senior prom in its gym. When we were in school, we had to follow the rules or see our prom cancelled. If we don't agree to follow eBay's rules, a safe and trusted eBay community can't exist.

Listing policies

eBay has some hard and fast rules about listing your items. You must list your item in the appropriate category, for example — that only makes sense. We highlight a few other rules in this section to keep in mind when listing. Remember that what we discuss here isn't a definitive list of eBay listing policies and rules. Take time to familiarize yourself with the Listing and Selling section of the User Agreement at the following:

```
pages.ebay.ca/help/policies/user-agreement.html
```

We recommend regularly checking the eBay User Agreement for any policy changes.

Choice auctions

Your auction must be for one item only: the item that you specifically list in your auction. It's against the rules to give the bidder a choice of items, sizes, or colours. eBay protects you with its Purchase Protection Program, which covers all online eBay transactions that are legitimate. When you give your bidders a choice, it's considered an illegal sale and isn't covered. Anything that's negotiated outside the eBay system can lead to either misrepresentation or fraud. You don't want to be caught up in that sort of grief and misery.

If eBay catches you offering a choice, they will end the auction and credit the insertion fee to your account.

Duplicate auctions

Remember the old supply and demand theory from your economics class? When people list the same items repeatedly on eBay, they drive down the item's going price, while ruining the opportunity for other members to sell the item during that time.

You can run ten identical listings simultaneously on eBay. If you're going to list the same item that many times, be sure to list it in different categories. That's a rule on eBay, but it also makes sense. Nothing drives down the price of an item faster than closing identical auctions, one after another, in the same category. eBay also requires that you list your auction in a category that's relevant to your item.

If you have multiple copies of something, a better solution is to run a Dutch auction for the total number of items you have for sale. You can also run two Dutch auctions in different (but appropriate) categories.

If you're caught with more than ten identical auctions, eBay may end the additional auctions and credit the insertion fees back to you.

Pre-sale listings

eBay doesn't like it when you try to sell something that's not in your hands (known as a *pre-sale listing*). Doing so is a dangerous game to play anyway. Often, being the first seller to put a very popular item up for sale can get you some pretty high bids. It's not illegal to run a pre-sale, as long as you can guarantee in your auction description that the item will be available to ship within thirty days of the purchase date or the day the auction closes. However, we don't recommend even attempting a pre-sale listing unless you're completely sure that you'll have the item in time.

Pre-selling: Not worth the hassle

A seller we once knew pre-sold Beanie Babies on eBay. She had a regular source that supplied her when the new toys came out, so she fell into a complacent attitude about listing pre-sales. Then her supplier didn't receive the shipment. Motivated by the need to protect her feedback rating (and by the fear that she'd be accused of fraud), she ran all over town desperately trying to get the beanies she needed to fill her orders. The beanies were so rare that she ended up spending several hundred dollars more than what she had originally sold the toys for, just to keep her customers happy.

If you know that you'll have the item to ship — and it won't be lost on its way to you — you may list an item with the following requirement: You must state in your auction description that the item is a pre-sale and will be shipped by the thirtieth day from the end of the listing or purchase. You'll also have to use a little HTML here; the text in the auction description must be coded with an HTML font size no smaller than three.

Before you set up a pre-sale auction, check out the perspective of Industry Canada's Office of Consumer Affairs at the following address:

```
http://strategis.ic.gc.ca/epic/internet/inoca-
           bc.nsf/en/ca01495e.html
```

Bonuses, giveaways, raffles, or prizes

Because eBay sells virtually anywhere in the world, it must follow explicit laws governing giveaways and prizes. Every government has its own set of rules and regulations, so eBay doesn't allow individual sellers to come up with their own promotions.

If your auction violates this rule, eBay might cancel it and refund your listing fee.

Keyword spamming

Keyword spamming is when you add words, usually brand names, to your auction description that don't describe what you're selling. (Describing a little black dress as Givenchy-style when Givenchy has nothing to do with it is a good example.) Sellers use keyword spamming to lure viewers to their auctions who have searched for a particular brand name. To attract attention to their listings, some sellers use "not" or "like" along with the brand name in phrases such as "like Givenchy."

eBay Giving Works (charity) auctions

Tens of millions of dollars have been raised on eBay for charitable organizations (see the figure below). If you represent a legitimate charity, you may run auctions on eBay to raise funds. Just follow these simple steps:

1. **Register your charity as an eBay member.**

2. **Prepare an About Me page describing your charity.**

   Explain what the charity is, what it does, where the money raised goes, and so on. Set up the page to "Show no feedback" and indicate for the page to "Show all items." eBay will link this page to the Giving Works area.

3. **E-mail all the following information to eBay at** `http://pages.ebay.ca/charity/`:

   ✔ The User ID and e-mail address you registered with on eBay

   ✔ The completed About Me page

✔ The charity registration number for your non-profit organization

✔ The time frame in which you expect to run your auction

✔ A brief description of your organization

✔ Some examples of the items you'd like to list

✔ The name, e-mail address, and telephone number of the organization's main contact person

✔ The Web site address for your organization (if it has one)

You'll hear back from eBay when your charity has been approved. Your charity will then appear on Giving Works, and you can start planning your charity auctions. The eBay Charity Fundraising page is directly accessible through the following URL:

`http://pages.ebay.ca/charity/`

Featured Canadian Charities

eBay Canada has recently enhanced its charity platform to further support the generosity of the eBay community via the eBay Canada Charity Fee Credit Policy. When a registered charity lists on www.ebay.ca for the purpose of fundraising, eBay Canada will credit the Insertion, Gallery and Final Value Fees back to the organization in the listing.

NEW! As of June 1, 2006, Registered Canadian charities must contact the eBay Canada Billing Support team in order to receive a free credit for their charity listings. Visit our FAQ page for Registered Canadian Charities to find out more.

Over the past ten years, more than US$59 million has been raised for charitable organizations through listings on the eBay Marketplace. eBay Canada is pleased to be able to offer additional support to charitable fundraising in Canada.

- More information about Charity Fundraising on www.ebay.ca
- Start fundraising now!

Charity FAQs

- FAQ for Registered Canadian Charities
- FAQ if you are not a Registered Canadian Charity

Helpful Links

- eBay Explained - Getting Started
- eBay Explained - Buying Basics
- eBay Explained - Selling Basics
- eBay Selling Fees
- Help Centre

Charity: SickKids Foundation

SickKids FOUNDATION

SickKids Foundation

Wendell Clarke signed Toronto Maple Leaf Collectable Teddy Bears, WWE Wrestling Fan Package, Canadian Olympic Coin Collection, and rare Disneyana. All proceeds benefit SickKids Foundation.

Charity: Kids Help Phone

KIDS HELP PHONE

Kids Help Phone

Bid on Exotic Hotel and Vacation Packages, Signed Movie and Sport Memorabilia, Awesome Electronics and Gadgets, Clothes and Watches, All in Support in Kids Help Phone!

Charity: Jacob's Ladder

More Charities

The Charity Store

Charity: Ontario March of Dimes

Ontario March of Dimes

On eBay, keyword spamming actually causes whatever you are selling to be classified as a "potentially infringing" item. Keyword spamming is a listing violation, and we mention it here because it affects all listings. The wording you choose when you run this kind of auction manipulates the eBay search engine and prospective bidders. For a complete discussion of keyword spamming and its complexities as an infringement of eBay's policies, see Chapter 4.

Linking from your auctions

Few issues cause sellers to argue more than the rules on linking your auction to other pages on the Web. We describe eBay's rules about linking in this section.

In your auction item description, you *can* use the following:

- ✔ One link to an additional page that gives further information about the item you're selling.

- ✔ One link that opens an e-mail window on the prospective buyer's browser so that the buyer can send you an e-mail.

- ✔ Links to more photo images of the item you're selling.

- ✔ Links to your other auctions on eBay and your eBay Store listings.

- ✔ One link to your About Me page, besides the link next to your user ID that eBay provides.

- ✔ Links to vendors' sites that help you with your auctions. eBay considers listing services, software, and payment services to be third-party vendors. You can legally link to them as long as the HTML font is no larger than size three; if you're using a logo, it must be no larger than 88 x 33 pixels.

  Most third-party vendors are well aware of these restrictions. They don't want their credits pulled from eBay, so the information they supply as a link generally falls within eBay's parameters.

In your auction description, you *cannot* link to the following:

- ✔ Any page that offers to sell, trade, or purchase merchandise outside the eBay site.

- ✔ Any area on the Internet that offers merchandise considered illegal on eBay. See Chapter 4 for information on illegal items.

- ✔ Any site that encourages eBay bidders to place their bids outside eBay.

- ✔ Any site that solicits eBay user IDs and passwords.

Linking from your About Me page

eBay rules are pretty much the same as the rest of the site when it comes to your About Me page. Because eBay gives you this page for self-promotion, you may link it to your own (e-commerce or personal). Be sure not to link to other trading sites or to sites that offer the same merchandise for the same or a lower price. Read more about the do's and don'ts of the About Me page in Chapter 3.

Chapter 3

Cool eBay Tools

*e*Bay offers you an amazing variety of tools. Because the site is constantly changing, very few of us know where these tools are, how to find them, or how to use them. We admit that we have fallen victim to the "Oh, you can do that?" syndrome. When poking around eBay it's always easy to find a new cool tool or neat shortcut and it's always an eye-opener!

Aside from the tools we tell you about in this chapter, the most important shortcut we can give you is a reminder to sign in and click the box that says "Keep me signed in on this computer unless I sign out" before you attempt to do anything on eBay. This one click will permit you to do most of your business on eBay without being bugged for your password at every turn.

If you have more than one user ID or you share a computer with other people, be sure to sign out when you're finished. The cookie system has been changed on eBay. Now, like other Web sites, eBay will permit your computer to hold your sign-in information until you sign out. For your protection, you still have to type your password. To specify the tasks for which you want eBay to remember your sign-in information, go to the Preferences area of the My eBay page.

Many eBay users frequently share with us some nuggets of information that have helped them along the way. In this chapter, we share these nuggets with you.

In addition, eBay has developed some incredibly useful features. My eBay, for example, allows you to customize eBay for your home page. Another feature, the About Me page, lets you tell the story of your business to the world and also, with a click of the mouse, find out about the people you plan to buy from. To get the lowdown on my favourite cool eBay tools, read on.

My eBay

A great place to start on eBay every morning is at My eBay, where you are greeted by your user ID followed by your current feedback rating. My eBay is no longer just a step-by-step list of what you're selling and bidding on — it is now a veritable Swiss Army knife of eBay tools.

Access the My eBay page by clicking the My eBay button above the eBay navigation bar. The navigation bar, shown in Figure 3-1, appears at the top of every eBay page. You can also click the <u>My eBay</u> link at the bottom of the eBay home or Search page. Why? We don't really know why anyone would take two steps instead of one, but it's there, and you can.

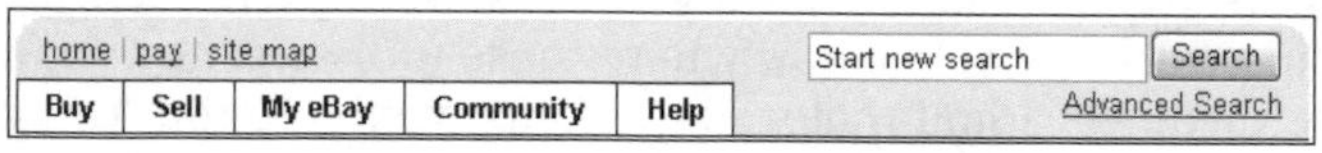

Figure 3-1:
The eBay navigation bar appears at the top of every eBay page.

home	pay	site map			Start new search	Search
Buy	Sell	My eBay	Community	Help		Advanced Search

When you arrive at your My eBay page, you'll see a summary of the business that you have in progress on the site (see Figure 3-2). Each comment has a link so you can investigate the progress of the transactions.

My eBay is divided into nine areas: My Summary, All Buying, All Selling, Want it Now, My Messages, All Favourites, My Account, My Reviews & Guides, and Dispute Console. Visit these areas by clicking links in the My eBay Views box on the left side of the page. The top link of each My eBay area presents you with a summary of the activity in that section. The links below the top link take you to specific data without forcing you to scroll through a lot of information.

At the bottom of My eBay Views are other boxes with convenient links to services and answers to questions you may have while doing business on eBay (see Figure 3-3). The task-specific pages of My eBay may show a <u>more</u> link in this box of additional links. Click the <u>more</u> link, and you're presented with a page of links related to what you were looking at first.

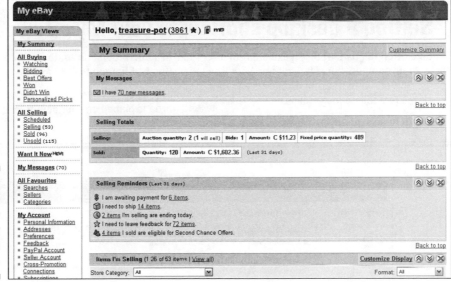

Figure 3-2:
A sample
My eBay
Summary
entrance
page.

Figure 3-3:
The Related
Links box
on the
My eBay
Selling
page.

The links in the Related Links box are different, depending on the page: The buying-related links are on the All Buying page, the selling-related links are on the All Selling page (see Figure 3-4), the account-related links on the My Account page, and the favourites-related links on the All Favourites page. When you have a question regarding an eBay procedure, you'll find these links very handy.

Setting a desktop shortcut to your My eBay page

People often tell us that they'd like a direct link from their computer desktop to their My eBay page. If you use Internet Explorer as your browser, just follow these steps:

1. Sign in and go to your My eBay page.

2. In your browser's toolbar, choose File⇨ Send⇨Shortcut to Desktop.

That's it. A clickable shortcut to your My eBay area is placed on your computer's desktop.

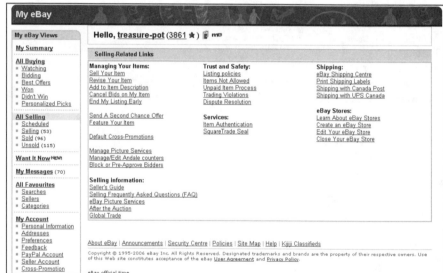

Figure 3-4:
Selling-related links on the All Selling page.

At the top of each of the Views is a mini tote board, giving you a snapshot of your financial business dealings. In the Buying area, it displays the number of items you're bidding on and the dollar amount of all your winning bids. In the Selling area, you see the number of items and the dollar amounts bid. The other views have a similar summary tote at the top of the page.

All Buying

Here it is: the hub for keeping track of your bids, your wins, items you're watching, and any items you didn't win. Although you plan to sell more than buy on eBay, we're sure you'll occasionally find something to buy, if only to turn around and resell it. Many a bargain item on eBay can be turned around and resold almost immediately at a profit. Plus, eBay can be a great place to purchase many of your shipping supplies. (In Chapter 17, we reference a few eBay sources with great prices and fast shipping.)

Buying Reminders

Buying Reminders are like a customized to-do list for your eBay buying activities. For example, you might check Buying Reminders to see how many items you still need to pay for or how many transactions still need your feedback.

Items I'm Bidding On

When you place a bid, eBay automatically registers it in the Items I'm Bidding On area, like the one shown in Figure 3-5.

Make the bidding page a daily stop on eBay so you can see the status of your bids. Here's how to read it:

- ✔ Bid amounts in green indicate that you're the highest bidder in the auction.

- ✔ Bid amounts in red indicate that your bid is losing. If you decide to increase your bid, simply click the auction title to go to the auction.

Figure 3-5: Keeping track of your bidding at My eBay.

✔ Dutch auctions appear in black. To determine whether you retain high bidder status in a Dutch auction, you have to view the actual auction.

✔ The My Max Bid column reminds you of the amount of your highest bid; if you see a bid that surpasses your own, you'll know it's time to throw in another bid.

✔ The Bidding Totals box, at the top of the Bidding page, lists the current dollar amount you're spending and the number of items you're currently winning in pending auctions. You'll see the total amount you've bid and a separate total representing auctions you're winning.

✔ As auctions on which you have bid end, the information is automatically transferred to the Won and Didn't Win pages, based on your success or failure in the bidding process.

You can make notations on your bidding or item-watching pages to, for example, help you organize your gift-giving. (See the note added in Figure 3-6.) Click to place a check mark next to the item you want to annotate, click the Add Note button, and then add the information.

Figure 3-6:
A Father's
Day notation
on a
particular
bid.

Items I Made Best Offers On

A relatively new feature on eBay, the Best Offer function allows you to make an offer to sellers who determine that they may be willing to accept less than the opening bid price for their items. A seller can choose to accept, decline, or make a counter-offer to your suggestion. If the seller accepts your offer, the item will automatically be moved to the "Items I've Won" section of the page.

Items I've Won

Clicking the Won link in the bidding area displays all the items you've won in the past sixty days. The default is thirty-one days, which should suffice for most transactions. The Items I've Won page is a great place to keep track of items that you're waiting to receive from the seller. It's also a convenient way to keep track of your expenditures, should you be buying for resale. Helpful features on this page include the following:

- **Check box:** Click the box to add a check mark, and you can indicate that you'd like to add a note to your record or remove it from the list.

- **Seller's user ID:** It always helps to remember the seller's name, and this link sends you to their Member Profile (feedback page) where you can send them an e-mail.

- **Auction title:** A link to the auction. We suggest using this when an item purchased arrives so that you can be sure that the item you receive is exactly as advertised.

- **Item number:** The auction number for your records.

- **Auction sale date:** A convenient way to see whether your item is slow in shipping. After a couple of weeks, it doesn't hurt to drop the seller an e-mail to check on the shipping status.

- **Sale price** and **quantity:** Help you keep track of the money you've spent. Works with the totals in the tote board.

- **Action:** Displays different commands based on the status of your transaction. You can click a link to pay for the item through PayPal, mark the item "paid" if you've used another method of payment, view your item's payment status, view items you've already paid for, or leave feedback once you've received the item and are satisfied that it's what you ordered.

- **Icons:** At the end of each item's listing are three icons that appear dimmed until the selected action is taken. A dollar sign indicates whether you've paid for the item, a star indicates that you've left feedback, and a quote bubble indicates that feedback has been left for you.

After you have received an item and left feedback, check the box next to it and then press the Delete Selected Items button to remove the completed transactions from view.

Items I'm Watching

Have you ever seen an auction that made you think, "I don't want to bid on this just now, but I'd like to buy it if it's a bargain"? Clicking the <u>Watching</u> link in the My eBay Views box will bring you to the Items I'm Watching page (see Figure 3-7).This is just the tool to help you, and one of the most powerful features of the My eBay area. The Items I'm Watching page lists each auction with a countdown timer ("time left"), so you know exactly when the auction will close. When an auction on your watch list gets close to ending, you can swoop down and make the kill — if the price is right.

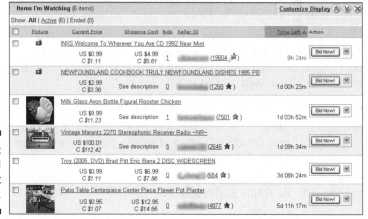

Figure 3-7:
Sit back and
observe at
My eBay.

Also a handy marketing tool, the Watching page allows you to store auctions from competitive sellers. That way, you can monitor the status of items similar to the ones you plan to sell later, noting whether they are selling high or low. Using the Watching page helps you to decide when it's a good time to sell.

You've probably seen the <u>Watch This Item</u> link at the top of each auction page. If you're watching items (eBay allows you to monitor 100 auctions at a time), you'll see a notation on the page indicating how many auctions you are keeping tabs on.

The number-one reason for using the Watch This Item function is that it allows you to keep your bargain hunting quiet. Everybody — including the competition — knows when you're bidding on an item, but nobody knows when you're watching the deals like a hawk. When you're looking for bargains to buy and resell, you may not want to tip off the competition by letting them know you're bidding.

All Selling

eBay provides some smooth management tools on your All Selling page. You can track items you currently have up for auction and items you've sold. It's a quick way to get a snapshot of the dollar value of your auctions as they proceed. Although the All Selling page isn't as good for marketing information (detailed counters are best — see Chapter 9), it's a pretty good way to tell at a glance how your items are faring.

Items I'm Selling

On the Items I'm Selling page, shown in Figure 3-8, you can keep an eye on your store items, your fixed-price sales, and the progress of your auctions. You can see how many bids your auctions have, whether your reserves have been met, and how long before the auction will close. By clicking an auction title, you can visit the auction to make sure your pictures are appearing or to check your counter.

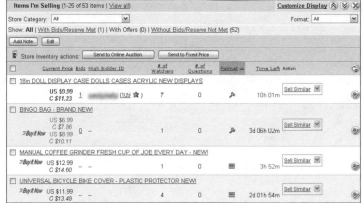

Figure 3-8:
Items I'm
Selling view
at My eBay.

Many people watch auctions and don't bid until the last minute, so you may not see a lot of bidding activity on your page. The Number (#) of Watchers feature can give you important information on the progress of your auctions.

The auctions that appear in green have received one or more bids (and met any reserves you've set). Auctions in red haven't received any bids, or the set reserve price hasn't been met. Dutch auctions aren't colour-coded and appear in black.

At the top of the Items I'm Selling area, eBay lists the current price of all items, including bidding on items that haven't met your reserve. The total dollar amount of the items that will sell when the auction is over appears beneath these totals. On the right side of your listings, eBay has a column for icons.

Items I've Sold

As you scroll down the All Selling page, you'll come to the Items I've Sold area. To avoid a lot of scrolling, you can reach an abbreviated version of this area (missing the detailed Selling Totals box) by clicking the Sold link in the Views box, under All Selling.

The Items I've Sold area keeps your sales in a concise place, as shown in Figure 3-9. It can be used in lieu of fancy auction management software. If you're selling hundreds of items, your list will probably be too long to monitor individual auctions — but you can easily view the total current price of the items that will sell.

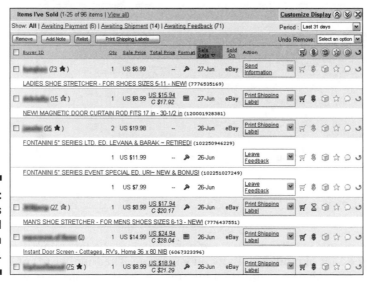

Figure 3-9: The Items I've Sold view in My eBay.

If you're selling more than twenty items a week, you might consider using eBay's Selling Manager as an even more complete auction management solution. See Chapter 9 for the lowdown on how to make this tool work for you.

The Items I've Sold page has the following features that we're sure you'll find helpful in completing your transactions:

- ✔ **Check box:** Click here to add a personal note to your record or to remove an item from your list.

- ✔ **Buyer's user ID** and **feedback rating:** The eBay ID of the winner of the sale. Click it to go to the user's Member Profile, where you can use eBay's e-mail service to contact the buyer.

- ✔ **Quantity:** If the sale was for multiple items, the number of items is displayed here.

- ✔ **Item title:** A direct link to the auction. You can click this link to check on your auction and see the other bidders, should you want to make a Second Chance offer.

- ✔ **Item number:** The auction number for your records.

- ✔ **Sale price:** The final selling price for your item.

- ✔ **Total price:** The final selling price plus the shipping amount.

- ✔ **Sale date:** Keep an eye on the end date so that you can be sure you get your payment as agreed.

- ✔ **Action:** Here's where you find a hidden, drop-down menu that works with the icons to the left and offers links to various actions that you can take:

  - • **Mark paid:** If the customer hasn't paid using PayPal, you can indicate their method of payment (after you receive it).

  - • **View payment status:** See a copy of the payment receipt if the buyer paid using PayPal or a notation you inserted regarding other payment methods.

  - • **Print shipping label:** You can print a shipping label from here. See Chapter 14 for more professional options.

  - • **Leave feedback:** Leave feedback with a single click once you've heard that the item arrived safely and your customer is happy. For more information on leaving feedback, check out the section "Feedback: Your permanent record," later in this chapter.

  - • **Mark shipped**: After you've shipped the item, click here to indicate that it's on the way.

  - • **Second chance offer:** Click here to make a second chance offer to one of your underbidders if you have multiple items for sale.

  - • **Relist:** Here you can relist your item on the site.

✔ **Icons:** My eBay has several icons that appear dimmed until you perform an action with the Action command. You may also click the icons at the top of the list to sort your listings by actions completed, although most sellers prefer to keep the listings in the default chronological order.

- **Shopping cart:** The buyer has completed checkout (supplying a shipping address and planned payment method).

- **Dollar sign:** The buyer has paid using PayPal, or you've used the drop-down menu to indicate that the buyer has paid with a different form of payment (such as a money order or a personal cheque).

- **Shipping box:** The item has shipped.

- **Star:** You've left feedback.

- **Comment bubble:** The buyer has left feedback. A plus sign (+) indicates a positive comment, and a minus sign (–) indicates a negative comment.

Want it Now

According to eBay, Want it Now is where buyers ask and sellers deliver. This part of eBay is still growing in popularity because it's a great place to post an ad for an item you want to buy. Hopefully a seller will view the posting and respond with a listing item number. The buyer then receives an e-mail from eBay with a direct link to the listing.

My Messages

In an effort to protect users from unwanted spam e-mail, eBay introduced My Messages as an online e-mail clearing house. All e-mails related to your eBay activities will appear here, including those from interested bidders who ask questions about your listings using the Ask the Seller form. Since all e-mails go through the eBay Email Forwarding System (EFS), your actual e-mail address is protected from those who might abuse the information.

Another great benefit of My Messages is in determining which e-mails you receive are actually from eBay and which are not. If you have been on the site for any period of time, you are probably familiar with the *phishing* e-mails that eBay users receive with increasing frequency. These e-mails are sent with the intention of securing the user's personal account and credit card information by intimidating them to believe that their eBay account is about to be closed. Many of these e-mails look extremely authentic, and it can be difficult for a novice to avoid being fooled. A quick visit to My Messages will reveal whether the e-mail in question is actually from eBay; if the questionable message does not appear in your Inbox, it is safe to discard it as spam. See Chapter 4 for more information about protecting yourself from phishing e-mails.

Reviews and Guides

Do you have an opinion on the latest digital camera? Some other expertise that you would like to share with your fellow eBayers? The Reviews and Guides section is the place where eBay allows you to share your wealth of knowledge — or express your opinion — on almost any type of product or service.

Dispute Console

Occasionally, transactions can go sour, and this is the place that eBay users can go to in an effort to reach a resolution. As a buyer, you can file a Significantly Not as Described claim with eBay if that antique chair you purchased arrives with only two legs. As a seller, your Unpaid Item disputes with non-paying buyers will congregate here as well. eBay added this haven for disputes aiming to increase communication between buyers and sellers, and also to help track, manage, and resolve user conflicts as quickly as possible.

All Favourites

If you sell and have an interest in a few categories, look no further than the My eBay All Favourites page of links for checking out what's hot and what's not. The All Favourites page helps you track trends and even find some bargains to resell on eBay.

Favourite Categories

eBay allows you to store hot links for four categories. These links allow you to quickly check out the competition.

Before you list some auctions on a popular item, estimate the date and hour that other auctions selling that item will close. Then go into the category and check to be sure that your auction won't be closing during a flood of auctions for the same item. Nothing kills profits more than closing an auction in the middle of a series of auctions selling the same thing. You can watch the final values drop one at a time.

Favourite Searches

Another tool that comes in handy for sellers as well as buyers is My Favourite Searches (see Figure 3-10). You can list as many as 100 favourite searches; when you want to check one out, simply click the <u>Search Now</u> link next to the item.

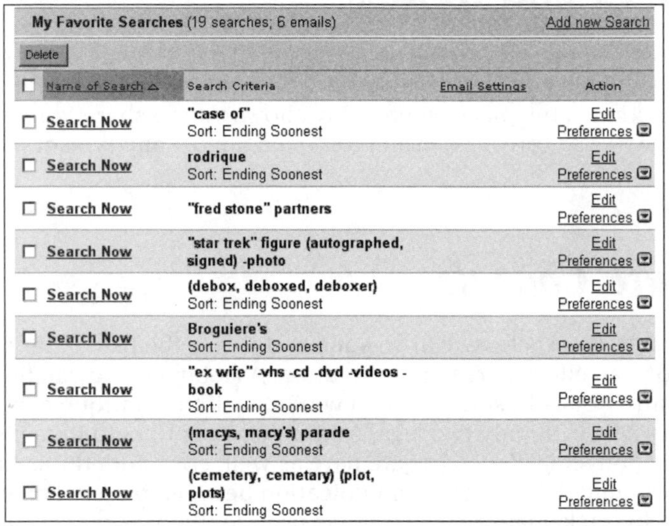

Figure 3-10:
A collection of favourite searches.

You can view saved searches, change them, delete them, or indicate that you'd like to receive e-mail notification when a new item is listed. To add an item to the list, run a search from any search bar on any eBay page and click the <u>Add to Favourites</u> link that appears at the top of the search results. The next time you reload your My eBay All Favourites page, your new favourite will be listed.

Keeping track of favourite searches is a valuable tool when you're looking for particular items to resell and want to find them at bargain-basement prices. Be sure to take advantage of asterisks (wildcard characters) and alternate spellings so you can catch items with misspellings in the title. These are your best bets for low prices because they will slip under the radar of your competitors. See Chapter 7 for the lowdown on how the eBay search engine can help your sales.

If you choose to receive e-mail when your search locates a new listing, you can request that you receive notification from seven days to a year from the time you submitted the request. You're allowed to receive new listing e-mails on 30 of your 100 searches. Just click the <u>Edit Preferences</u> link in the far-right column to set up the service (refer to Figure 3-10). eBay sends its robot to check listings each night, so you'll get notification of a new listing the next morning. This is an especially valuable feature when you are waiting for that rare collectible to come up for auction — eBay will check each day so that you don't have to.

Favourite Sellers

Favourite Sellers is where you can keep a list of people who sell items similar to what you sell. You can check up on them and see what they're selling, when they're selling it, and for how much. It's a helpful tool that can help you avoid listing an item right next to one of their auctions.

Favourite Sellers can be a very handy tool when your competition is selling an item that you plan to sell, but at a deeply discounted price. When that happens, don't offer yours until they sell out of the item, at which time the price will most likely go back up — supply and demand, remember? The Favourite Sellers area is also a great place to add quality wholesalers and liquidators so that you can easily search for lots that you can buy and resell at a profit.

To add a seller to your Favourite Sellers list, click the <u>Add New Seller</u> link in the upper-left corner of the page. On the page that appears, type the seller's user ID. You may add a maximum of thirty sellers to your list.

My Account

Your eBay account summary page (see mine in Figure 3-11) lets you know how much you owe eBay and how much they will charge your credit card that month. This is a quick and easy way to check your last invoice, payments and credits, and your account status; all the links are located in one area.

Figure 3-11:
The My
Account
summary
page.

You can also access your PayPal account to see, for example, when deposits were credited to your chequing account. (For a complete picture of how to sign up and use PayPal, visit Chapter 13.)

Personal Information

The Personal Information page holds all the links to your personal information on eBay. This is where you can change your e-mail address, user ID, password, and credit card information and edit or create your About Me page. You can also change or access any registration or credit card information that you have on file on eBay on this page.

The Personal Information page has a link for adding a wireless e-mail address for your cell phone or Palm. What a great idea — eBay can send End of Auction notices right to your WAP-enabled (*wireless application protocol*) cell phone. The trouble is, sometimes these messages are sent out hours, or even days, after the listing ends. So don't count on always getting immediate updates.

eBay Preferences

A nifty feature of the eBay Preferences page is the opportunity to customize how you see your My eBay pages (see Figure 3-12). You can show as many as 200 items on these pages — very useful if you are running many auctions simultaneously.

Preferences	Show all
Use Preferences to change your eBay settings for email, payment, selling, etc. To view your preferences, click the "Show" link.	
Notification Preferences	
Receive emails, wireless notifications and other communications from eBay.	Edit
Selling Preferences	
Sell Your Item form and listings Edit your Sell Your Item form preferences and other listing preferences.	Show
Payment from buyers Edit Checkout, PayPal, and other payment options you offer Buyers.	Show
Shipping and discounts Offer shipping discounts on combined purchases.	Show
Promoting Similar Items on eBay Pages and Emails Promote your items in emails and on item pages.	Show
Logos and branding Display your logo and send customized emails to Buyers.	Show
Buyer requirements Block certain eBay users from buying your items.	Show
eBay Express Include qualifying items on eBay Express	Show
Ask seller a question Customize what is displayed on the Ask a Question page	Show

Figure 3-12:
Your eBay
Preferences
page.

You can also customize your eBay Sign In activities by clicking the Change link in the eBay Sign In Preferences section of the screen. You may as well select everything so that you won't be constantly hammered for your password while conducting business on eBay.

The About Me Page

If you're on eBay, you *need* an About Me page. We hate to harp on this, but eBay is a community, and all eBay members are members of that community. Checking out the About Me pages of people you conduct business with gives you an opportunity to get to know them. Because eBay is a cyberspace market, you have no other way to let prospective bidders know that you're a real person. Don't you shop at some stores just because you like the owners or the people who work there? The About Me page takes a first step toward establishing a professional and trusted identity on eBay.

The About Me page enables you to personalize your business to prospective bidders. (See Figure 3-13 for an example.) Your About Me page also becomes your About the Seller page if you have an eBay store.

Figure 3-13:
An excellent example of an About Me page from eBay member NobleSpirit!

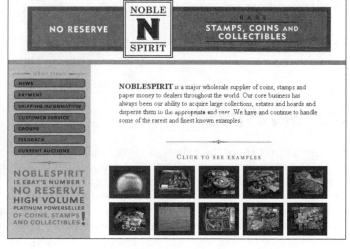

An About Me page also benefits you when you buy. Sellers usually like to know about their bidders to build confidence in their trading partners. If you've put up an About Me page, you're halfway there.

If you don't have an About Me page, put this book down and set one up immediately. It doesn't have to be a work of art; just get something up there to tell the rest of the community who you are. You can always go back later and add to or redesign it.

When you plan your About Me page, consider adding the following:

- ✔ Who are you? Where do you live?

- ✔ What are your hobbies? If you collect things, here's where to let the world know.

- ✔ Do you run your eBay business full-time? Part-time? Do you have another career? This is more integral information about you.

- ✔ What type of merchandise does your business revolve around? Promote it here — tell the reader why your merchandise and service are the best!

- ✔ Include a list of your current auctions and most recent feedback.

To create your page, click the Me icon next to any user's name, scroll to the bottom of the About Me page that appears, find the line that reads "To create your own About Me page, click here," and click. You can also click the About Me link on the Personal Information page on the My eBay page. Or, you can go to the following:

```
http://cgi3.ebay.ca/ws/eBayISAPI.dll?AboutMeLogin
```

Follow the simple preformatted template for your first page and then work from there.

eBay Seller Services

Most eBay users don't know the extent of eBay's seller-specific services. And sometimes sellers are so involved with their auctions that they don't take the time to find out about new helper tools. So we've gone deep into the eBay pond to dredge up a few excellent tools to help you with your online business. Even if you've used some of these before, it might be time to revisit them, because eBay has implemented quite a few changes in the past couple of years.

Bidder-management tools

Did you know that you don't have to accept bids from just anyone? Although many people include notices in their auction descriptions attempting to qualify bidders ahead of time, doing this doesn't always prevent the wrong people from bidding on your auction. Alas, part of the business of eBay is watching your bidders. With bidder-management tools, you can save yourself a good deal of grief.

Cancelling bids

You could have any number of reasons for wanting to cancel someone's bid. Perhaps an international bidder has bid on an auction in which you clearly state that you don't ship overseas. Here are a few other legitimate reasons for cancelling a bid:

- ✔ The bidder contacts you to back out of the bid; choosing to be a nice person, you let him or her out of the deal.

- ✔ The bidder has had a lot of negative feedback and hasn't gone through with other transactions that he or she has won.

- ✔ The bidder's identity can't be verified through e-mail or the phone.

- ✔ You need to cancel the auction for your own reasons (see the following tip, however).

We don't recommend cancelling an auction unless you absolutely have to because it's just bad business. People rely on your auctions being up for the stated amount of time. They may be planning to bid at the last minute, or they may just want to watch the action for a while. You may lose potential buyers by ending your listing early.

For whatever reason you're cancelling someone's bid, you should e-mail that person first and clearly explain why. Your bid cancellation appears in the auction's bidding history and becomes part of the auction's official record. For that reason, we recommend that you leave a concise, unemotional, one-line explanation on the cancellation form as to why you've cancelled the bid.

To get to the bid cancellation form, start on your My eBay All Selling page and scroll to Selling Links. You can also get to the cancellation form directly by typing the following in your browser:

```
http://offer.ebay.ca/ws/eBayISAPI.dll?CancelBidShow
```

End your listing early

Any number of reasons may make you decide to end a listing early. If any bids are on your auction before you end it, you'd be duty-bound to sell to the highest bidder. So before ending an auction early, it's polite to e-mail everyone in your bidder list explaining why you're cancelling bids and closing the auction. If an egregious error in the item's description is forcing you to take this action, let your bidders know whether you're planning to relist the item with the correct information.

After you've e-mailed all the bidders, you must then cancel their bids by using the bid cancellation form. For the link to this form, refer to the preceding section, "Cancelling bids."

Only after cancelling all bids should you go ahead and close your auction. To close your auction, use the <u>more</u> link at the bottom of your Selling Links box to get to the Managing Your Items box. Click the link there that says <u>End My Listing Early</u>. You can also go directly to

```
http://offer.ebay.ca/ws/eBayISAPI.dll?EndingMyAuction&ssP
ageName=STRK%3AMESRL%3A005
```

The following are some legitimate reasons for closing your auction:

- ✔ **You no longer want to sell the item.** Use this one carefully; your account may be subject to a Non-Selling Seller warning unless you really have a good reason. (See Chapter 4 for more details.)

- ✔ **An error occurred in the minimum bid or reserve amount.** Perhaps your wife said that she really loves that lamp and you'd better get some good money for it, but you started the auction at $1.00 with no reserve.

- ✔ **The listing has a major error in it.** Maybe you misspelled a critical keyword in the title.

- ✔ **The item was somehow lost or broken.** Your dog ate it?

Blocking buyers

If you don't want certain buyers bidding on your auctions, you can remove their capability to do so. Setting up a list of bidders that you don't want to do business with is legal on eBay. If someone that you've blocked tries to bid on your auction, the bid won't go through. A message will be displayed notifying the person that he or she is not able to bid on the listing and that they can contact the seller for more information.

You can block as many as 1,000 users from bidding on your auctions. However, we recommend that you use this option only when absolutely necessary. Situations — and people — change, and it's best to try to clear up problems with particular bidders.

You can reinstate a bidder at any time by going to the Buyer Blocking box and deleting the bidder's user ID at

```
http://pages.ebay.ca/services/buyandsell/biddermanagement
        .html
```

Pre-approving bidders

Suppose that you're selling a big-ticket item and want to pre-qualify your bidders. You can scroll through a user's bidding history to see the amounts they've successfully bid in previous auctions and whether the feedback on those transactions is okay. Although eBay gives you the tools, you still have to do the research to determine whether you deem particular bidders trustworthy enough to bid on your special auction. It's a good idea to build your own pre-approved bidder list; here's how:

- Decide which auction you want your bidders pre-approved for, and notify eBay of the auction number. Remember that your pre-approved bidder list is applicable only on an auction-by-auction basis.

- Ask bidders to pre-qualify for your auction by sending you an e-mail stating their intent to bid.

- Evaluate bidders' intentions and add the names of the bidders you feel comfortable with to the Pre-approved Bidders list. You can add approved bidders to the list right up to the close of the auction. Find the form here:

```
http://cgi3.ebay.ca/aw-cgi/eBayISAPI.dll?
        PreApproveBidders
```

Keep in mind that having a pre-approved bidder's list doesn't prevent people who are not on the list from bidding in your auction. When someone who isn't pre-approved tries to place a bid, eBay asks that person to contact you by e-mail for permission. After you've investigated the bidder to your satisfaction, you can add their name to your pre-approved bidder's list.

Feedback: Your permanent record

Just like your high school permanent record, your eBay feedback follows you forever. If you change your user ID, it's there. If you change your e-mail address, it's there.

When you click the feedback number next to a user's ID, the user's eBay ID card (see Figure 3-14) is displayed. The information shown will tell you a lot about your bidder.

Figure 3-14:
The eBay
feedback
page with
an overall
profile and
an ID card,
summariz-
ing recent
comments.

The most obvious tip-off to someone's feedback is the star you see next to the user ID. Different coloured stars are awarded as folks reach milestones in their feedback ratings. To decipher the star colours and see what they mean, click the <u>help</u> link and then type the word *star*.

Your feedback means a great deal to people who visit your auctions. By glancing at your feedback page, they can see

- Whether you're an experienced eBay user
- Your eBay history
- When you started on eBay
- How many bid retractions you've had in the past six months

This is valuable information for both the buyer and the seller because it helps to evaluate whether you're the type of person who would make a responsible trading partner.

Worried about negative feedback? If you do get saddled with a negative comment or two, there are a couple of ways exist for getting a negative feedback expunged from your record. You can file for mediation with SquareTrade (see Chapter 4 for how to do this). Or, if both you and the person who wrote the comment agree that it should be retracted, you can file for Mutual Feedback Withdrawal at

`http://feedback.ebay.ca/ws1/eBayISAPI.dll?MFWrequest`

Enter the item number of the auction in question and complete the rest of the form. eBay will ask the person who posted the feedback to allow its removal. If they agree, the comment will remain, but it will no longer impact your feedback score.

Leaving feedback

Everyone in the eBay community is honour-bound to leave feedback. Sometimes when you've had a truly dreadful experience, you hate to leave negative or neutral feedback, but if you don't, you're not helping anyone. The point of feedback is not to show what a great person you are, but to show future sellers or bidders where the rotten apples lie. So, when leaving feedback, be truthful and unemotional, and state just the facts.

Feedback is important, so you should be sure to leave some for every transaction you take part in. If several weeks have passed since you've shipped an item and you haven't heard from the bidder or seen any new feedback, drop that bidder an e-mail. Write a short note, such as "Thanks for your purchase. Are you happy with the item?" Also emphasize that you'll be glad to leave positive feedback after you've heard a reply, and ask for the same in return.

Never leave feedback on a sale until you're absolutely, positively sure that the buyer has received the product and is happy with the deal. Many inexperienced sellers leave feedback the minute they get their money, but experience can teach them that it ain't over till it's over. A package can get lost or damaged, or the bidder may be unhappy for some reason. A buyer may also want to return an item for no good reason, turning a seemingly smooth transaction into a nightmare. You get only one feedback per transaction, so use it wisely. You can't go back and say that the buyer damaged the product and then tried to return it.

eBay provides so many different links to leave feedback that we could probably write an entire chapter on it. But we don't want you to fall asleep while reading, so we'll only mention the most convenient methods:

- Go to your auction page and click the <u>Leave Feedback</u> link, which appears on the left.

- Click the number (in parentheses) next to the other user's name. When you're on that user's feedback page, click the <u>Leave Feedback</u> link.

- Click the <u>Leave Feedback</u> link next to the completed sale on your My eBay page.

- Visit the feedback forum (this link shows up on the bottom of every page) and click the link that shows you all pending feedback for the past 90 days. When you've fallen behind in leaving feedback, this is a super-fast way to catch up.

Responding to feedback

You may occasionally get feedback that you feel compelled to respond to. Did you know that you could? If the feedback is neutral or negative, we recommend that you cover yourself by explaining the situation for future bidders to see.

If you receive a negative feedback rating, a well-meaning admission of guilt would work. You could say something like this: "Unfortunately, shipping was delayed, and I regret the situation." Prospective bidders will see that you've addressed the problem instead of just letting it go.

To respond to feedback, follow these steps:

1. **In the My eBay Views box on your My eBay page, click the <u>Feedback</u> link under My Account.**

2. **On the feedback page, find Go to Feedback Forum at the top of the page, and click the <u>Reply to feedback received</u> link.**

   The Review and Respond to Feedback Comments Left for You page appears, as shown in Figure 3-15.

Figure 3-15: Review and respond to your feedback comments.

Feedback Forum: Reply to Feedback Received					

Enter a User ID or Item Number   Find Feedback

An important part of the Feedback Forum is sharing with the community your experience with other members. In addition to leaving feedback, there may be occasions where you want to reply to a comment another member has left in your member profile.

To reply to a comment, click the **Reply** link.

137 feedback received by ▓▓▓ from buyers and sellers(0 mutually withdrawn)   Page 1 of 6

Comment	From	Date	Item #	Action
Hope to have them at more of our aucitons in the future!! Thanks from: ▓▓	Seller ▓▓ (56313 ⭐)	12-Jun-06	4891275869	Reply
OUTSTANDING EBAYER!!! A++++ THANK YOU!!!	Seller ▓▓ (1301 ⭐)	08-Jun-06	9729066081	Reply
OUTSTANDING EBAYER!!! A++++ THANK YOU!!!	Seller ▓▓ (1301 ⭐)	08-Jun-06	9729065474	Reply
OUTSTANDING EBAYER!!! A++++ THANK YOU!!!	Seller ▓▓ (1301 ⭐)	08-Jun-06	9729066700	Reply
OUTSTANDING EBAYER!!! A++++ THANK YOU!!!	Seller ▓▓ (1301 ⭐)	08-Jun-06	9729066401	Reply
Thanks for the wonderful transaction	Seller ▓▓ (5304 ⭐)	03-Jun-06	7241975862	Reply
Fast payment, great communication, fast and friendly emails.	Seller ▓▓ (2290 ⭐)	31-May-06	9731034101	Reply
EXCELLENT EBAYER!!! A+++ THANK YOU AGAIN!!!	Seller ▓▓ (1301 ⭐)	30-May-06	9723871316	Reply
EXCELLENT EBAYER!!! A+++ THANK YOU AGAIN!!!	Seller ▓▓ (1301 ⭐)	30-May-06	9723871467	Reply
EXCELLENT EBAYER!!! A+++ THANK YOU AGAIN!!!	Seller ▓▓ (1301 ⭐)	30-May-06	9723871553	Reply

3. **Scroll to find the feedback comment that you want to respond to and click the <u>Respond</u> link.**

4. **Type your response, and then click the Leave Response button.**

Canadian sellers should be aware that they may be susceptible to more negative feedback as a result of slow shipping times. Many U.S. buyers often forget
that Canada and the U.S. are operating two independent postal systems and
find it hard to understand that it may take two weeks or more to receive their
purchase. Unfortunately, some buyers will leave negative feedback without
contacting the seller first. In those instances, polite communication with the
buyer is the key to having the negative feedback removed by mutual consent
(a great new eBay feature described earlier in this chapter). Although the
comment will remain, the red mark against your feedback is removed and
isn't calculated in your feedback score.

The eBay PowerSeller program

We're sure you've seen that big, giant PowerSeller logo on the auctions that
you browse. eBay PowerSellers are the users with the largest gross sales
users on eBay. The requirements for becoming a PowerSeller are as follows:

- ✔ You must have a gross monthly U.S. dollar volume of $1,000 (Bronze
  level); $3,000 (Silver level); $10,000 (Gold level), $25,000 (Platinum level),
  or $50,000 (Titanium level). To remain a PowerSeller, you must maintain
  your level's minimum gross sales for three months and keep current
  with all the other requirements. To advance up the PowerSeller chain,
  you must reach and maintain the next level of gross sales for an average
  of three months.

  If you miss your minimum gross sales for three months, eBay gives you a
  grace period. After that time, if you don't meet the minimum gross figures for your level, you may be moved down to the level below it or be
  removed from the PowerSeller program.

- ✔ You must have at least 100 feedback comments, and 98 percent must be
  positive. To calculate your feedback percentage, divide the number of
  positive feedback comments you have received by your total number of
  comments (negative and positive).

- ✔ You must have averaged a minimum monthly total of four listings for
  three months.

PowerSellers enjoy many benefits:

Level	Priority eSupport	Toll-free phone	Account Manager
Bronze	Yes	No	No
Silver	Yes	Yes	No
Gold	Yes	Yes	Yes
Platinum	Yes	Yes	Yes
Titanium	Yes	Yes	Yes

The best thing about being a PowerSeller is the awesome level of customer service you receive, called Priority eSupport. When a PowerSeller dashes off an e-mail to a special customer service department, a reply comes back at the speed of light — well, not quite, but pretty darn fast, compared to the service for regular eBayers.

eBay doesn't require you to show the PowerSeller logo in your descriptions when you become a PowerSeller. Some PowerSellers don't include the logo in their auctions because they'd rather be perceived as regular folks on eBay.

eBay auction software

eBay has developed a fantastic software program called Turbo Lister that is free and downloadable from the site. eBay also has an online Selling Manager to manage your auctions. For a breakdown of these software products and others that can ease the seller's burden, skip to Chapter 9.

eBay fraud protection

The minute an auction payment hits the mailbox, or the moment that a winner pays with an online payment service, eBay covers the buyer with its fraud protection program. The program covers the bidder for $200 U.S. of the final auction price, with a $25 deductible.

The eBay fraud protection plan covers only fraud, not lost or damaged packages. Canada Post, CanPar, UPS, and FedEx all offer insurance as an option. I guess this means that if your package arrives damaged and isn't insured, you may be out of luck. One exception to this problem is when the bidder has used PayPal, which has its own Buyer Protection program. PayPal provides strong remedies for buyers who are dissatisfied with the items they have purchased. The seller infrequently wins if the buyer can show that the item they received is "significantly not as described" — items damaged in transit will often fall into this category. The eBay fraud protection program covers eBay buyers only when they're defrauded, when the item is never shipped, or the item is significantly different from the auction description. eBay's fraud policy does *not* cover sellers for everything — so don't ship that item until you're darn sure the cheque has cleared! In most cases, due to the overwhelming popularity of PayPal, eBay's fraud protection program will defer to the PayPal program.

When you get down to the nuts and bolts of the eBay fraud protection program, it has a lot of "ifs." Buyers can apply only *if* they didn't pay with cash. Bidders, *if* they paid by credit card, need to first apply to their credit card companies to see whether the card company offers coverage. *If* the seller has a negative feedback rating, the insurance will not cover the bidder. Also, *if* the bidder has any more than three claims within a six-month period, they're out of luck.

eBay education

eBay offers many forms of training and education. No matter how advanced an eBay user you are, it's fun to take a refresher course on the basics. You can also find some cool online interactive tutorials as you make your way through eBay. Take a moment when you can to watch them — you might just see one or two new features that you didn't know about. More information about eBay education is available at the following address:

```
http://pages.ebay.ca/education/
```

eBay On the Road

The eBay travelling tent show tours across the country, hosting thousands of eBay members and spreading the word of eBay to the masses. At the show, you get a chance to meet some wonderful people who work for eBay and who enjoy answering questions. eBay On the Road follows three tracks:

- ✓ **Learn to Buy:** An introductory class designed for newbies
- ✓ **Basic Selling:** A beginning class for new sellers that lays out the basics so they can progress from there
- ✓ **Beyond the Basics:** A tutorial on eBay tools for advanced sellers

Live, in-person seminars

Education Specialists trained by eBay are located around the country and offer an advanced, personalized form of "The Basics of Selling on eBay." These instructors specialize in smaller classes so that you can readily get answers to all your questions. For the most part, Education Specialists are experienced sellers, and can help you get your eBay business off to a great start. You can visit the Education Specialists' Web site for a listing of instructors near you, or to see a schedule of future classes:

```
http://www.espcanada.com/ebay/index.asp
```

Online workshops

eBay also has ongoing online workshops that allow you to participate in a one-hour session through a chat screen. eBay records and archives many interesting classes in the eBay education area, so that you can see the classes after they premiere as well.

Chapter 4

Practising Safe Selling

• •

• •

A lot of *shoulds* exist in this world. You *should* do this and you *should* do that. We don't know who's in charge of the *shoulds,* but certain things just make life work better. You may or may not take any of the advice on these pages, but if you do, it will make your eBay business thrive with a minimum of anguish. If you've ever had an auction pulled by eBay, you know what anguish truly feels like.

In the real world, we have to take responsibility for our own actions. If we buy a television set for $25 from some guy selling them out of the back of a truck, who do we have to blame when we take it home and it doesn't work? You get what you pay for, and you have no consumer protection from the seller of a possibly "hot" TV. Responsible consumerism is every buyer's job. Lawsuit upon lawsuit gets filed — and some are won — when someone feels they've been ripped off. Our best advice is this: If you stay clean in your online business, you'll keep clean.

eBay is a community, and the community thrives on the following five basic values:

✔ We believe people are basically good.

✔ We believe everyone has something to contribute.

✔ We believe that an honest, open environment can bring out the best in people.

✔ We recognize and respect everyone as a unique individual.

✔ We encourage you to treat others the way that you want to be treated.

eBay is committed to these values, and it says so right on its Web site. eBay believes that community members should "honour these values — whether buying, selling, or chatting." So *should* we all.

Is What You Want to Sell Legal?

Although eBay is based in California and therefore must abide by California law, sellers do business all over the world. Therefore, items sold on eBay must also be subject to the laws of every other jurisdiction. As a seller, you're ultimately responsible for the legality of the items you sell and the way that you transact business on eBay. Yes, you're able to sell thousands of different items on eBay. But do you know what you aren't allowed to sell on eBay?

The eBay User Agreement outlines all eBay rules and regulations regarding what you can and can't sell, as well as all other aspects of doing business on eBay. If you haven't read the agreement in a while, do so. You can find it at the following address:

```
http://pages.ebay.ca/help/policies/user-agreement.html
```

The policies in the eBay User Agreement can change from time to time. As an active seller, you should make sure that you're notified of any changes. To request that you be notified when eBay makes changes to the User Agreement, or, for that matter, to control any correspondence you receive from eBay, follow these steps:

1. **In the My eBay Views section of the My eBay page, click the <u>eBay Preferences</u> link under My Account. Then, click the <u>Edit</u> link next to Notification Preferences.**

2. **Sign in with your user ID and password.**

   The Change Your Preferences page appears.

3. **Scroll down to the Legal and Policy Notifications area (see Figure 4-1). Check or un-check any option you want to invoke.**

   To receive important information that may affect how you run your auctions, be sure that you click the User Agreement Changes option and Privacy Policy Changes option.

Figure 4-1:
The Legal
E-mails and
Policy
Notifications
area of the
Change Your
Preferences
form.

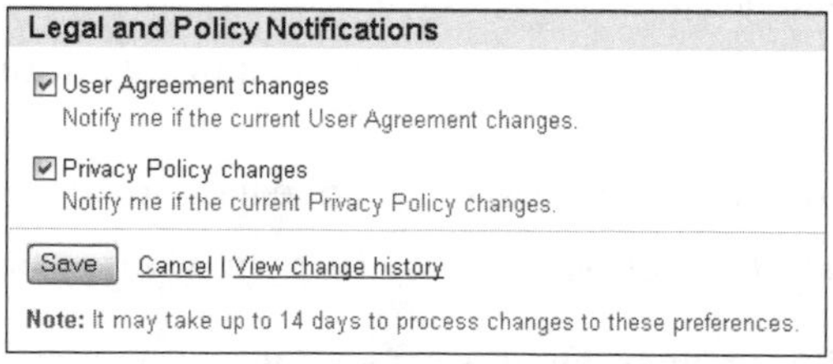

Legal and Policy Notifications

☑ User Agreement changes
   Notify me if the current User Agreement changes.

☑ Privacy Policy changes
   Notify me if the current Privacy Policy changes.

[Save]   Cancel | <u>View change history</u>

Note: It may take up to 14 days to process changes to these preferences.

By now, you should have a firm grasp of the rules and regulations for listing auctions (if not, check out Chapter 2). But in addition to knowing the rules for listing items, you must consider the items themselves. In this section, we detail the three categories of items to be wary of: prohibited, questionable, and infringing. Some items are banned, period — others fall in a grey area. You're responsible for what you sell, so you'd better know what's legal and what's not.

You may think you can give away a regulated or banned item as a bonus item with your auction instead of selling it. Think again. Even giving away such items for free doesn't save you from potential legal responsibility.

Prohibited items

A *prohibited item* is banned from sale on eBay. You can't sell a prohibited item under any circumstance. Take a look at the following list. A little common sense tells you there's good reason for not selling these items, including liability issues for the seller. (What if, for example, you sold alcohol to a minor? That's against the law.)

Here are some of the items prohibited as of this writing, so don't try to sell 'em on eBay:

Alcohol*

Animals and wildlife products

Catalogues (current issues) and Web sales

Counterfeit currency or stamps

Counterfeit items, replica, and unauthorized copies

Credit cards

Drugs and drug paraphernalia

Electoral votes

Federal, provincial, or locally prohibited plants and seeds

Firearms, ammunition, replicas, and militaria

Fireworks

Government IDs and licences

Human parts and remains**

Lock-picking devices

Lottery tickets

Mailing lists and personal information

Mod chips or game enhancers

Police-related items

Postage meters

Prescription drugs and devices

Recalled items

Satellite and cable TV descramblers

Stocks and other securities***

Stolen property

Surveillance equipment

Tobacco

Travel****

*Alcohol may be allowed if the value of the item lies in the collectible container (bottle), which exceeds the alcohol's retail price. The item should not be currently available at a retail outlet. The auction should state that the container has not been opened, and the seller should be sure that the buyer is over 21.

**Skulls, skeletons, and items that may contain human hair are permissible as long as they're used for educational purposes.

***Old or collectible stock certificates may be sold provided that they're cancelled or are from a company that no longer exists.

****All sellers listing airline tickets, cruises, vacation packages, or lodging must be verified by Square Trade.

Check the following address for updates:

```
http://pages.ebay.ca/help/policies/items-ov.html
```

Questionable items

A *questionable* item is, by definition, iffy — and determining whether or not you can sell it is tricky. Under certain circumstances, you may be able to sell the item on eBay. To fully understand when and if you can list a questionable item, visit the links that we highlight in Table 4-1.

Note: All URLs listed in Table 4-1 begin with `http://pages.ebay.ca/help/policies/`

Table 4-1	Questionable Items and Where to Find the Rules Regulating Them
Can I Sell This?	*Go Here to Find Out**
Alcohol	`/alcohol.html`
Artifacts	`/artifacts.html`
Autographed Items	`/autographs.html`
Batteries	`/batteries.html`
Contracts and tickets	`/contracts.html`
Electronics equipment	`/electronics.html`
Event tickets	`/event-tickets.html`
Food	`/food.html`
Hazardous materials	`/hazardous-materials.html`
International trading — sellers	`/international-sellers.html`
Items or entertainment for mature audiences	`/mature-audiences.html`
Offensive material	`/offensive.html`
Pesticides	`/pesticides.html`
Police-related items	`/police.html`
Pre-sale listings	`/pre-sale.html`
Slot machines	`/slot-machines.html`
Used clothing	`/used-clothing.html`
Used medical devices	`/medical-devices.html`
United States embargoed goods from prohibited countries	`/embargo.html`
Weapons and knives	`/weapons.html`

* All URLs begin with `http://pages.ebay.ca/help/policies/`

When alcohol becomes collectible

Many people collect rare and antique bottles of liquor or wine. For instance, we recall a bottle of Korbel champagne designed by Frank Sinatra that sold on eBay in 1998. Korbel bottles have featured artwork by designer Nicole Miller and comedienne Whoopi Goldberg, as well as designs by Tony Bennett, Frank Sinatra, and Jane Seymour.

People also collect Jim Beam bottles, Dug decanters, and miniature liquor bottles that are even more valuable when they're full. You *can* sell these on eBay as long as you fulfill the following requirements:

- ✔ The value of the item is in the collectible container, not its contents.

- ✔ The item must not be available at any retail outlet, and the container must have a value that substantially exceeds the current retail price of the alcohol in the container.

- ✔ The auction description should state that the container has not been opened, and that any incidental contents are not intended for consumption.

- ✔ The buyer of collectible alcohol bottles must be of lawful age in both their own and the

seller's jurisdiction — the seller should take steps to ensure that this requirement has been met. (The legal age to buy alcohol varies from province to province and from state to state; a safe guideline is 21 years old.)

Potentially infringing items

Potentially infringing items follow a slippery slope. If you list a potentially infringing item for sale, you may conflict with existing copyrights, trademarks, registrations, or the like. Get the idea? These items are prohibited for your own protection.

Items falling under the *potentially infringing* category are generally copyrighted or trademarked items, such as software, promotional items, and games. Even using a brand name in your auction as part of a description (known as keyword spamming) may get you into trouble.

The Chanel-style purse

We recall a seller who listed a quilted leather women's purse that had a gold chain strap, which was described as a Chanel-style purse. Within two hours of beginning the auction, the seller received an informational alert from the eBay listing police. Although the purse was described reasonably, it was deemed to be a potentially infringing item. The use of the brand name *Chanel* caused the auction to come under the violation of keyword spamming. In its informational alert, eBay described the violation:

"Keyword spamming is the practice of adding words, including brand names, which do not directly describe the item you are selling. The addition of these words may not have been intentional, but including them in this manner diverts members to your listing inappropriately."

Oops! You can see how an ingenuous listing was actually a violation of policy. Think twice before you add brand names to your auction description. Thankfully, the eBay police judge each violation on a case-by-case basis. Because the seller's record was clear, she merely got a reprimand. Had the violation been more deliberate, she may have been suspended.

To see the Chanel USA statement on violations, visit its About Me page. The violations apply to many items that may be listed on eBay. Here's the link:

```
http://members.ebay.ca/about
     me/chanelusa/
```

Keyword spamming manipulates the eBay search engine by including an unrelated item in the listing for a copyrighted or trademarked item and then diverting bidders to an auction of other merchandise. This is frustrating to the person trying to use the search engine to find a particular item and unfair to members who've properly listed their items.

Keyword spamming can take many forms. Some merely mislead the prospective bidder while others are legal infringements. A few of the most common are

- Superfluous brand names in the title or item description
- Auction titles or item descriptions including phrases like "not brand X"
- Improper trademark usage
- Lists of inappropriate keywords
- Drop-down boxes
- Hidden text — white text on a white background or hidden text in HTML code. The white text resides in the auction HTML, so it shows up in the search but is not visible to the naked eye. Sneaky, eh?

The eBay Verified Rights Owners program

eBay can't possibly check every auction for authenticity. But to help protect trademarked items, it formed the Verified Rights Owners (VeRO) program.

Trademark and copyright owners expend large amounts of energy to develop and maintain control over the quality of their products. If you buy a "designer" purse from a guy on the street for $20, it's probably counterfeit, so don't go selling it on eBay.

eBay works with VeRO program members to educate the community about such items. They also work with verified owners of trademarks and copyrights to remove auctions that infringe on their products. If eBay doesn't close a suspicious or blatantly infringing auction, both the seller and eBay are liable for the violation.

To become a member of the VeRO program, the owners of copyrights and trademarks must supply eBay with proof of ownership. To view the VeRO program information and download the application for membership, go to

```
http://pages.ebay.ca/help/community/notice-infringe2.pdf
```

Note: eBay cooperates with law enforcement and may give your name and street address to a VeRO program member.

To view a list of other VeRO members' About Me pages, go to

```
http://pages.ebay.com/help/community/vero-aboutme.html
```

To get the latest on eBay's keyword spamming policy, go to

```
http://pages.ebay.ca/help/policies/keyword-spam.html
```

Repeating various un-trademarked keywords can get you into trouble as well. eBay permits the use of as many as five synonyms when listing an item for sale. A permissible example of this might be: purse, handbag, pocketbook, satchel, and bag. Adding many un-trademarked keywords would cause the auction to come up in more searches.

Trading Violations

Both buyers and sellers can commit trading violations by attempting to manipulate the outcome of an auction or sale. Many of the violations aren't necessarily buyer- or seller-exclusive, but apply to both. Regardless of the nature of a violation, such behavior violates everyone who's part of the eBay community.

As a valued member of the eBay community, it's partially your responsibility to look out for violations so that eBay continues to be a safe community in which to do business. Should you see a violation, report it immediately to the eBay Security Centre (see "eBay's Security Centre" later in this chapter). In this section, we detail many common violations so that you can be on the lookout for them — and we'll just assume that you won't be committing any yourself.

We need to be watchdogs to protect the other users in our community. Don't feel like a squealer if you make a report. Remember that it takes just one rotten apple to spoil the basket, so if you see a violation, do your duty and report it.

When the competition doesn't play fair

Unfortunately, you may sometimes encounter non-community-minded sellers who interfere with your auctions or sales. This interference can take on several forms, such as sellers who illegally drive up bids or "steal" bidders.

Again, should you fall victim to bad deeds, be sure to report the bad-deed-doer's actions immediately. (Check out "Taking Action: What to Do When Someone Breaks the Rules" later in this chapter.) eBay will take some sort of disciplinary action. Penalties range from formal warnings and temporary suspension to indefinite suspension. eBay reviews each incident on a case-by-case basis before passing judgment.

Shill bidding

Shill bidding is the practice of placing a bid on an item to artificially inflate the final value. Every eBay user, whether buyer or seller, hates this because it undermines community trust. Shill bidding is immoral, illegal, and not something to be toyed with!

The practice of shill bidding has been a part of auctions from their beginnings. To prevent the suspicion of shill bidding, people in the same family, those who share the same computer, and folks who work or live together should not bid on each other's items.

Should you ever even dream of participating in any sort of auction manipulation, we urge you to think twice. You might think you're smart by using another e-mail address and username, but that doesn't work. Every time you log onto your ISP, your connection carries an IP address. So no matter what name or computer you use, your connection will identify you. eBay can use this number to track you through its site.

Shill bidders are fairly easy to recognize, even for the eBay user who isn't privy to things such as IP addresses. By checking a bidder's auction history, you can easily determine a user's bidding pattern. A bidder who constantly bids up items and never wins is suspicious.

Spurious sellers often employ shill bidding to increase the number of bids on an item, making it seem like a very sought after item. This doesn't mean that all auctions with numerous bids are products of shill bidding — it means that, due to the herd mentality, hotly contested auctions are often more desirable and pull in lots of extra bids. Rogues recognize this, and will often bid on their own auctions to create a false impression.

Transaction interference

Have you ever received an e-mail from an eBay seller offering you an item that you're currently bidding on for a lower price? This is called *transaction interference,* and it can prevent sellers from gaining the highest bid possible.

Transaction interference also occurs when a troublemaker who "has it in" for a particular seller e-mails bidders participating in the seller's current auctions to warn them away from completing the auction. Tales of woe — and much bitterness — usually accompany such e-mails. If a bidder has a problem with a seller, that bidder can — and should — both file a report with eBay and leave negative feedback for that seller. Sending a barrage of e-mails about a seller you dislike can be perceived as libel, and isn't a safe thing to do. If you receive an e-mail that sounds like what we've described, ignore its message and report it to eBay.

Transaction interception

They say the criminal mind is complex; when it comes to *transaction interception*, it certainly is! Transaction interception occurs when an eBay scalawag keeps track of closing auctions and then, when the auction is finished, e-mails the winner as if the scalawag were the seller. The e-mail often looks official and is congratulatory, politely asking for payment. Interceptors usually use a post office box for such mischief. This behavior is more than a trading violation — it's stealing.

The best way to protect yourself from intercepting miscreants is to accept payments through a payment service, such as PayPal, that offers a <u>Pay Now</u> link. For more about setting up a payment service account, see Chapter 13.

Fee avoidance

Basically, *fee avoidance* is just what it sounds like — the practice of manipulating the eBay system to evade paying appropriate fees. You can commit fee avoidance in many ways — sometimes without even realizing it. Read this section carefully so that you don't fall into this violation by mistake.

You're guilty of fee avoidance if you

- Use information that you've received from an eBay member's contact page in an attempt to sell a listed item off the system

- Close your auction early because a user e-mailed you to offer to buy an item you were auctioning and you accepted the offer

- End your auction before it legally closes by canceling bids so that you can sell the item to someone who has e-mailed you with an offer of a higher price

- Use an eBay member's contact information to sell an item from one of your closed auctions off the eBay site in which the reserve wasn't met

- Offer duplicates of your item to the unsuccessful bidders in your auction, unless you use the Second Chance option

Take a look at the discussion on listing policies in Chapter 2 for other violations that might fall into this category.

Non-selling seller

Refusing to accept payment from the winning bidder or refusing to complete the transaction is simply wrong. Very, very bad form! You are legally and morally bound to complete any transaction into which you enter.

Baaad bidders

Nothing can ruin a seller's day like a difficult bidder, such as someone who asks questions that are clearly answered already in your auction description, or someone who asks you to close the auction so that he or she can buy the item offline. Sheesh — you'd think no one read the rules. From the non-paying bidder to the unwelcome and shady, you might encounter the buyers we describe here.

Bid shielding

When two or more eBay members work together to defraud you out of real auction profits, they're guilty of *bid shielding*. One member, lets call him Joe, places an early bid on your item with a proxy bid. Immediately, the accomplice, we'll call her Sharon, places a very high proxy bid to drive it to the max or beyond. If legitimate bidders bid, they only ratchet up the second bidder's bid — they don't outbid the high bidder's proxy. When the auction is coming to a close, the high bidder (Sharon) retracts her bid, thereby granting the winning bid to her buddy (Joe), the original low bidder. The ultimate point of bid shielding is that it increases the bid to such a high level that normal bidding by authentic bidders is discouraged.

This illegal bidding process is not only used to get bargain-priced merchandise, but also to drive bidders away from competitors' auctions by artificially inflating the high bid level.

Unwelcome bidder

In this business, you might think that you couldn't possibly regard anyone as an *unwelcome bidder,* but you just might. Remember how you painstakingly explain the terms in your auction description? That's lost on people who don't take the time to read those descriptions or choose to ignore them. Consider the following examples of bad bidder behaviour:

✔ You state in your description that you ship only within North America, but you see a bidder with an e-mail address that ends in .jp (Japan), .au (Australia), .uk (United Kingdom), or whatever.

✔ You state in your description that you don't want bidders who have a negative feedback rating of more than one negative in a six-month time span. Still, someone fitting that description bids on your auction.

✔ You decide to cancel a bid for one of the previous two reasons, but the bidder continues to bid on your auction.

✔ You've blocked a particular bidder (see Chapter 3) who's now using a secondary account to bid on your auctions.

If you encounter any of the previous situations, contact eBay immediately to report the unwelcome bidder (see "eBay's Security Centre" later in this chapter). Still, in the first two cases, culprits might be inexperienced users. Before bringing in the authorities, you may want to e-mail each bidder immediately to clarify what they don't understand about the eBay system. For example, in the first case, re-emphasize your shipping policy. In the second, make sure the bidder understands the legal connotations of making a bid.

Non-paying buyer

If there's one thing that just ain't tolerated on eBay, it's a non-paying buyer (NPB). eBay reminds all bidders, before they place a bid, that "If you are the winning bidder, you will enter into a legally binding contract to purchase the item from the seller." You'd think that was clear enough, but sadly, many people out there think that bidding on eBay is a game. If you see a high bidder on your auction who has negative or a very low number of feedback comments, dropping them a line to reiterate eBay policy never hurts.

How you, as a seller, communicate with the high bidder is also important. Many times, a well-written, congenial, businesslike e-mail can cajole the bidder (who is most likely a decent person) into sending payment. To see some samples of correspondence that get the job done, drop by Chapter 12.

As long-time sellers on eBay, we've come to recognize that certain categories of products may be more susceptible to non-paying buyers. Marsha has been selling and buying on eBay for more than five years. During that time, she's had to file only five non-paying buyer alerts. (For how to do this, see the steps a bit later in this section.) She's noticed that non-paying buyers tend to bid on certain types of items, and after you've seen some NPBs, you'll get an idea of which items to stay away from. Gas-powered scooter, video game, MP3 player and Beanie Baby sellers all seem to get more than their fair share of NPBs. On the other hand, serious collectible or business items infrequently cause the same problems.

To reduce the number of non-paying buyers, eBay has established that all eBay users are indefinitely suspended if they have three non-paying buyer alerts filed against them. An *indefinite suspension* is a suspension of members' privileges to use the eBay site for more than sixty days, with no definite reinstatement date. If users attempt to re-register on eBay and under a new ID, they risk being referred to the authorities for criminal prosecution. (The authorities change depending on the sale particulars. Within Canada, complaints could be forwarded to the RCMP or the provincial or local police. In the U.S., complaints could be forwarded to U.S. postal inspectors, the FBI, or local police. eBay determines what level of enforcement it prefers to work with depending on the circumstances.)

Before filing a non-paying buyer alert, give the winner a second chance to send payment. If you still don't receive payment, follow these steps to recoup your Final Value fees and be eligible for the non-paying buyer relist credit:

1. **As soon as you have a winner, contact him or her.**

2. **If you don't hear from the winner within three days of the auction's end time, send a payment reminder:**

   a. **Go to the My eBay Views area on the My eBay page. Under Selling, click the <u>Sold</u> link.**

   b. **Click the <u>View Payment Status</u> link next to the pertinent auction.**

   c. **Click the <u>Send a Payment Reminder</u> link.**

   You may send a reminder between three and thirty days after the auction closes.

If you still don't hear from or receive money from your high bidder, swing into action by filing an Unpaid Item Dispute.

You must file the dispute no earlier than seven days and no later than forty-five days after the auction has ended.

Follow these steps to file an Unpaid Item Dispute:

1. **In the My eBay Views area of your My eBay page, click the <u>Dispute Console</u> link. In the Dispute Console page that opens, click the <u>Report an Unpaid Item</u> link.**

2. **Supply eBay with the item number for the unpaid transaction.**

    Once the number is supplied to eBay, click <u>Continue</u> and the process is under way. eBay will e-mail the buyer and suggest that they communicate with you in an effort to resolve the dispute.

Eight days after filing an Unpaid Item Dispute, you may apply for a Final Value Fee credit if you have not heard from the buyer, or if payment has still not been received (see Figure 4-2). To receive your Final Value Fee credit, click the Dispute Console link in the My eBay Views area of the My eBay page. You can select the transaction in question by clicking on the <u>View Dispute</u> link.

On the View Dispute screen that opens, you are offered a choice of three options to resolve the dispute:

✔ **We've completed the transaction and we're both satisfied.**

    With this option, the seller does not receive a Final Value Fee credit and the buyer does not receive an Unpaid Item strike.

✔ **We've agreed not to complete the transaction.**

    With this option, the buyer does not receive an Unpaid Item strike, the seller receives a Final Value Fee credit, and the item is eligible for a relist credit.

✔ **I no longer wish to communicate with or wait for the buyer.**

    With this option, the buyer receives an Unpaid Item strike, the seller receives a Final Value Fee credit, and the item is eligible for a relist credit.

You can view the entire Unpaid Item process in greater detail here:

```
http://pages.ebay.ca/help/tp/unpaid-item-process.html
```

You must file for your Final Value Fee credit within sixty days of the auction's close.

When you close a dispute and file for the Final Value Fee credit, you also have the option of blocking the non-paying buyer from your auctions.

If you work things out with the winner, eBay sends an e-mail to that person notifying them that the dispute has been resolved, and that no Unpaid Item strike has been levied against them. This is important to buyers because on eBay, as in baseball, three strikes and yer out!

View Dispute

ⓘ **Resolution Tip:** Avoid threats and insults, as they almost always backfire. See some suggestions for communicating with buyers.

Transaction: Instant Door Screen - Cottages, RV's, Home 36 x 80 NIB (#6008196246) sold to ▒▒▒▒ on 13-Jun-2006 filed on 20-Jun-2006.

Dispute status: Other party has not responded.

Enter your response

500 characters left. No HTML or javascript allowed.

[Submit Response]

Previous messages

eBay   20-Jun-06

An Unpaid Item dispute has been opened for the following item: Instant Door Screen - Cottages, RV's, Home 36 x 80 NIB (#6
Reason given for Unpaid Item: We have both agreed not to complete the transaction.
Buyer actions reported by seller: The buyer purchased item in error.

Figure 4-2:
The View
Dispute
screen.

Not knowing who's who

Most eBay members prefer to be contacted through their user IDs rather than exposing their e-mail addresses for all to see. However, you must supply eBay with accurate contact information. When you register on eBay, its software immediately checks the area code of your primary phone number against your postal code to verify that the two numbers are from the same city. If you've supplied incompatible codes, the eBay servers will recognize that and ask you to re-input the correct ones. Be aware that eBay will reveal your contact information to any buyer or seller who requests it, as long as the two of you are involved in a transaction. On the flipside, you too can find other members' phone numbers and e-mail addresses by following these steps:

1. **Click the Advanced Search option on any eBay page.** The Search page appears.

2. **Select Find Contact Information in the Members section on the left of the page.**

3. **Input the transaction number and the member's User ID and click the Search button.**

   Within moments, eBay send e-mails with the other person's contact information to both you and the other member. You can't request another user's information without eBay sending them your own.

To be on the up-and-up on eBay (and to keep others honest, too), make sure that you

✔ **Provide eBay with your current phone number:** If a bidder can't reach you by phone, you're in violation of the False Contact Information policy and you *can* be disciplined.

Don't be lured by phishing

Fraudulent e-mail has become a common occurrence. Without warning, a request for confirmation of your personal details arrives from a source claiming to be your bank, your Internet service provider, your credit card company, PayPal, or even eBay. These e-mails are *phishing* for your personal information and passwords to defraud you of your money or your identity.

Phishing e-mails look just like legitimate e-mails from the company that holds your data. If you follow the links in the e-mail to "update" your information, you'll be brought to a Web page that duplicates a legitimate Web page. Sneaky!

How can you protect yourself from these scammers?

✔ **Look for personalization.** Your bank, eBay, or PayPal will address the e-mail to your proper name, and not, for example, to *Dear PayPal Member.*

✔ **Never follow the link in the e-mail to the Web site in question.** Open up a new browser and type the URL that you normally use to enter the site. After you log in, you'll know whether there's actually a problem with any of your information.

✔ **Always look for secure Web site information.** If you're logged onto a secure Web site, the URL will begin with `https://` rather than the standard `http://`. You'll also see a lock symbol in the status bar at the bottom of your browser window.

✔ **Regularly log onto your Internet accounts.** By keeping in regular contact with your providers, you'll know about issues with your accounts before they have a chance to cause a problem.

✔ **Report suspicious e-mail to the company they are mimicking.** If you receive an e-mail supposedly from PayPal, forward the e-mail to `spoof@paypal.com`. Forward an e-mail claiming to be from eBay to `spoof@ebay.com`.

You can take things into your own hands by checking the questionable message's underlying code. Using Internet Explorer or Outlook, open the e-mail, right-click it, and choose View Source. When you view the HTML code, you may be able to see the actual URL of the site that would get your response if you clicked the link, as shown in the figure.

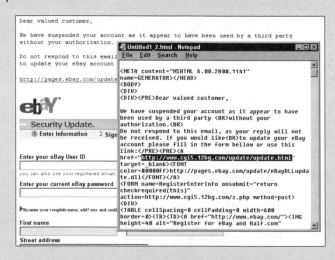

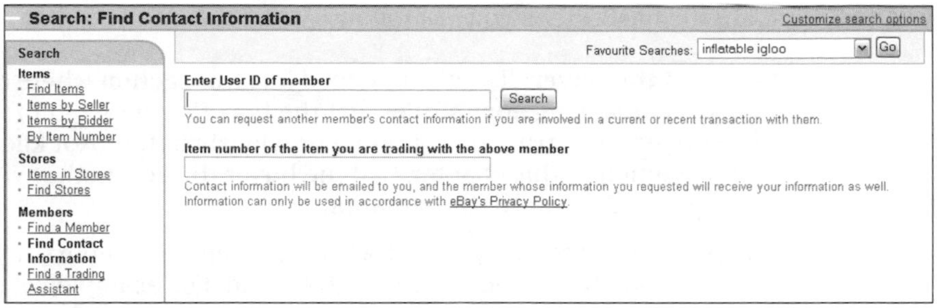

Figure 4-3:
eBay's Find
Contact
Information
form.

- ✔ **Keep your e-mail address current with eBay:** If your bidder continually gets e-mail bounced back from your e-mail address, you could get in big trouble.

- ✔ **Report all underage bidders:** If you suspect that a bidder in one of your auctions is underage (younger than 18, by eBay's rules), eBay may suspend or close the account. Underage bidders may be using their parent's credit card without permission, or perhaps even a stolen card, to become an eBayer.

- ✔ **Verify e-mail allegedly sent by an eBay employee:** If someone e-mails you claiming to work for eBay, be sure to check the e-mail carefully before replying. When eBay employees conduct personal business on the site, they have to use a personal, non-company e-mail address for their user registration — it's a company policy. If you suspect someone is impersonating an eBay employee for harmful purposes, contact the Security Centre.

Taking Action: What to Do When Someone Breaks the Rules

You need to take a business-like approach to problems on eBay, whatever those problems may be. In previous sections of this chapter, we have outlined eBay's many rules, as well as the bad deeds — and bad seeds — you're likely to encounter while doing business on eBay.

As a member of the eBay community, you have a responsibility to know and abide by eBay's rules and regulations. This responsibility includes notifying eBay when someone tries to sell an illegal item (refer to "Is What You Want to Sell Legal?," earlier in this chapter) or reporting it when you suspect someone is committing fraud. Looking out for bad apples is an integral part of keeping eBay a safe and lucrative place to do business. In this section, we discuss who to call when someone breaks the rules and what to do when a third party is necessary.

Here are the basic steps you can follow:

- ✔ **Contact the buyer:** If you're involved in a transaction where the other party is breaching eBay's rules, get the buyer's contact information by following the instructions outlined previously in the "Not knowing who's who" section of this chapter. Call the buyer to see whether you can diplomatically resolve the situation.

- ✔ **Seek out eBay security:** Use the Security Centre to report any shady actions, policy violations, or possible fraud. For example, let someone know if you suspect that a community member is impersonating an employee, or if you're aware of a suspicious auction. Likened to the front desk at your local police station, eBay's Security Centre report form gets results. Click the <u>Security Centre</u> link that appears at the bottom of most eBay pages. Then, click the <u>Report a Problem</u> link. Alternatively, you can go directly to

```
http://pages.ebay.ca/securitycentre/
```

  You'll find an all-purpose security form on this page to help you in your eBay transactions. After they are filled out, these forms are routed to the right department for action.

- ✔ **Apply for online resolution:** SquareTrade offers online dispute resolution services and mediation for eBay members. See the following section on how to involve SquareTrade.

- ✔ **Contact Reporting Economic Crime Online (RECOL):** If you feel you've become a victim of fraud, be sure to file a report through eBay channels first. But to really bring down wrath on your nemesis, report them to RECOL by calling 1.888.495.8501.

- ✔ **Contact local law enforcement:** If you become the target of a cheque-bouncer, contact the local law enforcement agency in your bidder's hometown. eBay will supply any information necessary to help the authorities clear the world of fraud. Provide eBay with the name of the local law enforcement agency, its telephone number, and the case number or police report number for the incident. Also include the offending user's ID and the auction item's number. Criminal penalties exist for those that purposely write rubber cheques.

SquareTrade to the rescue

Threats of suing each other, filing fraud charges, and screaming back and forth don't really accomplish anything when you're in the middle of an eBay dispute. Back in the olden days of eBay when you weren't able to respond to feedback, users threw negative feedback back and forth willy-nilly — needless to say, this resulted in some vile flame wars.

These days, you have SquareTrade, one of the best services available to you as a seller. When you're selling regularly on eBay, you will undoubtedly run into a disgruntled buyer or two. SquareTrade, a Web-based dispute resolution company, waits in the wings to pull you out of the most difficult situations.

If you find yourself in an inexorably difficult situation with one of your bidders and you'd like to take the situation up a notch, go to the following page, shown in Figure 4-4:

```
http://www.squaretrade.com/cnt/jsp/odr/overview_odr.jsp?m
            arketplace_name=ebay&campaign=EBY_OD_2
```

After you click the <u>File a Case</u> link on this page and answer a few questions about the situation, SquareTrade generates and sends an e-mail to the other party containing instructions on how to respond. From this point, the case information and all related responses appear on a private, password-protected page on the SquareTrade site.

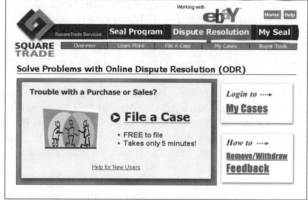

Figure 4-4:
Square
Trade
Dispute
Resolution
start page.

SquareTrade offers three main services to eBay members, which we discuss in this section:

- ✔ Online dispute resolution through direct negotiation
- ✔ Professional mediation
- ✔ SquareTrade seal

Online dispute resolution

Online dispute resolution is a fast, private, and convenient way to resolve your auction disputes — and it's *free*. Both you and the buyer work together through the SquareTrade Web-based system. Online dispute resolution (ODR) works whether your transaction is in Canada, the United States, or another country. Every day, more than 400 buyers file cases with the ODR service.

The SquareTrade Web-based negotiation tool is automated, and you and the other party get to communicate on neutral ground. When (and if) the buyer responds, the two of you can work out the situation online and without human interaction. If you're unable to reach a solution, you need to move on to professional mediation (see the following section).

SquareTrade states that problems are usually solved in ten to fourteen days, and 85 percent of all cases are resolved without going to mediation. The process will run a quicker course if both people in the transaction are at their computers and answer e-mail during the day.

Participation in ODR is voluntary. If a buyer is set on defrauding you, he or she probably isn't going to engage in a resolution process. If you get no response to your ODR, report your situation to the Security Centre.

Professional mediation

If push comes to shove, and in auction disputes it certainly may, you might have to resort to professional mediation. A *mediator,* who is neither a lawyer nor a judge but an impartial professional, works with both parties to bring the situation to a convivial conclusion. This service is available for a reasonable fee of $29.95 USD per issue.

If both parties participating in dispute resolution agree to mediation, each party communicates with only the assigned mediator, who communicates with each party individually through the same case page. Your case page shows only your communications with the mediator. The mediator reviews both sides of the story to find a mutually acceptable solution to the problem. He or she tries to understand the interests, perspectives, and preferred solutions of both parties, and tries to help both parties understand the other's position.

The mediator is there to disperse highly charged emotions commonly associated with disputes, and recommends a resolution only if both parties agree to have the mediator do so. By using the mediation service, you do not lose your right to go to court if things aren't worked out.

SquareTrade seal

A SquareTrade seal lets prospective bidders know that you deal with customers promptly and honestly. Should you choose to get a SquareTrade seal, the symbol is inserted into your auctions automatically. (Each seal icon contains a digital watermark with an encrypted expiration date.) You can use the seal in your auctions only if SquareTrade approves you.

Your Square Trade seal approval is based on several points:

- ✓ **Identity verification.** SquareTrade will verify your identity using the information you provide through a third party.

- ✓ **Superior selling record.** SquareTrade runs your eBay feedback history through five individual checks. It has an advanced system based on its extensive experience of dispute resolution that allows it to evaluate the quality and quantity of your eBay feedback.

- ✓ **Dispute resolution.** SquareTrade checks whether you have a history of resolving disputes.

- ✓ **Commitment to standards.** You pledge to meet the SquareTrade standards regarding selling and to respond to disputes within two business days.

After you are given a seal, you must continue to uphold SquareTrade standards and maintain an acceptable feedback rating. If approved, the nifty little personalized seal icon will appear on each of your auctions. Users can click the icon to access their own Seal Display page on the SquareTrade site.

A study conducted by SquareTrade of 623 SquareTrade seal members compared their feedback for the four months after they became a seal member to their feedback in the prior four months. They found that once a seller became a SquareTrade seal member, negative feedback was reduced by 43 percent. The ratio of negative to positive feedback went from 1 in 60 before certification to 1 in 280 after.

The SquareTrade seal (shown in Figure 4-5) currently costs around $9.50 USD per month — an affordable and good idea if you're in this business for the long run. The seal tells prospective buyers that you care about good customer service and don't tolerate fraudulent activity. It also says that you abide by the SquareTrade selling and customer service standards, which dictate that you will

- ✓ Disclose your contact information and credentials

- ✓ Provide clear and accurate descriptions of goods and services in your auctions

- ✓ Clearly disclose pricing, including all applicable fees

- ✓ List clear policies on after-sales services, such as refunds and warranties

- ✓ Maintain privacy policies

- ✓ Conduct transactions on secure sites only

- ✓ Respond to any disputes filed against you within two business days

Figure 4-5:
The Square
Trade seal.

To provide an additional security feature for your buyers, you can bond your auctions. Doing so also protects you. See Chapter 10 for more information.

eBay's Security Centre

The Security Centre is eBay's version of the RCMP. By rooting out evil-doers, it serves and protects — and puts up with an immense amount of e-mail from users.

If you see an item on eBay that isn't allowed (refer to "Is What You Want to Sell Legal?," earlier in this chapter), be sure to make eBay aware of the auction. The Community Watch team then takes over and investigates the item. When necessary it will end the auction and warn the seller.

When you click the Security Centre link (at the bottom of most eBay pages), you'll see the page shown in Figure 4-6. Click the Report a Problem button to make sure justice is served.

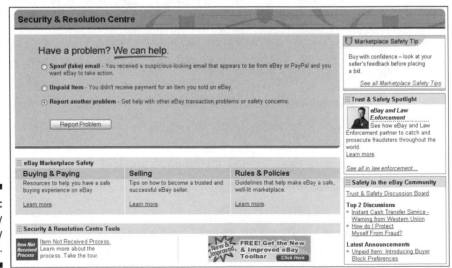

Figure 4-6:
The eBay
Security
Centre.

You then fill out a step-by-step customer service report, which is shown in Figure 4-7.

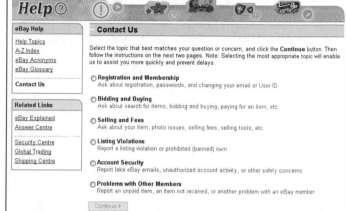

Figure 4-7:
The
Customer
Service
reporting
form.

Alternatively, you can find the Security Centre customer service reporting form at

```
http://pages.ebay.ca/help/contact_us/_base/index.html
```

Chapter 5

Your Very Own eBay Store

*I*f you're doing well selling your items on eBay auctions, why open a store? Have you used the eBay Buy It Now feature in one of your listings? Did it work? In an eBay store, all items are set at a fixed price and are kept online for at least thirty days or until you cancel them. So your eBay store is kind of like a giant collection of Buy It Now featured items. Get the idea?

When you're opening a store, you have just three main rules to remember: location, location, location. Say you were opening a brick-and-mortar store. You could open it in the corner strip mall, a shopping center, or somewhere downtown, depending on where you think it would do best. Location also affects online stores. You have tons of locations to choose from when planning your online store, including online malls (when you can find them) and sites such as Amazon.com, Yahoo!, and, of course, eBay.

You do have to pay rent for your online store, but opening and running a store online isn't nearly as expensive as a store in the real world. No overhead costs like electrical and maintenance bills exist. Plus, the ratio of rent to sales makes the decision to start an online store a much easier financial decision, and your exposure can be huge.

In this chapter, we show you step-by-step how to hang out your virtual shingle and get business booming by opening your own eBay store.

Online Stores Galore

Amazon.com, Yahoo!, and eBay make up the "big three" of online stores. They're the top locations and get the most visitors. According to comScore Media Metrix, in April 2004 these sites garnered an astounding number of *unique* visitors (that counts all of one person's visits to the sites just *once* a month):

- **Yahoo!: 113,190,000 unique visitors.** Because it's a search engine, many people must hit this site ten times a day — though it seems they rarely visit the auctions.
- **eBay: 60,016,000 unique visitors.**
- **Amazon.com: 39,083,000 unique visitors.** This site sells books, CDs, DVDs, and lots of other merchandise, but how many of these people are actually going to the zShops?

No doubt feeling competition from Yahoo! and Amazon, in July 2001, eBay launched its own feature for sellers who wanted to open their own stores. Fixed-price stores were a normal progression for eBay in its quest to continue as the world's marketplace. And eBay stores make sense: They're a benefit to all current eBay sellers as they open the doors to new shoppers who don't want to deal with auctions.

eBay is an online store that specializes in selling *your* stuff, not *theirs*. It doesn't stock a stick of merchandise, and it isn't in competition with you. eBay not only attracts a staggering number of visitors to your store — it also offers you the most reasonable rent. To see what we mean, check out Table 5-1.

Table 5-1	Online Starter Store Monthly Costs		
	eBay	*Yahoo Shopping*	*Amazon zShops*
Basic rent	$15.95	$39.95	$39.99
Listing fee	$0.02	0	$0.10 after 40,000 items
High final value fee	8%	1.5%	$0.025 + 5%

For more information on current rankings, search for eBay on the comScore Web site at www.comscore.com. This site keeps a monthly scorecard of unique visitors to the top fifty Internet sites. Visit it now and then to see where the online shopping industry is going.

You probably don't need a rocket scientist to convince you that having an eBay store is a way better bargain than setting up shop elsewhere (see Figure 5-1). Used to eBay auctions? Don't be deterred — Buy It Now items are just as easy to handle. Review prices and rules before opening your store here:

```
http://pages.ebay.ca/storefronts/seller-landing.html
```

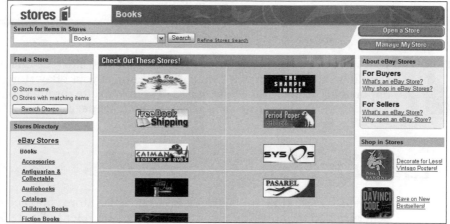

Figure 5-1: eBay Stores opening page.

Naming Your eBay Store

You've decided to take the plunge and open an eBay store. Do you have an eBay user ID? Have you thought of a good name for your store? Your store name doesn't have to match your eBay user ID, but they're more recognizable if they relate to each other. You can use your company name, your business name, or a name that describes your business. We recommend that you use the same name for your eBay store that you plan to use in all your online businesses. Creating an identity (or a *brand*, as the pros call it) that customers will come to recognize and trust is valuable.

Mind your underscores and hyphens

If you want to use your eBay user ID for your store name, you can — unless it contains a hyphen (-) or an underscore (_). Remember how eBay recommends that you break up words in your user ID with a dash or an underscore? Uh oh, that's no good for an eBay store name. Marsha's in that situation. Her user ID is marsha_c; without the underscore, it translates into a user ID that someone else has already taken! Even though marshac hasn't been used since 1999, someone else has it, which means she can't use it. (marsha_c is probably a crummy name for a store anyway!)

A favorite seller of ours — mrswarren — realized that mrswarren isn't a good name for a store either. So she named her store *Pretty Girlie Things,* which suits her merchandise to a T.

Your online eBay store should not replace your Web site (see Chapter 8); it should be an extension of it. When people shop at your eBay store, take the opportunity to make them customers of your Web site through your store's About the Seller page (the same as your About Me page on eBay). Good deal!

Setting up Shop

Now you can get down to business. Go to the eBay Stores hub and click the Sellers link in the upper-right corner of the screen (refer to Figure 5-1). This takes you to the Seller's hub of eBay Stores, as shown in Figure 5-2. Click any of the links you see here, and you get the eBay company line about how good an eBay store can be for your business. You already know that, so skip the propaganda and get started (but don't forget to check for any policy changes that may affect your store's operations).

Before you click that link to open your store, ask yourself two questions:

- ✔ **Can I make a serious commitment to my eBay store?** A store is a commitment. It won't work for you unless you work for it. You have to have the merchandise to fill it and the discipline to continue listing store and auction items. Your store is a daily, monthly, and yearly obligation. When you go on vacation, you need someone else to ship your items or your customers may go elsewhere. You can close your store temporarily, but eBay will reserve your store name for only 30 days. After that, you have to come up with a new name (and your competition may have taken over your famous store name!).

Figure 5-2:
The Seller's welcome page to eBay Stores.

> ✔ **Will I work for my eBay store even when I don't feel like it?** You have to be prepared for the times when you're sick or just don't feel like shipping, but orders are waiting to be shipped. You have to do the work anyway; it's all part of the commitment.

eBay gives you the venue, but you have to make your mercantile efforts a success. If you can handle these two responsibilities, read on!

If you're serious and ready to move on, click the <u>Open a Store</u> link in the upper-right corner of the page (refer to Figure 5-2). Because you're always signed in on your home computer (presuming that's where you're working), eBay escorts you to a page reminding you that eBay stores share the same User Agreement you agreed to when you began selling on eBay. Click the <u>Continue</u> button to access the Build Your Store pages (see Figure 5-3).

You need to make a few decisions to create a good store. Read through the following sections carefully before you start building your personal retail space. When you're ready, follow these steps:

1. Choose a colour theme.

eBay provides some elegant colour and graphics themes. You can change the colour scheme or layout of your store later, so choose one of the sample layouts to use for now — later you can go hog-wild and design a custom masterpiece. eBay offers fourteen of these clearly organized layouts, either predesigned or with easily customizable themes. Don't select something overly bright and vibrant; you want a scheme that's easy on the eyes to create a comfortable viewing — and selling — environment.

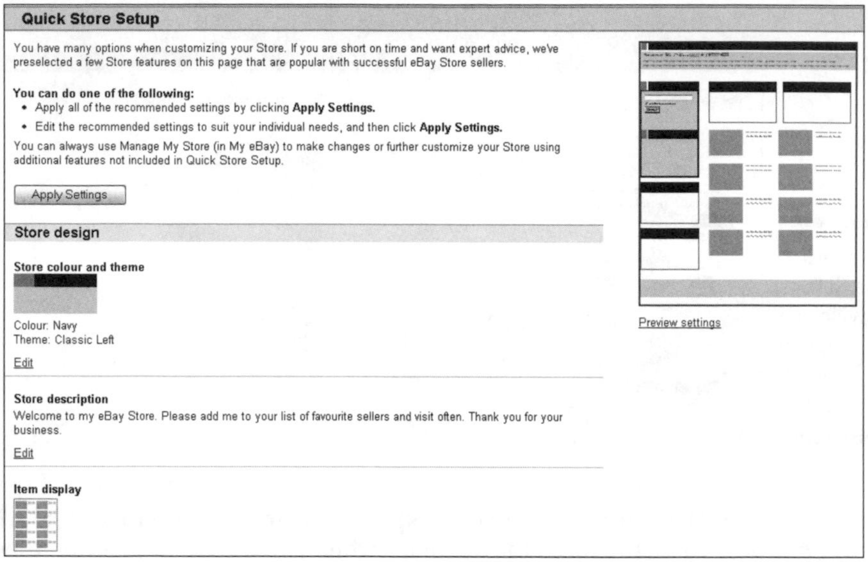

Quick Store Setup

You have many options when customizing your Store. If you are short on time and want expert advice, we've preselected a few Store features on this page that are popular with successful eBay Store sellers.

You can do one of the following:
- Apply all of the recommended settings by clicking **Apply Settings**.
- Edit the recommended settings to suit your individual needs, and then click **Apply Settings**.

You can always use Manage My Store (in My eBay) to make changes or further customize your Store using additional features not included in Quick Store Setup.

[Apply Settings]

Store design

Store colour and theme

Colour: Navy
Theme: Classic Left

Edit

Store description
Welcome to my eBay Store. Please add me to your list of favourite sellers and visit often. Thank you for your business.

Edit

Item display

Preview settings

Figure 5-3:
Select the
store theme.

You have the option of selecting a store theme that doesn't require you to insert a custom logo or banner. We highly discourage this. You need to establish a unifying brand for your online business.

2. Click Continue.

3. Type your new store's name (see Figure 5-4).

You've decided on a store name, right? Your eBay store name can't exceed thirty-five characters. Before you type it, double-check that you aren't infringing on anyone's copyrights or trademarks. You also can't use any permutation of eBay trademarks in your store's name.

4. Type a short description of your store.

When we say short, we mean *short.* This paragraph is 308 characters — you have only *300* characters to give a whiz-bang, electric description of your store and merchandise. You can't use HTML coding to doll up the description, and you can't use links. Just the facts, please, and a little bit of dazzle.

This description is hugely important. Choosing the right keywords can make a big difference in the number of customers that are directed to your store as they search eBay stores and descriptions. Also, if the store header contains your description (the Classic style themes offer this), search engines such as Google and Yahoo! will use that text for key-words to classify and list your store.

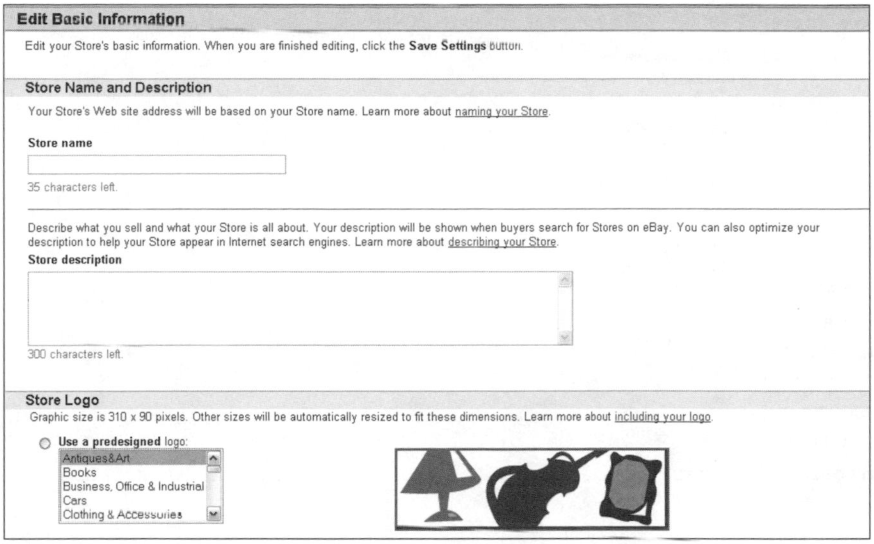

Edit Basic Information

Edit your Store's basic information. When you are finished editing, click the **Save Settings** button.

Store Name and Description

Your Store's Web site address will be based on your Store name. Learn more about <u>naming your Store</u>.

Store name

35 characters left.

Describe what you sell and what your Store is all about. Your description will be shown when buyers search for Stores on eBay. You can also optimize your description to help your Store appear in Internet search engines. Learn more about <u>describing your Store</u>.

Store description

300 characters left.

Store Logo

Graphic size is 310 x 90 pixels. Other sizes will be automatically resized to fit these dimensions. Learn more about <u>including your logo</u>.

○ **Use a predesigned** logo:

Antiques&Art
Books
Business, Office & Industrial
Cars
Clothing & Accessories

Figure 5-4:
Type your
store's
name and
description.

Write your copy ahead of time in Word. Then, highlight the text and use the program's *Word Count* feature by clicking Tools➪Word Count. You can see the number of words in your selection and the character count with spaces to be sure your text fits.

5. Select a graphic to jazz up the look of your store.

You can use one of eBay's clip art-style banners or create a custom one, up to 310 x 90 pixels in size. If you use one of eBay's graphics, you must promise (hand over heart) that you won't keep it there for long — be creative! (See the text after this set of steps for info on designing your own graphics — or hiring someone else to do it.)

6. Click Continue.

Now you're getting somewhere. At this point, your eBay store looks something like what you see in Figure 5-5. You are about to open an eBay storefront (drum roll, please).

7. Sign up for the basic store ($15.95 a month) , and click the Start My Subscription Now button.

Your store is now live on the Internet with nothing up for sale — yet.

8. Click the link "Manage My eBay Store" from your "My eBay" page to get in the trenches and customize your store further.

Subscribe to Stores: Choose Your Subscription Level

Choose your subscription level:

○ **Basic Store** (C $15.95 per month, free 30-day trial*)
An ideal solution for lower-volume sellers who already sell on eBay but want to take the next step with an easy-to-use, customizable Web store.

stores

○ **Featured Store** (C $64.95 per month, free 30-day trial*)
All of the benefits of a Basic Store plus more advanced customization and business tools. A more comprehensive solution for small to medium-sized sellers who want to aggressively grow their online business.

○ **Anchor Store** (C $649.95per month)
All of the benefits of a Featured Store plus increased marketing support, making it an optimal solution for larger-volume sellers who are looking for maximum exposure on eBay.

Special Offers

○ **Basic Store and Selling Manager** (C $15.95 per month, free 30-day trial*)
Subscribe to a Basic Store and get Selling Manager **free**.

More special offers...

* Free trial for first-time subscribers only.

Choose a Store Name

35 characters remaining.
Learn more about naming your Store.

[Continue >] Cancel

Figure 5-5:
Verify your choices and become a store owner.

If you're wondering what category your store falls under on the eBay Stores homepage, it's all up to you. eBay files your store items as you list them in the standard eBay category format. For example, if you have six books listed in the Books: Fiction and Nonfiction category and five items in the Cameras & Photo category, your store will be listed in both of those categories. Your custom store categories (read on) will be used to classify only items you are selling in your store.

If you use one of eBay's prefab graphics, people shopping in your eBay store will know that you aren't serious enough about your business to design a simple and basic logo. This is what we were getting at in Step Five. After many years of experience in advertising and marketing, we can tell you that a custom look will beat out clip art any day. Your store is special — put forth the effort to make it shine.

If you have a graphics program, design a graphic with your store's name. Start with something simple; you can always change it later when you have more time. Save the image as a GIF or a JPG, and upload it to the site where you host your images (your own Web site, your ISP, or a hosting service).

A bunch of talented graphic artists make their living selling custom Web graphics on eBay. If you aren't comfortable designing, search eBay for *web banner* or *banner design*. Graphic banners on eBay sell within the $10 to $40 USD range — certainly worth the price in the time you'll save.

Running Your Store

You can customize your store at any time by clicking the <u>Seller Manage Store</u> link, which is at the bottom of your store's page and in the upper-right corner of the eBay Store's hub page. The page shown in Figure 5-6 appears, with headings describing important tasks for your store.

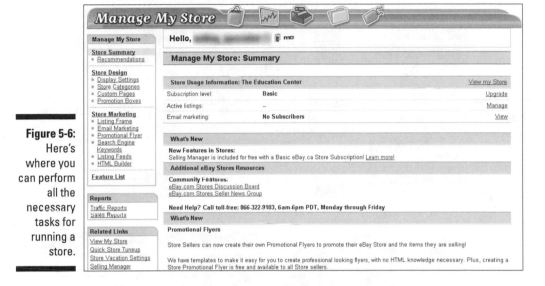

Figure 5-6: Here's where you can perform all the necessary tasks for running a store.

Store design and marketing

In the Store Editing/Branding list, you can perform the major tasks required for your store:

✔ **Store Builder:** You can go back to Store Builder (the original store setup area) to change the name of your store or the theme of your pages. You can also change the way your items are displayed: Gallery view (as in Figure 5-7) or List view (as in Figure 5-8). Neither view is inherently better, but we like the Gallery view because it shows the thumbnails of items being offered.

In Store Builder, you can also select the order in which your items will sort. Choose between Highest priced first, Lowest priced first, Items ending first, or Newly listed first. We like Items ending first for sorting, so that buyers can get the chance to swoop in on items closing soon.

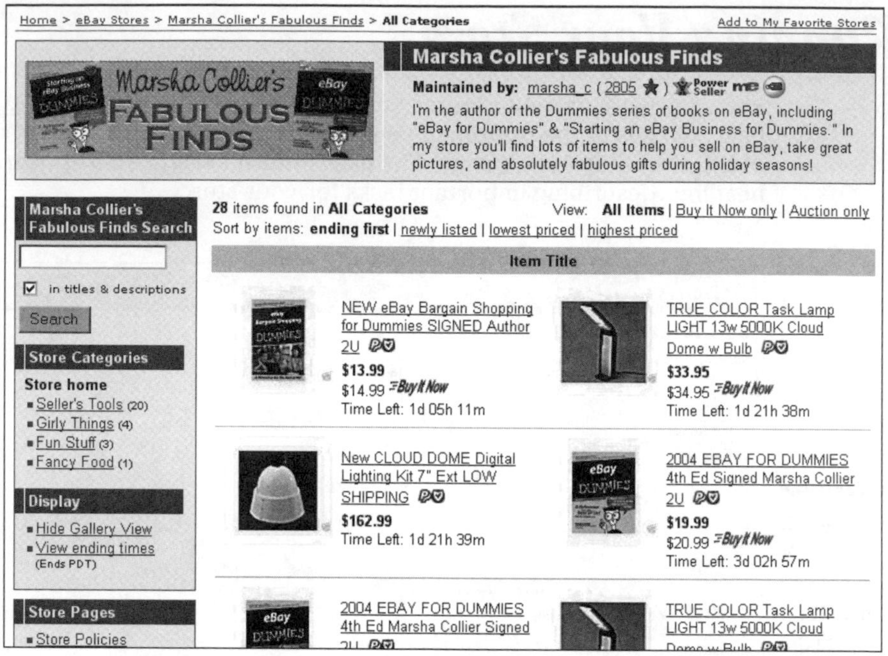

Figure 5-7: An eBay store in Gallery view.

Figure 5-8: Noblespirit's eBay store in list view.

 Custom pages: Most successful eBay sellers hav
Figure 5-9 shows you the one for my store. Whe
page, eBay supplies you with a choice of layou
New Page link to choose a template, as shown
out if you don't know HTML; eBay helps you
HTML generator, the same one offered on the b

Figure 5-9:
An eBay
store
policies
page.

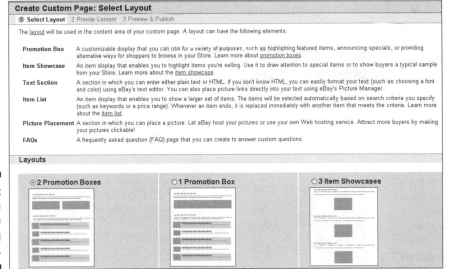

Figure 5-10:
eBay Store
page
customizing
templates.

Following are some important policies to include:

- Indicate what locations you ship to.

- Specify the taxes you plan to collect. If you don't collect Provincial Sales Tax, GST, or HST, leave the tax area blank. If you do, indicate the proper amount of sales tax. Most provinces don't require you to collect sales tax unless the sale is shipped to your home province. See Chapter 15 to verify your provincial sales tax regulations.

- State your customer service and return policy. Explain how you will handle refunds, exchanges, and so on. If you're a member of SquareTrade (see Chapter 4), mention here that you subscribe to its policies. Be sure to include whatever additional store information you think is pertinent.

You can also set up a custom homepage for your store, but it's not a popular option. Letting your visitors go right to the page that lists what you're selling is a better idea, don't you think?

✔ **Custom categories:** Here's where you really make your store your own. You may name up to 300 custom categories that relate to the items you sell for your store. These categories can then be broken down further into sub-categories.

✔ **Custom listing header:** Do this. Don't ask questions, just do it. The custom listing header display is one of the best tools you can use to bring people into your store. Click the link and select the Show option to display your custom listing header on all your eBay auctions and fixed-price sales. This will encourage shoppers to visit your eBay store when they browse your eBay listings.

When customizing, be sure to include your store logo as well as a store search box. In Figure 5-11, you can see how the store header looks at the top of an eBay listing.

Figure 5-11:
Super promotion for your eBay store: add a link from your auctions and allow customers to search the store.

Create an About the Seller page

If you haven't already created an eBay About Me page, do it now! The About Me page becomes the About the Seller page in your store. This page is a primary tool for promoting sales. (See Chapter 3 for more on About Me pages.) You can put an About Me page together in about ten minutes — max — with eBay's handy and easy-to-use templates!

Manage your items

We've all listed items on eBay, so we don't plan on boring you with another tutorial on how to do it. (We do give you some listing and photo image tips in Chapter 11, though.) Following are the most important ways that listing an item in your store differs from listing an auction on eBay:

- ✔ You have to assign each item in your store to one of the categories that you designated while setting up your store. If your new item falls into a category that you haven't defined, you can always go back to your store and add a category or put it in the eBay-generated Other Items category. (You can have up to 300 categories.)

- ✔ You don't place a minimum bid or a reserve price on your store items because everything you list in your eBay store is a Buy It Now item.

- ✔ You can keep your listings up in an eBay store for 30 days or post that they are GTC (good till cancelled). The listing fees are shown in Table 5-2.

- ✔ Finally, you can buy something for six cents!

Table 5-2	Store Inventory Insertion (Listing) Fees
Item Value	*Insertion Fee*
C$0.01-C$29.99	C$0.06 per 30 days (or every 30 days if Good Till Close option selected)
C$30.00 and higher	C$0.12 per 30 days (or every 30 days if Good Till Close option selected)

The items you list in your eBay store don't *necessarily appear* in a title search on the regular eBay site. Whether the items do or not is determined by the number of regular auction or fixed-price items that are similar and already available on the site. Your store items *will* be seen if one of your buyers does a Seller or Stores search from the eBay Search page. That's why you pay only two cents per listing for thirty days. You *must* put a link in your auctions to your eBay store (see the next section) to tell the auction browsers that you have more stuff for them that they "can't find in a regular eBay search."

Promotions

Some excellent new ways to promote your store have been added to eBay. As a store owner, you have access to promotional tools that other eBay sellers can't use. The most valuable tool that you've now got your hands on is cross promotions — and it's free of charge! The Cross-Promotion box appears after a buyer purchases or bids on an eBay seller's item, directing them to more items for sale.

The beauty of having a store is that the cross-promotion box appears *twice*: once with your regular listings and again, with a different assortment of items (if you want), after someone buys an item. Best of all? You get to select which items are shown with your individual auctions.

Figure 5-12 shows you a cross-promotion box that appears when someone views one of Marsha's auctions.

Figure 5-12:
A cross promotion in an eBay auction.

You can set up the promotions so that they default to show other items from related store categories, or you can go in and set them up yourself for individual auctions. Again, every listing has two sets of options: one for when a user views your listings, and the other for when someone bids or wins your item.

Marketing Your Wares

eBay has even more tempting features that you can use to spruce up and draw attention to your store items. They work exactly like the one eBay offers for your auctions (see Chapter 10). When choosing whether to use these features, remember that your eBay store items only appear when someone searches in the eBay stores. Because eBay store items don't appear in a regular eBay search, we recommend you use the Gallery display option at this time for maximum results. Check out Table 5-3 for a rundown of fees for these optional features.

Table 5-3	eBay Optional Store Features	
		Price
Feature	**30 days**	**or Good 'Til Cancelled**
Feature item in store search	$25.95	$25.95 / 30 days
Item subtitle	$0.03	$0.03 / 30 days
Gallery	$0.01	$0.01 / 30 days
Listing Designer**	$0.12	$0.12 / 30 days
Highlight title	$5.90	$5.90 / 30 days
Boldface title	$1.20	$1.20 / 30 days

**Listing Designer fees are waived if you subscribe to Selling Manager Pro.*

Making a Sale

From the buyer's point of view, shopping at an eBay store is much different than winning an auction. eBay stores feature fixed-price sales; the buyer will get the merchandise as soon as you can ship it, instead of waiting for the auction to run its course. Even though your auctions show up on your store's homepage, all regular listings in your eBay store are Buy It Now items.

When a buyer makes a purchase from an eBay store, here's what happens:

1. The buyer clicks the Buy It Now button on the listing page. The Review Payments page appears, where the buyer can review the purchase. This page contains the shipping amount that you specified when you listed the item.

2. The buyer's shipping information is included on the page by default, but that buyer can change it later if they want the item shipped to another address — that happens a lot around Christmas. When eBay notifies you that a sale has been made, you have all the information you need. You don't have to scurry around looking for the return address on the envelope when the payment arrives.

3. The buyer reviews the transaction and then clicks the Confirm button. The information about the sale is e-mailed to you, and the buyer receives confirmation of the sale.

Your eBay store will be an essential backup to your auctions. You can put out-of-season items, accessories for the items you sell actively, and even consignment items in your store between relisting so that they are always available for sale. Because having an eBay store is so inexpensive, you have to make only a few sales per month to pay for it — and when your sales start to build, your efforts will be greatly rewarded!

Part II
Setting Up Shop

The 5th Wave   By Rich Tennant

Did I mention that I ran across a balloon animal storefront on eBay recently?

In this part . . .

Your hobby is what you love, and we're betting you have a houseful of duplicate items — the perfect stuff to sell on eBay! Or why not buy from other collectors locally and become a specialist on eBay? Or perhaps you'd like to sell inventory from an existing business or from others on consignment. Or maybe you are ready to start buying wholesale merchandise from importers or manufacturers.

As you can see, the options are countless. In this part, we talk about how to find merchandise to sell, the best ways to sell it, and how your ever-important Web site can help.

Chapter 6

Stocking the Store

· ·

In This Chapter

▶ Going to dollar stores

▶ Checking out closeout wholesalers

▶ Joining discount club stores

▶ Prowling garage sales

▶ Researching going-out-of-business sales

▶ Going, going, gone: Traditional auctions

▶ Visiting resale shops

▶ Finding freebies

▶ Selling salvage

▶ Buying by the case

▶ Searching eBay

▶ Selling by consignment

· ·

*Y*ou're probably wondering just how you can possibly get enough merchandise to list as many as twenty items a day. You're thinking that enough sources can't possibly exist out there to fulfill that kind of volume. Success on eBay isn't easy. Many hours and a good deal of perspiration — along with loads of inspiration — are necessary to make a good living selling online. You *can* do it — if you apply the same amount of effort to acquiring merchandise as you do to selling.

 One of our mottoes is "Buy off-season, sell on-season." You can get great bargains on winter merchandise in the heat of summer. January's a great time to stock up on holiday decorations, and the value of those trendy vintage aluminum trees doubles in November and December. Cashmere sweaters, too! In the winter, you can get great deals on closeout summer sports merchandise. It's all in the timing.

How are you going to acquire the products you need? We've spent hours, days, weeks — okay, even months — trying to work out the best ways to stock an eBay business. Ultimately, this depends on you, your personality, and the type of merchandise you plan to sell. We've tried many of the tactics that we discuss in this chapter, as have some eBay sellers that we know. Here we pass on all the secrets and caveats each of us has discovered along the way.

Dollar Stores

Dollar stores come in all shapes and sizes and can now be found in virtually every corner of the country. They can be filled with junk or treasure, and it takes a practised eye to separate the wheat from the chaff. Try going in with a teenager, and see whether he or she reacts to any of the items for sale. Sometimes only one in five visits works out, but you'll know when you see the item — and at these prices, you can afford to go deep! Stock at these stores doesn't stay on the shelf for too long; if you pass on an item, it may not be there when you return for it the next day. Maybe another savvy eBay seller picked up the values.

Closeout Wholesalers

Closeout wholesalers are bricks and mortar businesses that generally make their living buying and reselling a wide variety of distressed inventory from manufacturers, importers and distributors at fire sale prices. Be prepared to buy in larger quantities as they will usually have a minimum order requirement of several hundred dollars. For the most part, a closeout wholesaler will sell only to other businesses and will not sell to the general public. This means you'll have to get your provincial resale license before they will consider selling to you (you can find out more about resale licenses in Chapter 15).

Goren Sales

Goren Sales Ltd. is one of Canada's largest and oldest closeout companies. Their business is to buy and resell manufacturer and importer overstocks, end-of-line items, and heavily discounted premiums. It's a great place to stock up on smaller-ticket items — most of their merchandise is priced under ten dollars. You will need a reseller's permit (again, see Chapter 15) to do business with Goren Sales Ltd., and they do have a $500 minimum order, but the savings make it worthwhile. Buying from this company is made simple by shopping on their Web site at www.gorencatalogue.com.

RetailBuyers.ca

Another great online source for heavily discounted merchandise is www.retailbuyers.ca. Registration with a reseller's permit is required to gain entrance, but once inside, you'll find items for sale at a discount from the wholesale price. Most of what's available on RetailBuyers.ca is end-of-season or closeout stock. Many of Canada's leading manufacturers and importers of gift and tableware offer merchandise on the site. Because all dealings are first-hand with the manufacturer or importer, using the site is also a great way to make valuable business connections. Each company tends to have its own minimum purchase requirements.

Offerings on RetailBuyers.ca run the gamut from tabletop and linens to giftware and candles. Through this site, Bill connected with one importer to purchase thousands of dollars' worth of Seraphim Classics collectable angels, still in their original packaging. He bought the whole lot for a mere 25 percent of the retail selling price. All of the figurines were long retired but were in very hot demand by North American collectors who missed them the first time around. The entire inventory of angels took months to sell, but the healthy profit it brought was worth it.

When shopping the RetailBuyers.ca site, remember that most of the items shown are in very limited supply. Visit frequently to get the best deals before they are snapped up by another eBay seller.

Although some closeout wholesalers allow you to shop online, it doesn't hurt to talk to them directly. A casual conversation to discuss the types of merchandise you prefer to purchase may go a long way toward securing early notice when new items arrive. Being friendly with personnel at the order desk can translate into profits when you get first dibs on fast-selling merchandise.

Discount Club Stores

Warehouse stores originally made their mark by selling items in bulk to large families, clubs, and small businesses. In case you haven't noticed, these stores have recently upscaled and now sell just about anything you could want. Their shelves are brimming with current merchandise ripe for the picking.

Sam's Club

Sam's Club has begun expansion into Canada. In case you haven't heard the name before, it's a part of the Wal-Mart empire that was created to compete with the large "members only" discount chain Costco. If you're fortunate enough to have one close by, it's a great place to buy new on-season merchandise at a fraction of the retail price that can often be resold.

Costco

Believe it or not, one day Marsha was wheeling her cart around Costco to buy her monthly ration of meat, and right in front of her was a huge display with women jumping and grabbing at the merchandise. She glanced above to read the sign: Fendi Baugette Handbags $199.99. With the help of her daughter, she elbowed her way through the crowd (in a not-too-ladylike fashion) and saw the purses, regularly priced at $450, stacked like lunchmeat. In those days, the Baugette was new, and sold on eBay for around $350. Needless to say, she bought all that her credit cards could handle.

In the first edition of this book, Marsha talked about a special on the Costco Web site, www.costco.com, for a new *Snow White & the Seven Dwarfs* DVD. For $18.49, you could pre-order the Snow White DVD and get a second Disney DVD for *free*. When there's an offer like this, you can often sell two items on eBay for the price of one. A smart eBay seller would buy a case at this price and hold some for future sales. It seems that Disney movies are released for a limited time only. For a period of time after Costco offered the two-for-one deal, the original *Snow White & the Seven Dwarfs* DVD set sold on eBay for around $40 USD.

When an item is new but has some collectibility, we suggest you buy in bulk, sell some of the item off to make up your investment, and save the balance for later. This has paid off for Marsha a good many times with Disney films, Barbies, and Andy Warhol dinnerware.

Garage Sales

What can be better than getting up at 6 a.m. to troll the local garage sales? We say nothing — if you're prepared and motivated to find lots of good eBay merchandise. Buy the newspaper or check your local paper's online classifieds (just run a Google search for the name of the paper) for times and locations of sales. Also, print maps of the locations from MapQuest or Yahoo! You know the neighbourhoods in your town, so you can make a route from one sale to the next that makes sense — and that figures in bathroom stops and coffee breaks.

Neighbours often take advantage of an advertised sale and put out some stuff of their own. Bring a friend; you can cover more ground faster if two of you are attacking the sales.

A few tips on shopping garage sales:

- ✔ Fancier neighbourhoods have better stuff than poor or middle class ones. We know that sounds unfair, but we know for sure that rich folks' trash is better than ours.

- ✔ Look for sales that say "Early Birds Welcome," and make them the first on your list so you can get them out of the way. It seems like a universal bell goes off somewhere and all garage sales start at 8 a.m. *sharp!*

- ✔ The stuff you find at estate sales is often of a higher quality. These sales feature things that have been collected over many, many years.

- ✔ Keep an eye out for "moving to a smaller house" sales. These are usually held by people who have raised children, accumulated a houseful of stuff (collectibles? old toys? designer vintage clothes?), and want to shed it all so that they can move to a condo in Florida.

- ✔ Marsha usually puts sales that feature "kids' items and toys" at the end of her list, and will go only if she's not too tired. These are generally young couples (with young children) who are trying to raise money or are moving. More often than not, the family is keeping the good stuff and is simply shedding the excess. On the other hand, *any* toys people are selling while downsizing are usually good ones.

Bill's best garage sale find was a vintage Marantz stereo receiver that the owner insisted was not working, and so he was willing to part with it for $5. Bill initially planned to break it down for parts, but, instead, decided to find out what was wrong with it. A small amount of electronic cleaning solvent, a few mini-lamp bulbs, and a generous amount of cleaning and polishing were all that was required to restore the highly sought-after receiver to its former glory. It sold for a whopping $524 USD on eBay — at a time when the exchange rate was getting a premium of fifty cents on the U.S. dollar!

Going-Out-of-Business Sales

Going-out-of-business sales can be a bonanza, but be careful not to be misled. Provincial laws generally require retailers that are putting on a going-out-of-business sale to purchase a special licence that proves the store is *really* going under. Some store ads may read "Going Out for Business" or some similar play on words, so you need to be sure that you're going to the real thing. When a retailer is liquidating its own stock, you're going to get the best buys. A retailer will often run the sale week by week, offering bigger discounts as time goes by. If a company is really going out of business, don't be afraid to make an offer on a quantity of items.

When a very large Canadian catalogue sales company went bankrupt, Bill managed to purchase many thousands of dollars' worth of inventory for a fraction of the original price. These items were then resold on eBay for often ten times their liquidated cost, and sometimes more. One good example of how Bill's purchase turned out to be lucrative concerns a children's inflatable igloo that originally retailed for $89 CAD. During the final days of the bankruptcy sale, Bill bought 150 of these at $2.50 each. During the following holiday shopping frenzy, he sold almost every one for a very profitable $59.99 USD each. Deals like this don't happen every day, so be ready to capitalize on them when they do.

Auctions

Two types of auctions where you can pick up bargains are liquidation auctions and estate auctions. (We also discuss charity auctions, where bargains may be found while you donate to a good cause.) You'll find perfectly saleable and profitable items at either type of auction, though each has its idiosyncrasies. Before you go to any auction, double-check the terms of payment: Must you bring cash, or can you pay by credit card? Also, before you bid on anything, find out the *hammer fee,* or *buyer's premium.* Auction houses add these fees — a percentage of what is offered — to the winner's bids, and he or she is responsible for paying them.

Liquidation auctions

When a company gets into serious financial trouble, its debtors (the people to whom it owes money) obtain a court order to liquidate the company, or force it to convert its assets into money, in order to pay its bills. The liquidated company then sells its stock, fixtures, and even real estate. Items sell for just cents on the dollar, and you can easily resell many of these items on eBay. A special kind of auctioneer handles liquidation auctions. Look in the phone book under Auctioneers for ads that mention liquidation services, then call and ask to be put on the agency's mailing list. This way, you'll always know ahead of time when something good comes up for sale.

Estate auctions

Estate auctions are like estate garage sales, but at a higher level. Fine art, antiques, paper ephemera, rare books, and collectibles of all kinds can be found there. Aside from the larger estate auctions held there less frequently, most auction houses also hold composite auctions on a monthly basis where groups of merchandise from various small estates are sold. Find out when these auctions are being held and mark them on your calendar.

Have you seen this headline before?

"Make Hundred$ of Thou$ands in Profits by Reselling Items from Government Foreclosure Auctions!" Yes, we've seen this headline, too. You send someone money, and they let you in on the big "secret."

Here's the secret. You can find out about many government auctions on these sites:

✔ **www.pwgsc.gc.ca/text/fact sheets/seized_property-e.html**. This site gives information on how the Canadian government disposes of seized and forfeited items. The Seized Property Management Directorate (SPMD) of Public Works and Government Services Canada (PWGSC) stores these items in regional facilities around the country prior to sale by auction. The site is updated with future auctions and also posts the bid results for previous auctions so you can get an idea about the selling price of various lots.

✔ **http://crownassets.pwgsc.gc.ca/text/index-e.cfm**. The Crown Assets Distribution Centres (CADC), part of Public Works and Government Services Canada, dispose of surplus materials through six regional warehouses around the country by way of public auction. The CADC auctions just about everything from electric razors to drywall, so check the Web site frequently. The goods sold are often retired from government service, but new items will also frequently appear. Out collecting their tax money!

✔ **www.bcsolutions.gov.bc.ca/wair/Default.htm** . This is the official link to the Province of British Columbia Asset Investment Recovery site. It lists surplus provincial and some Crown Corporation items on an ongoing basis for sale by tender. The province also holds "Cash and Carry" auction sales of surplus goods at various locations — more details can be found at **www.bcauction.ca/open.dll/welcome**.

✔ **http://surplus.gov.ab.ca**. Like BC, Alberta also offers its surplus by either tender or auction. This Web site is not as detailed as some others, offering only very basic information on upcoming offerings. Fortunately, they do provide staff contact information to help you research the true value of the goods available.

✔ **www.governmentauctions.org/**. This is a private company specializing in liquidation auctions for the Canadian and U.S. governments. Membership to the site costs $39.95 USD per year and permits access to detailed listings for government auction sales on both sides of the border. The site is heavily dominated by U.S. listings but with a little patience you may come up with some real opportunities within Canada.

To find other government auction sites, run a Google search for *seized property*, *tax sales*, *confiscated property*, *provincial auctions*, and *government surplus* (results for the latter include tons of links to individual U.S. state-seized property auctions). Remember, if you're asked for payment to get information about the auctions, it's not an official site

Estate auctions are attended mostly by dealers, who know the local going rate for each item they bid on. But because they're buying to sell in a retail environment, their highest bids will generally be the wholesale price for the items in your area. If a particular item is flooding your market, the high bid may be low. We've seen some incredible bargains at estate auctions near our homes. When you're in a room full of local dealers, they're buying what's hot to resell in your city — not what's going to sell across the continent. With some help from eBay, that entire market could be yours.

Charity silent auctions

We're sure you've been to your share of silent auctions for charity. A school or an organization will persuade everyone from the largest corporation to the local gift shop to donate items. The goods are then auctioned off to the highest bidder, usually in a silent format.

You can find many a great item at charity silent auctions. Aside from new merchandise, collectors may feel good about donating some collection overflow to a charity. Marsha purchased the keystone of her Star Trek action figure collection at a charity auction: the very rare tri-fold Borg (one of perhaps only 50 in existence). This figure has sold for as much as $1000 USD on eBay, but she paid just $60 USD, and donated to a charity at the same time. (Okay, now it's only selling on eBay for about $400 USD — but heck, it was *still* a deal!)

Goodwill, Salvation Army, and Resale Shops

Participating in a charity such as Goodwill or the Salvation Army is a powerful thing with many benefits. You don't have to worry about having a garage sale to get rid of unwanted stuff (no need to have strangers trodding all over the lawn, crunching the daisy borders while sniffing around at the stuff for sale), and a lot of items exist that you can pretty much write off as a charity tax deduction. It's simple: You just load the goods into your car and take 'em to the store. It's a win-win-win situation. The extra win is you acquiring valuable pieces at bargain-basement prices.

At resale stores, such as Goodwill and the Salvation Army, you'll sometimes uncover treasures — other times, you'll find only junk. We recommend befriending the manager, who sees the merchandise as it comes in, will know just what you're looking for (because you mentioned it in a friendly conversation), and will call you before the items hit the floor. This type of relationship can save you from making fruitless trips to the store.

Some stores receive merchandise from a central warehouse where donations are initially sent for minor rehabilitation and cleaning. Other, smaller operations process items in-house with the store manager supervising. The resale store is a business that runs on a schedule. Ask the manager (who is now your friend) when the delivery truck regularly comes in. Being there when it arrives enables you to view items before the general public.

A sharp seller Marsha knows is always at his local Salvation Army when the trucks come in. One day as workers unloaded the truck, he saw a plaque-mounted baseball bat. Withholding his excitement, he picked it up and found that it was a signed Ty Cobb bat with a presentation plaque. Although uncertain of its real value, he took a gamble and brought it to the cash register, where he paid $33, minus the senior citizen's discount. He took the bat to his office and made a few phone calls, later discovering that it was indeed a rare Louisville Slugger bat that had been presented to the Georgia Peach, Ty Cobb. He knows now that it's very valuable, but he'll never sell it; it's his good luck bat, and it now hangs above the desk in his warehouse.

Goodwill Industries is definitely an opportunity for inventory at rock bottom prices. You can find their locations and store hours at `www.goodwill.on.ca/`.

Freebies

Freebies come in all shapes and sizes, and — best of all — they're free, of course! Freebies are usually samples or promotion pieces that companies give away to introduce a new product, service, or, best of all, a media event. Even carefully trimmed ads from magazines can fetch high prices from collectors.

When you go to the cosmetic counter and buy a way-too-expensive item, be sure to ask for tester-sized samples. Name-brand cosmetic and perfume samples of high-priced items sell very well on eBay. Also, look for *gift with purchase* deals. If it's a specialty item, you can usually sell it on its own to someone who'd like to try a sample themselves, rather than plunge headlong into a large purchase. Less special items can be grouped together as lots. Be sure to put the brand names in the title.

Remember the talking Taco Bell Chihuahua giveaway? Those cute little dogs were all the rage, and sold for big money on eBay. It almost seems foolish to remind you of the McDonald's Teenie Beanie Baby giveaways; moms, dads, and dealers were driving in circles through the drive-thru, purchasing as many of the Happy Meals as each store would allow. They'd then drive to the next McDonald's to purchase a different toy. In Marsha's house alone they had frozen hamburgers for three months!

When *Return of the Jedi* was re-released in 1997, the first 100 people to enter each theatre got a Special Edition Luke Skywalker figure. These figures are still highly prized by collectors, and if future parts of the Star Wars saga are released, you can bet the prices on this figure will rise yet again.

In 1995, the Paramount network premiered a new show, *Star Trek Voyager*. In selected markets, Paramount sent a promotional microwave popcorn packet as a Sunday newspaper insert. These are still selling well (when you can find them), although the value rises and falls according to current interest in Star Trek.

Before you pass by a freebie, consider its possible resale value in the future.

Salvage: Liquidation Items, Unclaimed Freight, and Returns

The easiest buy of all, *salvage merchandise* is retail merchandise that has been returned, exchanged, or shelf-pulled for some reason. Generally, this merchandise is sold as-is — and "where-is" — and it may be in new condition. To buy salvage merchandise, you must have your resale permit. Also, be prepared to pick up the items or pay for shipping to your location — unless you're buying them on eBay.

Available all over the country, liquidation businesses have been thriving as a well-kept secret for years. As long as you have space to store salvage merchandise and a way to sell it, you can acquire it for as low as ten cents on the dollar. When we say you need storage space, we mean *lots* of space. To buy this type of merchandise at bottom-of-the-barrel prices, you must be willing to accept truckloads — full 12–16-metre eighteen-wheelers, loaded with approximately 22–24 10 x 10 x 15 (or 17)-centimetre pallets — of merchandise at a time. Often each truckload has a *manifest* (document containing the contents of the shipment) listing the retail and wholesale price of each item. If you have access to the more than 3,048 square metres of warehouse space that you'll need to unpack and process this much merchandise, you're in business.

Several types of salvage merchandise are available:

- **Unclaimed freight:** When a trucking company delivers merchandise, a manifest accompanies the freight. If, for some reason, a portion of the shipment arrives incomplete, contains the wrong items, or is damaged, the entire shipment may be refused by the merchant. The trucking company is now stuck with as much as a full truckload of freight. The original seller may not want to pay the freight charges to return the merchandise to his or her warehouse (or accept blame for an incorrect shipment), and so the freight becomes the trucker's problem. The trucking companies forge agreements with liquidators, who then buy this freight from the truckers and store it at one of their several locations around the country. Because the liquidators have so many locations, truckers are never far from a place where they can dump, er, drop off merchandise.

- **Returns:** Did you know that after you buy something, decide that you don't want it, and then return it to the store or mail-order house, it can never be sold as new again? (This is true in most jurisdictions, anyway.) The merchandise is, instead, generally sent to a liquidator, who agrees in advance to pay a flat percentage of the retail price for goods. The liquidator must then move the merchandise to someone else. All major retailers liquidate returns, and much of the resulting merchandise ends up on eBay or in closeout stores.

  If you're handy at repairing electronics or computers, you'd probably do very well with a specialized lot. You may easily be able to revitalize damaged merchandise using parts from two or more unsaleable items to come up with one that you can sell in like-new working condition.

- **Liquidations:** Similar to the liquidation auctions we mention earlier in this chapter, liquidation companies buy merchandise by the truckload to sell off in smaller lots. The merchandise comes from financially stressed or bankrupt companies that need to raise cash quickly.

- **Seasonal overstocks:** Remember the motto, "Buy off-season, sell on-season"? Often, a store finds its shelves overloaded with seasonal merchandise (such as swimsuits in August) that it must get rid of to make room for the fall and winter stock. These brand-new items become salvage merchandise because they're seasonal overstocks.

- **Shelf-pulls:** When you're shopping, have you ever passed up one item in a display for the one behind it because its box was in better condition? Sometimes the plastic wrap or the package on a product is dented, and you'd rather have a pristine one. That box you just passed up may become a *shelf-pull*. The item inside may be in perfect condition, but it's cosmetically unsaleable in the retail environment.

Drop-shipping to your customers

Middlemen, wholesalers, and liquidators can specialize in selling to online auctioneers through a *drop-ship service.* Some crafty eBay sellers make lots of money selling lists of drop shipping sources to other users of eBay — we hope not to you. Dealing with a drop shipper means that you don't ever have to take possession of (or pay for) the merchandise you order. You're given only a photo to sell with; once the item is sold, you give the vendor the address of the buyer. They charge your credit card for the item plus shipping, and then they ship the item to your customer for you.

This way of doing business costs *you* more and lowers your profits. If you're in business, your goal is to make as much money as you can.

Because the drop shipper is in business, too, they'll mark up the merchandise they sell to you (and the shipping cost) to make their profit.

Be careful when using a drop shipper. Ask for references. See whether a zillion sellers are offering the same merchandise on eBay — and not getting any bites. Also, what happens if the drop shipper runs out of an item that you've just sold? You can't just say "oops!" to your buyer without getting some nasty feedback. Your online reputation is at stake. If you find a solid source and believe in the product, order a large quantity of the item and have it shipped to your door. Don't pay someone else's mark-up for giving them the privilege to ship to your customers.

We scoured the Internet and found tons of liquidators. Most are found in the U.S., so be prepared to import. The following are some sites that stood out and offered a wide variety of deals:

http://eis.net/lib/start.cgi/atlanticsurplus/listings.html

http://chli.ca/

www.wholesalecentral.com

www.salvagecloseouts.com

www.amerisurplus.com

www.amlinc.com

www.tdwcloseouts.com

Be careful before signing up for a newsletter on one of these sites. Your spam woes can grow to massive proportions after doing so. To preserve your privacy, sign up for a free Yahoo! or Hotmail account to use exclusively when dealing with liquidators.

A proportion of liquidation items, unclaimed freight, and returns may not be saleable for the reasons that we discuss in the rest of this section. Although you'll acquire many gems that stand to bring you profit, you'll also be left with a varying percentage of useless items from each lot that you purchase. Read on carefully.

Items by the pallet

Some suppliers take the risk of purchasing salvaged merchandise by the truckload. Then, they break up each truckload and sell the merchandise to you one pallet at a time. You'll probably find some local liquidators who offer this service; you can also go online to find one. Here's the rub: finding the right person to buy from takes some effort.

 As in any business, you'll find both good-guy liquidators and bad-guy liquidators. As you know, the world is full of e-mail scammers and multi-level marketers who are in business to take your money. No one trying to sell you merchandise can possibly *guarantee* that you'll make money, so beware of liquidators who offer this kind of promise. We don't care who they are or what they say. Carefully research whomever you choose to buy from. Use an Internet search engine to search for the words ***salvage, liquidation,*** **and** ***pallet merchandise***.

Some liquidation sellers sell their merchandise in the same condition that it arrives at their location, so what the buyer gets is a crapshoot. You may lose money on some items while making back your money on others. Other sellers who charge a bit more will remove less desirable merchandise from the pallets. Some may even make up deluxe pallets with better-quality merchandise. Hand-sorted loads cost more, but if they're filled with the type of merchandise that you're interested in selling, you'll probably write better descriptions for the items and subsequently do a better job selling them.

 Getting a pallet of goods shipped to you can cost a bundle, so finding a source for your liquidation merchandise that's close to your base of operations is a good idea. You'll notice that some liquidation sites have several warehouses; using one translates into lower shipping costs for the buyer. (Having a lot of warehouses also serves the company by allowing them to accept merchandise from diverse locations.) You might see FOB (freight on board) and a city name listed in the liquidation company's description, which means that when you buy their merchandise, you own it in the city listed. You're responsible for whatever it costs to ship the merchandise to your door. Search around; you may have to go through many sources before you find the right one for you.

When you find a source from which you want to buy merchandise by the pallet, check out a few things before spending your hard-earned cash:

- ✔ Do they sell mostly to flea marketers (remember, you're looking for *quality* as well as a low price) or closeout stores (in this case, the seller may be more retail-oriented).

- ✔ Did you get a reply within twenty-four hours after calling or e-mailing?

- ✔ Does anyone you speak to appear to care about what you want to sell?

- ✔ Are the available lots within your budget?

- ✔ Are the lots general or have they been sorted to include only the type of merchandise that you want to sell?

- ✔ How long has this liquidator been in business, and where does its merchandise come from?

- ✔ Does the source guarantee that you *will* make money, or say that you *can* make money by buying the right merchandise? Remember: No one can guarantee that you'll make money.

- ✔ Does the supplier offer references on its Web site that you can contact to find out valuable information about the items for sale, such as the approximate percentage of unsaleable goods in each box or pallet?

- ✔ Is a hard sell involved? Or is it a matter-of-fact deal?

Before you are dazzled by the low, low price of a lot and click the Buy It Now button, check the shipping cost. Many so-called wholesalers will lure you in with bargain-basement prices, only to charge you three times the normal shipping costs. Do your homework before you buy!

Job lots

Manufacturers often have to get rid of merchandise, too. Perhaps a particular company made 5 million bobble-head dolls and then sold only 4 million to retailers. It has to quickly unload the leftover merchandise (known as a *job lot*) so that it'll have the cash to invest in next season's array of items. Job lots often consist of hundreds or thousands of a single item. If you purchase a job lot, you'd best enjoy what you're selling, because you'll be looking at it for a while.

Remember supply and demand — don't ever flood the eBay market. Otherwise, your item will become valueless.

Many Web sites specialize in job lots, but you have to visit them often because the deals are constantly changing. One worth checking out is Liquidation.com, shown in Figure 6-1. Numerous sellers in Canada list merchandise on this site, and much of it is for sale *exclusively* in Canada. (Fewer people bidding on the item may mean lower costs to you.) Visit them at www.liquidation.com.

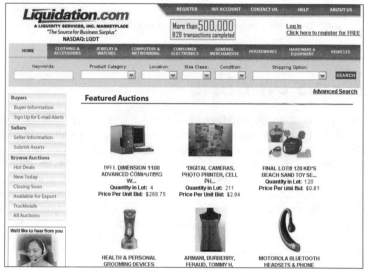

Figure 6-1:
Liquidation.
com con-
stantly offers
desirable
lots of
liquidation
merchan-
dise.

Wholesale Merchandise by the Case

Purchasing wholesale merchandise may require that you have a provincial resale licence, which identifies you as a professional. Be sure that you have one before you try to purchase merchandise directly from another business. Also, when you have a resale licence and conduct a business-to-business (B2B) transaction (in your case, purchase merchandise), you won't be charged provincial sales tax. Go to Chapter 15 to find out how to get that magic resale licence — it's a valuable thing.

When you have your resale licence, you can buy merchandise from whom-ever you like. If you want to buy directly from a manufacturer, you can. Unfortunately, manufacturers often have a monetary minimum for the amount of your order, which may be more than you want to spend. (Also, you could be stuck with more of one item than you know what to do with.) To avoid receiving and paying for more of a product than you need, see whether you can find some independent retailers who buy in quantity that might let you in on some of their orders.

Sometimes the liquidators that we discuss in the preceding section receive full cases of perfectly saleable goods. Many cases make up a pallet, and liquidators will often sell each case individually on eBay. What a great way to acquire goods for your eBay business — we know of several eBay sellers who consistently buy their merchandise this way.

Resale Items on eBay

We'll keep this eBay buying technique short and sweet: Use the magic search engine! But be careful; many a get-rich-quick schemer will use boldface keywords in their auctions to attract your attention. Look only for good quality merchandise to resell. Remember that the only way to make a living on eBay is to sell quality items to happy customers so that they'll come back and buy from you again. Be sure to search eBay auction titles for the following keywords: **resale**, **resell**, **"case of"** (see Figure 6-2), **"case quantity," "lot of," "pallet of"** (see Figure 6-3), **closeout**, and **surplus**. Be sure to use the quotes anywhere we've included them here — this forces the search engine to find the words in the exact order you write them.

Figure 6-2:
Results of a
"case of"
search on
eBay.

| | | All Items | Auctions | Buy It Now | | | | | |

Figure 6-3:
Results of a "pallet of" search on eBay.

Also, be sure to check out the wholesale categories on eBay. After noticing how many sellers were buying from other sellers, eBay set up wholesale sub-categories for almost every type of item. You can find the wholesale items in the category list on the left side of the page after performing a search. Or, just go to the eBay home page, scroll down the list of categories, and click Wholesale. You'll be brought to the Wholesale hub page, shown in Figure 6-4. Just click the category of your choice to find some great deals.

Figure 6-4:
eBay's Wholesale hub page.

Consignment Selling

Consignment sales are the up-and-coming way for you to help newbies by selling their items for them on eBay. Lots of sellers do it, and several retail locations base their business exclusively on this practice. This is how it works: You take possession of the item from the owner and sell it on eBay. You're responsible for taking photos of the item and marketing the auction, on eBay — for a fee. In addition to the money you earn selling on consignment, you also get excellent experience for future auctions of your own merchandise.

Become an eBay Trading Assistant

After you have fifty feedback comments under your belt on eBay (and have sold at least four items in the past thirty days), you can become a registered eBay Trading Assistant. Check out `http://tradingassistant.ebay.ca /ws/eBayISAPI.dll?TradingAssist ant&page=main` (shown in the figure) to get all the details.

eBay publishes a directory of consignment sellers that you can search by telephone area code, postal code, or country. Check out who in your area is a registered Trading Assistant. Read their terms and fees. Consignment sellers charge varied amounts based on their geographic location (some areas can bear higher fees than others).

To set up your business for consignment sales, you should follow a few guidelines:

1. **Design a consignment agreement (a contract) and send it to the owners of the merchandise.**

   Do this before you receive any items. Setting up all policies in advance minimizes any questions that can otherwise arise after the transaction has begun.

2. **Have the owners sign and send the agreement to you (the consignor) along with the item.**

3. **Research the item based on past sales so that you can give the owners an estimated price range of what the item might sell for on eBay.**

4. **Photograph the item carefully (see Chapter 11 for some hints) and write a thoughtful, selling description.**

5. **Handle all e-mail inquiries as though the item were your own; after all, your fee is generally based on a percentage of the final sale.**

What do you charge for your all your work? We can't give you a stock answer for that one. Many sellers charge a flat fee for photographing, listing, and shipping that ranges from $5 to $10, plus a commission of up to 30 percent on the final auction total (this will absorb eBay's fees). Other sellers base their fees exclusively on the final sale amount. They charge on a sliding scale, beginning at 50 percent of the total sale, less eBay and payment service fees. When deciding how much to charge for your services, you must consider how much you think you can make on an item.

Traditional auction houses handle consignment sales in a similar fashion.

When you've reached the next level of your eBay enterprise and are looking to spend some serious money on your merchandise, check out Marsha's book *eBay Timesaving Techniques For Dummies* (Wiley). There, she delves into the type of wholesale-buying secrets normally reserved for the big-time retailers.

Chapter 7

Knowing the Value of What You're Selling

• •

• •

*1*f you don't know what your item is worth, you may not get the highest price in any market. If you don't know how to make your item easy to find, it may not be noticed by even the hardiest of collectors. If you don't know the facts or what to say, your well-written title and detailed description (combined with a fabulous picture) may still not be enough to get the highest price for your item.

Knowing your item is a crucial part of successful selling on eBay. This is why we suggest in Chapter 1 that you specialize in a small group of items, allowing you to stay on top of ever-changing trends. An item may be appraised or listed in a book as very valuable, but what you care about is the price at which the item will actually sell. Imagine someone uncovering a hoard of your item and, not knowing the value of it, dumping it on eBay for a low Buy It Now price. This scenario would drive down the value of the item within a couple of weeks.

The values of collectibles go up and down. Star Wars items are a perfect example; values skyrocketed during the release of the latest movie, but now prices have settled to a considerably lower level. A published book of value listings is only truly valid at the *moment* the book is written. If you stay on top of the market for a few favourite items, you'll be able to see how the market fluctuates. If you're looking for the highest price instead of looking to liquidate excess inventory, we'd hold any special collectibles — such as Star Wars items — until they become popular again.

Because you no doubt *will* purchase the occasional gem, and *will* want to make the most money possible, in this chapter we examine the different ways you can find out just how much something is worth. We start with the easiest and most accurate method and progress to the most laborious. We hope you can get your answer the easy way.

The Easy Way: eBay Search

Who woulda thunk it? The best tool for evaluating your items is right under your nose. The eBay search tool is the best and quickest link to finding the pricing information you need. To see how items like yours have been selling, search recently completed auctions. Searching auction results also helps you determine the best categories to list your products in and when, judging by the time of day that high bidders for your type of item were active during the auction.

Every type of item has a different type of bidder. This makes sense, right? Would a person searching for collectible dolls have the same shopping habits as a coin collector? Probably not. Collectible coins can be far more expensive than collectible dolls. Although generalities can be dangerous, *profiling* your item's buyer is worthwhile. After you check out the completed auctions for items like yours, you'll be amazed at how the buying patterns of shoppers in different categories become crystal clear. After you arm yourself with this knowledge, you'll know not only how much your items should go for, but also when to end your auction.

If you're selling a common item, check to see how many other sellers are selling the same thing, and when their auctions close. Nothing can kill your profits like being the second or third auction closing with the same piece of merchandise. You have to space your auctions apart from the others, or the law of supply and demand will kick in — and kick you in the wallet.

The way the search system works has changed drastically over the years, so be sure that you know how to use this valuable tool. Almost every eBay page has a small box for searching. Initially, you may find it easier to go to the search page, but if you know the search engine *syntax,* or shorthand, you can pinpoint your items with amazing accuracy.

Here are some pointers to help you get the most out of the eBay search engine:

✔ The search engine isn't case sensitive, so don't worry about using capitalization in your search.

✔ To find more needles in the haystack, be sure to select the Search Titles and Descriptions option.

✔ To find historical pricing (what the item has sold for in the past), be sure to check the box to search completed listings.

✔ If you're looking for a popular item, don't search only auction titles and descriptions; search by category, too. For example, suppose that you're searching for a Winnie the Pooh baby outfit. Type ***Pooh outfit,*** and you'll get a ton of results. Look to the left of the page and see the category that more closely matches your search. In Figure 7-1, the matching category is Clothing, Shoes & Accessories. Click the link below for the Infants & Toddlers subcategory. Now you'll see the search results in the appropriate category — we guarantee that, with this method, you'll find exactly what you're looking for.

✔ In your search, don't use conjunctions (***or, and***) or articles (***a, an, the***); the search engine might misconstrue these *noise* words as part of search. Some sellers use the ampersand (&) in place of the word ***and***, so if you include ***and*** in your search, you won't find auctions that use the ampersand. In addition, some sellers, due to the fifty-five-character limit, may not place ***the*** in their title; the same goes for ***a, or,*** and ***and***.

Figure 7-1:
The eBay
search
results
with the
Matching
Categories
refinement
box.

Advanced searching methods

If you need to pinpoint a particular item or just want to weed out bogus responses, you can try a variety of advanced search methods, shown in Table 7-1. You can use these shortcuts in any of eBay's search windows.

Table 7-1	Advanced Search Syntax	
Symbol	*Effect*	*Example*
Quotes (",")	Limits search to the exact phrase in the quotes	**"American Staffordshire"** yields auctions relating only to this breed of dog
Asterisk (*)	Works like a wild card in poker	**196* fashion** displays auctions that relate to 1960s fashion
Parentheses (()) and comma (,)	Finds items related to either word	**(shipperke,schipperke)** finds items spelled both ways
Minus sign (-)	Excludes words	**watch -digital** gets you a lovely analog watch
Minus sign (-), parentheses (()), and comma (,)	Excludes more than one word	**Packard -(hewlett,bell)** finds those rare Packard auto collectibles
At (@) and number 1	Searches two out of three words	**@1 new purse shoes dress** gets you a nice new outfit

Now that you know how to finesse the search engine, head to the search page and see if you can work some magic.

If you have the item number, you can type or paste it into any of the eBay search boxes to find that item quickly.

Using eBay Advanced Search

By clicking <u>More Search Options</u> at the bottom of the Search>Find Items page, you can access eBay's advanced search options. With the advanced search, you can narrow your search to check out the competition (who else is selling your items). In the basic search, you also have few options:

✔ **View results:** You can choose to see a mini gallery of photos if you like. Although, ordinarily, this may not help your research, information is key; you might just see a variation of the item in photos that you didn't know about from the text description.

✔ **Search in categories:** You can narrow your search to one of the twenty-three major categories on eBay. If your product is made for men, women, or children, you may get more efficient results by looking in one of those categories. Strangely, when searching for a ladies' watch, we found the following synonyms and abbreviations for *ladies: lady's*, *ladys*, *lds*, and *femmes*.

✔ **Completed listings only:** Check this box to go directly to completed listings for your item research.

✔ **Sort by:** You can find items by asking the search engine to sort results by which auctions are ending soonest (this is the default), which items were listed most recently, which items are new, which items have the lowest prices, or which items have the highest prices. In each option, the results will be listed in descending order.

When you click the Advanced Search link, you can narrow your search even further:

✔ **Payment:** You can isolate your search to only those sellers who accept PayPal. This may enlighten you as to whether buyers of this product pay higher prices if they choose to pay using a credit card. (Although searching for sellers who accept PayPal excludes references to other methods of payment, it still speaks strongly for credit card users.)

✔ **Locate items near you:** If you're selling something big that you can't (or don't want to) ship, you want to deliver it or have the buyer pick it up. Using this option allows you to check out the competition within a limited distance of an entered postal code or in your closest eBay trading area (usually a major metropolitan centre) only.

✔ **Multiple item listings:** This option allows you to search by quantity or lot.

So how can you search completed auctions to find bidding patterns on items like yours? Here's a way to dig out all the details you need.

Use the Basic Search Options page to perform a search on the item you want information about. When the results appear (see Figure 7-2), you'll see how many other sellers are offering your same item. This information will help you judge whether it's the right time to sell. (If all active auctions for your items have high bids, it's definitely time to sell — just be sure not to list your auction to end at a similar time as another one.)

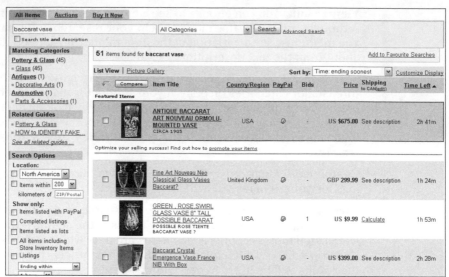

Figure 7-2:
Results of an investigatory search.

A search for historic pricing will also help you make wise decisions about your auction. For tips on how to price your own items based on past auctions, perform a Completed Listings search from the Advanced Search options page:

1. **Click the link on the basic Search page to expand the advanced options.**

2. **Click the Completed listings only option box in the options area at the top of the page.**

3. **To sort by price, go to the Sort By drop down menu at the bottom of the page and click the Price: highest first option.**

4. **Click Search.**

   The results of completed auctions of your particular item for the last fourteen days appear sorted by highest prices first. Now you're at the heart of the matter (see Figure 7-3). Pull out your calendar and make note of which days your item landed the highest bids. More often than not, you'll find that a pattern appears. Your item may see more action on Sunday or Monday or Thursday or whenever. After you figure out the days that your item gets the highest bids, pull out a copy of the eBay time chart that appears on the Cheat Sheet (at the front of the book) and evaluate what time of day your high bidders like to bid.

Figure 7-3:
The
Completed
Auctions
search
results,
sorted by
highest
prices first.

There you have it: the method that will get you the most information eBay can possibly give you on the sales trends for your item. It's money in the bank. Use it!

If you can't find any auctions for your item, you have a few more options. You're not gonna believe we're saying this, but try searching `auctions.yahoo.com`, or go to `auctions.amazon.com`. At least you'll see whether someone else in the world is selling an item like yours. None of the cool search features that we discuss previously will work on these other sites, but hey, they ain't eBay.

eBay also has a superior tool for checking your competitors' auctions. After a while, you will be able to identify the sellers that frequently offer items similar to yours. Aside from keeping them in the My Favourite Sellers section of your My eBay page (for more on that, see Chapter 3), here's a quick way to see whether one of your competing sellers has an item like yours up for sale:

1. **Go to the Search area, then click the <u>Items By Seller</u> link on the left.**

2. **Enter the seller's user ID in the box provided.**

   To search the seller's completed listings, select what time frame you want to search. To search only their current listings, just go to the bottom and click the Search button.

Useful Publications

So what if your item isn't for sale on eBay and hasn't been for thirty days? What's the first thing to do? Check out your local newsstand for one of the many publications devoted to collecting. Go over to Yahoo Yellow Pages at yp.yahoo.com. Enter your city and province or postal code to limit the search to your part of the country, then type a search for **Magazines — Dealers** in your area. Let your fingers do the walking and call the newsstands in your city to ask whether they have publications of the type you are looking for. If none are listed nearby, visit the local bookstore.

Here's a list of some popular reference publications:

- *Action Figure Digest*: Find out who's hot in the action figure biz in this monthly magazine. Its Web site sells back issues; go to www.tomart.com.

- *Antique Trader*: This magazine has been the bible of the antique collecting industry for more than 40 years. Visit its online home on the Web at www.antiquetrader.com/ for more articles and subscription information.

- *Autograph Collector*: This magazine gives the lowdown on the autograph business, as well as samples of many autographs for identification. Its Web site, www.autographcollector.com, features links to the price guides it publishes.

- *Barbie Bazaar*: The official Mattel magazine is packed with everything Barbie! Here you'll find news on what's hot in Barbie collecting and see all the new dolls put out by the Barbie team at Mattel. Visit the site at www.barbiecollector.com/ for subscriptions and news.

- *Collector Editions*: You'll find information on plates, figurines, glass, prints, cottages, ornaments, and dozens of other contemporary decorative collectibles in this monthly magazine.

- *Doll Reader*: The Ultimate Authority Doll Reader has been dishing out the scoop on collectible dolls of all sorts for more than 25 years. It's the place to go to catch the trends on the latest in doll collecting. At www.dollreader.com, you'll get an idea of what's in this very informative magazine.

- *Goldmine*: The magazine for CD and record collecting. The Web site, www.goldminemag.com, has many sample articles and provides information from its issues.

- *Canadian Coin News*: Another standard collector's magazine, *Canadian Coin News* has been around for more than forty years. Check them out on the Web at www.canadiancoinnews.ca .

- *Sports Collectors Digest*: This publication takes sports collectibles to the highest level. Visit its Web site at www.sportscollectorsdigest.com/ and sign up for a free e-mail newsletter.

✔ *Linns*: The world's largest weekly newspaper for international stamp collectors, this publication also has a great Web site loaded with quality information. Check them out online at `www.linns.com`. Alternatively, you can visit their associated site at `www.zillionsofstamps.com` for stamp pricing information found in a huge database of dealers from around the world.

✔ *Teddy Bear Review*: Since 1986, this review has offered pages of information on bear collecting. For a free trial issue, go to `www.teddybear review.com`.

It seems that every leading magazine has its own Web site. In the next section, we mention some more useful Web sites to help you reference pricing.

Online Sources of Information

Because you're all so Internet savvy (what's better than getting the information you want at a millisecond's notice?), we assume you plan to visit the magazine Web sites that we mention in the preceding section. In this section, we suggest a few more fun online sources where you can find information about your items.

Web sites

Many Web sites devoted to specific types of collectibles list the final selling prices of items at auctions that were recently completed. These auctions are the best evaluation of an item's value because they're usually directed towards specialists in a single item or group of items. Most of the participants in these auctions *really* know their stuff.

You may have to poke around the following Web sites to find the prices realized at auction, but when you do, you'll have the holy grail of estimated values. Look for links that point to auction archives. Many of these sites also offer to consign your item from you and sell it to their audience. Check out some of these great resources for specific collectable items:

✔ **Antiques, art, all kinds of rare stuff:** `www.sothebys.com`

✔ **Art auctions:** `www.artprice.com`

This site charges for its searches by artist, but has an immense database.

✔ **Autographs, movie posters, and comic books:** `www.heritage auctions.com`

✔ **Coins and sports memorabilia:** `www.collectors.com`

✔ **Collectible advertising glasses:** `www.pgcaglassclub.com`

(You've got to see this stuff!)

✔ **Currency auctions:** `www.lynknight.com`

✔ **Entertainment memorabilia:** `www.heritageauctions.com/entertainment`

✔ **Rare coins:** `www.bowersandmerena.com`

✔ **U.S. coin price guide:** `www.pcgs.com/prices/`

Online appraisals

Marsha has had a bit of personal experience with online appraisals, which seem quite tempting at first glance. Unfortunately, at second glance, she realized that unless the person doing the appraisal can actually *see* and *feel* the item, an accurate appraisal can't be performed. Also, you have no guarantee that the "appraiser" you are dealing with online is really an expert on the value of your item.

Marsha's story is that she had a few items *e-appraised* by a very prestigious (now defunct) online appraisal company. The appraisals seemed a bit off, so she took one of the items, a painting, to Butterfields (now Bonhams) in Los Angeles, where she was told the painting was worth ten times what she was quoted in her e-appraisal.

The bottom line here is that if you suspect — or know — that you have an item of real value that's worth appraising, the item deserves to be appraised in person. Most large cities have auction houses, and many of those auction houses offer *consignment clinics* on a monthly basis. (Consignment clinics are a way for auction houses to get merchandise for their future auctions.) If you bring your item to an auction house, you aren't legally bound to let the house sell your item for you; still, it may not be a bad idea. You'll get a free verbal appraisal out of the deal. The auction house won't fill out any official paperwork or anything, but at least you'll get an idea of what your item is worth. (Real appraisals are expensive, are performed by licensed professionals, and come with a formal appraisal document.)

Authentication Services

Some companies provide the service of *authenticating* your item (verifying that it's the real deal) or authenticating and *grading* (determining a value based on the item's condition and legitimacy). To have these services performed on your items, you'll have to send them to the service and pay a fee.

Following are a few excellent sites for grading coins:

- **Professional Coin Grading Service (PCGS):** www.pcgs.com.
- **American Numismatic Association Certification Service (AMNACS) —** sold to Amos Press in 1990: www.anacs.com.
- **Numismatic Guaranty Corporation of America (NGCA):** www.ngccoin.com/ebay_ngcvalue.cfm. The site offers eBay users a discount and features a mail-in grading and certification service for your coins.
- PCI Coin Grading Service (PCI): **www.pcicoins.com.**

Stamp collectors (or those who have just inherited a collection from Uncle Steve) can get their stamps "expertized" (authenticated) by the Roya Philatelic Society of Canada (http://www.rpsc.org/) or the American Philatelic Society. Visit www.stamps.org/services/ser_aboutexpertizing.htm for more information about authentication from the U.S. site.

For comic books, Comics Guaranty, LLC (CGC) www.cgccomics.com/ebay_comic_book_grading.cfm will seal (enclose in plastic to preserve the quality) and grade your items at a discount for eBay users.

A bunch of authentication services exist for sports cards and sports memorabilia. If you got your autograph or memorabilia direct from the player or team, you can assure its authenticity. Having the item authenticated may or may not get you a higher price on eBay. Try these sites:

- **Professional Sports Authenticator (PSA):** Offers eBay users a discount at www.psacard.com/cobrands/submit.chtml?cobrandid=23.
- **Online Authentics:** Reviews autographs by scans online or by physical review. Look at its services at www.onlineauthentics.com.

The best way to find a good authenticator in your field is to search the items on eBay for the most prominent authenticator listed in the descriptions. For example, note in the coins area that certain grading services' coins get higher bids than others. To find an authenticator for coins, you can also type the keywords **coin grading** into an Internet search engine (Google or Yahoo). You'll come up with a host of choices; use your good sense to see which one suits your needs.

Remember that not all items need to be officially authenticated. Official authentication does add value to an item, but if you're an expert on what you own, you can comfortably rate them in your auctions using your own judgment. People will know from your description whether you're a specialist. Your feedback will also work for you by letting the prospective bidder or buyer know that your merchandise from past sales has been top-drawer.

Chapter 8

Establishing a Base of Operations: Your Web Site

● ●

In This Chapter

▶ Finding free Web space

▶ Choosing a host

▶ Deciding on the perfect name

▶ Registering your domain name

▶ Marketing your piece of the Web

● ●

*Y*our eBay store is important to your business, but it doesn't replace your own e-commerce Web site when it comes to generating publicity and encouraging sales. You want to establish your own presence on the Web. And although you can — and are advised to — link your site to eBay, don't underestimate what links to other sites on the Internet can also do for you.

You don't have a Web site yet? The Web has so many sites with pictures of people's dogs and kids that we just assumed you had your own site, too. The space for a Web site comes *free* from your ISP (Internet Service Provider). (Marsha even has one embarrassing site with family pictures.) A personal Web space makes a great practice site for your business. Take down pictures of the baby and post pictures of the items you're selling. Or, at the very least, install the eBay Merchant Kit (see Chapter 2).

You do have a Web site? Have you taken a good look at it lately to see whether it's up to date? Does it link to your eBay auctions, eBay store, and the gallery that we discuss in Chapter 5?

Whether or not you have a Web site, this chapter has something for you. We provide a lot of detail about Web sites, from thinking up a name to choosing a host. If you don't already have one, we get you started on launching a site; if you do, we give you some pointers about finding the best host. For the serious-minded Web-based entrepreneur (that's you), we also include some ever-important marketing tips.

Free Web Space — a Good Place to Start

Although we love the word *free,* in real life it seems like nothing is *really* free. *Free* generally means something won't cost you too much money — but may cost you a bit more in time. When your site is free, you aren't able to have your own direct URL (Universal Resource Locator) or domain name. Most likely, a free Web site has an address such as one of the following:

```
www.execulink.com/~membername/
www3.ns.sympatico.ca/membername/
members.aol.com/membername
```

Having some kind of site at least gives you the experience of setting one up. When you're ready to jump in for real, you can always use your free site as an extension of your main business site.

From the first time you accessed the Internet, you had to sign on with an ISP, which means you more than likely already have your own Web space. Most ISPs allow you to have more than one e-mail address per account. Each e-mail address is entitled to a certain amount of free Web space. Through the use of *hyperlinks* (small pieces of HTML code that, when clicked, route the clicker from one place to another on the page or on other Web site), you can combine all the free Web space from each e-mail address into one giant Web site. Take a look at Table 8-1, where we compare some popular ISPs.

Table 8-1	ISPs That Give You Free Web Space	
ISP	*Number of E-Mail Addresses*	*Total Space per Account*
Rogers Express*	9	15MB per e-mail address (135MB)
Cogeco High Speed Pro	7	10MB per e-mail address (70MB)
Shaw High Speed	10	20MB per e-mail address (200MB)
Sympatico DSL	11	5MB in total
Execulink DSL	5	20MB in total
SureNet DSL	2	5MB in total
Primus DSL	4	20MB in total
AOL Canada Broadband	7	20MB per e-mail address (140MB)

*Offered through Yahoo! GeoCities, which isn't an ISP, but is a reliable online community that gives each member online Web space. Membership is free. Extra megabyte space is available for purchase.

If America Online (AOL) Canada is your Internet provider, you may already know that AOL often has some serious issues regarding its users getting e-mail from the rest of the Internet. You can't afford to run a business in an area that has e-mail issues. Your AOL account gives each of your seven screen names 20MB (megabytes) of online storage space per screen name (refer to Table 8-1). You can best utilize this space by using it to store images for eBay, not to run a business site. Each screen name, at 20MB, can store 500 images, if each is 40kb (kilobytes). (For more information on how to use this space for your extra images, see Chapter 11.)

Many ISPs have their own page-builder (HTML-generating) program that's free to their users.

Poke around your ISP's homepage for a <u>Community</u> or <u>Your Web Space</u> link. For example, after poking around the Road Runner ISP's homepage (`www.rr.com`), Marsha found the <u>Member Services</u> link, which led her to a page offering various options. She finally found a <u>Personal Home Page</u> link, which took her to a page that would walk her through setting up her own homepage. All she had to do to get started was agree to the site's Terms of Service and log on. Also, Road Runner offered her the option of using Microsoft FrontPage, which is one of the best and easiest Web-building programs around.

We highly recommend FrontPage, but if you want all its benefits, you'll need a site that uses FrontPage *extensions* (portions of the FrontPage program that reside on the server and enable all the HTML magic to happen automatically — you don't have to write in the code). Save FrontPage extensions for *hosted* Web sites (the ones you pay for) when you have a good deal of allotted space. Installing Microsoft FrontPage extensions on a small Web site like the one that Road Runner provides will take up too many of your precious megabytes. (Yahoo!, on the other hand, has them installed for the GeoCities sites, and doesn't count them as part of your allotted megabyte count.)

Instead of getting involved with a huge (and expensive) program such as FrontPage, you might want to consider using a quick and easy HTML generator such as CuteHTML. If you're not looking to get extra fancy, this is the program for you. We often use CuteHTML to put together our eBay auctions when using tables (to put pictures next to the text). You can download a free trial, and the price to buy the program is only $19.99 USD. You can find it on the GlobalSCAPE Web site at

```
www.globalscape.com/cutehtml/
```

If it's offered, use FTP (File Transfer Protocol) to upload your pages and images. You can still design pages in Microsoft FrontPage — just don't use the fancy features. If your ISP doesn't supply an FTP program for you, go to the following and download a free trial of CuteFTP:

```
www.globalscape.com/cuteftp/
```

TIP

Why learn HTML when Web page editors can do it for you?

If you need some help designing those first pages (neither of us consider ourselves proficient in HTML; we still depend on software to design our sites), try looking for inexpensive HTML Web software. I just checked eBay, and an older version of Corel Web Designer was selling for $9.99 USD. Another program, Web Easy 5 Professional Edition, is also selling for less than $20 USD. Lots of Web page editors are available; the key is to find one that includes a graphical WYSIWYG (what-you-see-is-what-you-get) interface that allows you to preview your pages as you design them. You can also use an older version of Microsoft FrontPage (without the extensions) to design simple Web pages.

CuteFTP is a small, simple program that will help you get the pages and images up on your site. Your first Web pages may be simple, and that's okay. You have to get used to having a Web site before you can really use it for commerce. Put up a homepage that links to your eBay auctions and a few product-related pages, and — voila — you're in business. If you're feeling more adventurous about your Web site, check out the next section, where we describe a handful of Web site hosts.

Paying for Your Web Space

If you've been on the Internet for any length of time, you've been bombarded by hosting offers through your daily spam. A Web hosting company houses your Web site code and electronically doles out your pages and images to Web page visitors.

REMEMBER

If you take advantage of PayPal's free Pay Now buttons or Shopping Cart, you can turn a basic-level hosted site into a full-on e-commerce store without paying additional fees to your hosting company. The PayPal tools are easily inserted into your pages with a snippet of code provided by PayPal. Find out more about this later in the chapter.

Before deciding to spend good money on a Web hosting company, thoroughly check it out. Go to that company's site to find a list of features they offer. If you still have questions after perusing the Web site, look for an 800 number to call. You won't find any feedback ratings like you find on eBay, but the following are a few questions to ask — don't hang up until you're satisfied with the answers!

✔ **How long have they been in business?** You don't want a Web host that has been up and running only a few months and operates out of their basement. Deal with someone who's been around the Internet for a while and hence knows what they're doing. Is the company's Web site professional looking? Or does it look like your neighbour's kid designed it? Does the company look like it has enough money to stay in business? You wouldn't want it disappearing mysteriously with your money.

✔ **Who are some of their other clients?** Poke around to see whether you can find links to sites of other clients. Take a look at who else is doing business with them and analyze their sites. Do the pages and links on their clients' sites come up quickly? Do all the images appear in a timely manner? Web sites that load quickly are a good sign.

✔ **What is their downtime-to-uptime ratio?** Does the Web host guarantee *uptime* (the span of time its servers stay operational without going down and denying access to your site)? Expecting a 99 percent uptime guarantee is not unreasonable; you're open for business — and your Web host needs to keep it that way.

✔ **How much Web space do you get for your money?** MSN (Microsoft Network Internet access service) gives you 30MB for free; you'd better be getting a whole lot more if you're paying for it!

✔ **What's their data transfer limit?** *Data transfer* is a measurement of the amount of bytes transferred from your site on the server to the Internet. In July 2001, Marsha's site had 93 thousand hits; in July 2004, it had more than 500 thousand. Each hit transfers a certain amount of bytes (kilobytes, megabytes) from your host's servers to the viewer's computer.

✔ **How easy is it to reach their technical support?** When something goes wrong with your Web site, you need it fixed immediately. You must be able to reach tech support quickly without hanging around on the phone for hours. Is their tech support line toll-free? Does the Web host have a technical support area on its Web site where you can troubleshoot your own problems (in the middle of the night)?

Whenever you're deciding on any kind of provider for your business, take a moment to call their tech support team with a question about the services. Take note of how long you're put on hold and how courteous the techs are. Before plunking down your hard-earned money, be sure the provider's customer service claims aren't merely that — just claims.

✔ **What's the policy on shopping carts?** In time you're probably going to need a shopping cart interface on your site. Does your provider charge extra for that? If so, how much? In the beginning, a convenient and professional-looking way to sell items on your site is to set up a PayPal shopping cart or PayPal Pay Now buttons, but when you're running your business full-time, a shopping cart or a way to accept credit cards is a must.

✔ **What kind of statistics will you get, and how will they be presented?** Visitors who go to your Web site leave a bread crumb trail. Your host collects these statistics so you can find out which are your most and least popular pages. You can know how long people linger on each page, where they come from, and what browsers they're using. How your host supplies these stats to you is important. One of the best reporting formats is provided from a company called WebTrends (www.webtrends.com).

✔ **What hidden fees exist, if any?** Are they charging an exorbitant amount for setup? Charging extra for statistics? Imposing high charges if your bandwidth suddenly increases?

✔ **How often will the Web host back up your site?** No matter how redundant a host's servers are, a disaster may strike, and you need to know that your Web site won't vapourize. *Redundancy* is the safety net for your site. You may be interested in how many power backups a company has for the main system. Perhaps it has generators (more than one is good) and more.

If you have a Web site and you're like us, you're always looking for other hosts that offer more bang for your buck. It takes time to look behind the glitzy promotional statements to find out the facts behind each company. Go to http://ca.tophosts.com and click the link to their current Top 10 Web Hosts in Canada. You can also view the top twenty-five in the U.S. at www.tophosts.com. You might want to also check out www.webhostdir.com/webhostawards. They review U.S.-based Web hosting companies monthly. Take a look at who's listed and then go to check out the host's own Web site.

Table 8-2 provides a comparison of some Canadian host service costs. In the rest of this section, we explain in more detail the services that each company in the table (NetNation, Canaca, Microsoft Small Business Centre, and Yahoo! Web Hosting) provides. Make sure you check out each company's Web site as well to get the most current information.

Table 8-2	Comparing Entry-Level Hosting Costs*			
Feature	*NetNation*	*Canaca*	*Microsoft*	*Yahoo! Web Hosting*
Monthly plan cost	$11.95	$6.95	$12.95	$11.95
Yearly discount rate	$126.24	$59.40	$119.40	N/A
Disk Space storage	150MB	80MB	100MB	5MB
Data transfer/month	Unmetered	800GB	5GB	200GB
24/7 Toll-free tech support	Yes	Yes	Yes	Yes

Feature	NetNation	Canaca	Microsoft	Yahoo! Web Hosting
E-mail aliases	Unlimited	5000	15	200
Set-up fees	$14.95	None	$20.00	$25.00**
FrontPage capability	Yes	Yes	Yes	No

*All prices shown are in U.S. dollars.
** Currently waived.

Keep in mind that 200MB disk storage space can host as many as 6000 HTML pages.

NetNation.com

Here's a company consistently ranked as one of the top ten in Canada by `http://ca.tophosts.com`. NetNation.com (see Figure 8-1) has been hosting Web space since 1996 with more than 300 thousand customers in over 130 countries. For details, check out

`www.netnation.com/products/sharedhosting`

Figure 8-1: The NetNation.com homepage.

Canaca.com

Canaca offers great, inexpensive starter packages, and their site is easy for novices to navigate. In business since 1998 and based in Toronto, they boast a "direct connection to Toronto's main carrier hotel using optimum dark fibre lines." (That means that they provide a fast and stable connection to the Web.) Uptime is guaranteed by their own generators, capable of supporting their system for up to a week without standard utility power.

One of their added features is a series of online tutorials that walk you through the process of getting your Web site up and running — a great bonus for first-timers.

For little guys, Canaca (see Figure 8-2) offers *shared hosting,* and that's probably what you'll be using for quite a while. With shared hosting, your site resides with others on a single server, sharing all resources.

Figure 8-2:
The
Canaca.com
homepage.

If your Internet sales gross more than $100 thousand a year, you might have to look into *dedicated hosting,* in which your site is on a server of its own and is managed by the technical experts at your hosting company.

Microsoft Small Business Centre

If NetNation is big, Microsoft is gargantuan; it's the leader in everything related to personal computing (as if you didn't know that). To grab a piece of the e-commerce market, Microsoft is making a strong push with its improved Small Business Centre site (see Figure 8-3), which has always been a home for business Internet utilities and has now come full circle to hosting Web sites and promoting e-commerce. Microsoft Canada does not yet offer Web hosting services, although their Small Business Corner is still a great resource for your Internet business.

Figure 8-3:
The
Microsoft
Small
Business
Centre Web
Hosting
page.

Availing yourself of Microsoft's U.S.-based Web hosting services is an easy procedure. You can find out the details of their current offerings at

```
http://www.microsoft.com/smallbusiness/online/web-
            hosting/detail.mspx
```

Microsoft Small Business Centre FTPs your pages through the use of Microsoft FrontPage, which must be purchased separately. Design your own pages in FrontPage, then take advantage of the many promotional and commerce-enabled options offered on the site.

Getting your Web site off the ground

Web hosting companies offer many levels of entry. Basic do-it-yourself packages are available, like those listed in Table 8-2. You can also choose a plan offering a crack team of professional Web designers at your service to help you get up and running, if you prefer. When you're just starting out, having the assistance of a professional always helps.

Most professional Web designers will give you the use of their own FTP service and an online easy-to-use WYSIWYG Web site Content Manager (so you don't have to invest in extra software). You can add all the pages you want to your professionally formatted site. By shopping around, you can view some custom designs that have been produced for small businesses and get a better idea of what you want for your own site.

 Microsoft Small Business Centre also has a Traffic Builder program for banner advertising on its LinkExchange Network. Banner ad campaign prices range from $50–$500 USD. Rates rise as you target your advertising and specify where you want the ad to appear. See the section "Marketing Your Web Site (More Visitors = More Business)," later in this chapter, for more tips on getting the word out about your Web site.

Yahoo! Web site services

Yahoo! is trying to do a little bit of everything these days. We're never sure in which direction it's going. Yahoo! took over GeoCities (one of the original free Web site hosts) a few years back, so Marsha's family Web site became a free Yahoo! site. Considering that its sites are free, we must admit it — the services Yahoo! offers have been top-drawer, disproving the notion that you get what you pay for. But then again, Marsha's not running a business from the site; it's just a bunch of family pictures.

When you subscribe to one of Yahoo!'s Web hosting plans, you can download their free SiteBuilder software, which lets you get a basic site up and running quickly. Thank goodness you don't have to know any HTML to use it! The download includes access to more than 300 stock templates that you can customize any way you want. If you don't want to use SiteBuilder, you can use good old Microsoft FrontPage to design your site.

If you're looking for a store solution, you can subscribe to a do-it-your
featured e-commerce site from Yahoo! for $39.95 USD a month. This site in
product merchandising templates, order management systems, thirty days
free consulting, and more. Check out their award-winning offerings at

```
smallbusiness.yahoo.com
```

What's in a Web Site Name:
Naming Your Baby

What to name the baby, er, Web site? It's almost as much of a dilemma as
deciding on your eBay user ID or eBay store name. If you don't have an existing company name that you want to use, why not use the same name as your
eBay store? (Check out Chapter 5 for details about eBay stores.) Lock it up
now so you can keep your brand forever.

Select a name for your site that identifies what you do, what you sell, or who
you are. And be sure you like it, because once it's yours and you begin operating under it — and establishing a reputation — it'll be with you as long as
you're selling online, even if that's twenty years from now. A few Web sites
offer wizards to help you decide your domain name. A particularly intuitive
one can be found at the following:

```
www.namesarecheap.com/wizard.shtml
```

In a small, Web-based form, you input your primary business type and
some keywords that describe your business. Then, the wizard displays
a large number of options and lets you know whether they are available.
Very convenient.

Before you attempt to register a name, check to be sure no one else has it
trademarked. To search an updated list of registered Canadian trademarks,
use the electronic trademark search system located here:

```
http://strategis.ic.gc.ca/app/cipo/trademarks/search/tmSe
        arch.do?language=eng
```

Or, for a search of U.S. registered trademarks, go to:

```
www.trademarksearchforfree.com
```

Once you find a good site name that isn't already taken, you may want to trademark it. NameProtect.com is an online service that can help you with that. Online trademark applications and referrals to an attorney (if you'd like to use one) are available — just visit their site for more information.

Registering Your Domain Name (Before Someone Else Takes It)

Talk about your junk e-mail. We get e-mails every day advising us to "Lose 40 pounds in 40 days" and "Accept credit cards now." Of course, those that shriek "REGISTER YOUR NAME NOW!" also exist, and are particularly jarring. This last scam seems to be geared to obtaining e-mail addresses for other junk mail lists rather than trying to help register a Web site. Choosing a select *registrar* (the company handling the registration of your site name) is as important as choosing the right Web host. Remember that the Internet is still a little like the Wild West; the James gang (or, false service providers) might be waiting to relieve you of your hard-earned cash. One way to protect yourself is understanding how the registry works — knowledge *is* power, so read on.

In Canada, the domain registration business has been controlled since 1998 by CIRA (the Canadian Internet Registration Authority), a not-for-profit corporation responsible for operating the dot-ca country code. CIRA, in turn, controls the certification of registrar companies. Although many companies may offer registration, all domains are eventually registered by certified registrars. A quick Web search reveals literally hundreds of companies that are more than happy to register your domain. Bill chose to allow his Web hosting service to register his domain names as they were competitive and it just made things so much easier to keep it all under one roof.

In most cases it is preferable to secure domains with a dot-com ending but that us becoming more and more difficult as more and more companies secure their presence on the Web. If the dot-com domain you want is already spoken for you may have to settle for the dot-ca alternative. Keep in mind though that you want potential buyers to find you easily and not confuse you with a similarly named Web site.

Before you decide on a registrar for your domain name, take a minute to see whether the registrar is accredited by ICANN (the Internet Corporation for Assigned Names and Numbers — the international governing body for domain names) or is reselling for an official ICANN-accredited registrar. (You'll have to ask who they register with.) The Accredited Registrar Directory is updated constantly, so check the following for the most recent list:

```
www.internic.com/regist.html
```

For a comparison of registration fees, see Table 8-3.

Table 8-3	Comparing Yearly Domain Name Registration Fees	
Registrar	**Registration Fee (*USD)**	**URL Forwarding**
namesystem.com	$12.00*	included
enom.com	$29.95*	included
domainpeople.ca	$17.95	included
tera-byte.com	$19.95*	included

You'll usually get a substantial discount from the more expensive registrars when you register your domain name for multiple years — not a bad idea if you plan on staying in business. Also, if you register your name through your hosting service, you might be able to cut the prices in Table 8-3 in half! The only drawback is that your prepaid registration goes out the window if you choose to change hosting companies.

If you're registering a new domain name but already have a site set up with your ISP, you need a feature called URL, or Web address, forwarding. This feature redirects any hits from your existing URL address to your new domain name. Some registrars offer URL forwarding as part of a package, but beware of any company that offers it for free. Remember, nothing's truly free — in this case, the price you will most likely pay is having a big, fat banner at the bottom of your homepage. You also want your registrar to have some available tech support. Troubleshooting DNS (distributed name service) issues is a job for those who know what they're doing! Sometimes you get what you pay for, so it may be worth paying for a service that includes these features.

Domain parking

Suppose that you've come up with a brilliant name for your site and you get really big and famous. Then someone else uses your Web site name, but registers it as a .net — while yours is a .com. When you're ready to register your site, take action to prevent this: register both domains (.com and .net) and park them with your registrar. For example, www.ebay.net and ebay org are registered to (guess who?) ebay.com. You can check the owner of any domain name on any of the Web hosting or registrar sites.

...keting Your Web Site (More
...tors = More Business)

After you set up your Web site, you can let the world know about it. Having spent many years in the advertising business, Marsha can spot businesses that *want* to fail. They open their doors and expect the world to beat a path to them and make them rich. This doesn't happen — ever.

You must take an active approach to letting the world in on the goodies you have for sale. This means spending a good deal of time promoting your site by running banner ads and getting your URL into a search engine. No shortcuts exist.

About a trillion people out there want to take your money to advertise your Web site. Knowing who you're dealing with is key in this situation, as in all business regarding your Web site. If you want to run your banner on someone else's site, don't spend money; ask to do an exchange. The more advertising you can get for free, the better. If you decide you want to pay for advertising, we recommend waiting until after you've made a profit selling merchandise from your site.

A simple link to your Web site from your About Me page on eBay will draw people to your site initially. You'll be pleasantly surprised.

Making your personal information private

ICANN requires every registrar to maintain a publicly accessible WHOIS database displaying all contact information for all domain names registered. Interested parties (or fraudsters) can find out the name, street address, e-mail address, and phone number of the site owner by running a *whois* search on the domain name. You can run a whois search by going to www.whois.net and typing in the domain name in question.

This information can be very useful to just about anyone who is up to no good, including identity thieves, stalkers, and spammers who cloak their identity by pretending their return address is your address. See the difference between private and public registrations by running a whois search on Marsha's Web site, www.coolebaytools.com, and then on www.ebay.com.

Registrars such as networksolutions.com offer private registration for an additional $9.00 USD a year. Check to see whether your registrar offers this service.

Banner ad exchanges

The way banner ad exchange services work is simple: you design a banner ad in your graphics program, following designated size requirements and other standards that are outlined in the following list. The service then displays your banner on other sites. When Web surfers click your banner, they're taken to your Web site, where they'll see all the great stuff you have for sale. You can even target what type of sites you want your banner to appear on. But that's only half of the deal — remember that this is, essentially, a swap. Someone else's banner will appear on your pages in exchange for showing yours on other sites.

The standard specs for a banner ad are as follows:

468 pixels wide by 60 pixels high

GIF format (no JPEGs)

Nontransparent

File size less than 10K (10,240 bytes)

If animated, the animation stops at seven seconds and doesn't include loops

Banner design

If you think that designing an eye-catching banner ad is beyond your graphic talents (see the one Marsha uses for her company in Figure 8-4), you'll be happy to know that many excellent graphic artists on the Internet can produce one for you. Type *banner design* into any search engine, and a ton of listings will come up. To find a designer who matches your needs, look at samples (and pricing) on their Web sites.

On eBay, search for *web banner* or *banner design*. We found 96 listings of banner ad designers with reasonable prices; we're sure you'll find one who meets your needs.

Figure 8-4:
One of
Marsha's
animated
banner ads.

Microsoft Banner Advertising

Microsoft Banner Advertising is one of the largest and most effective networks on the Net. They rotate your banner throughout their 400 thousand sites and give you great stats on how often your banner is viewed and how often your page is visited. Then, these stats are combined to calculate your *clickthrough ratio* (the number of times your banner is displayed versus the actual number of times people click it to visit your site).

Getting your URL into a search engine

For people to find your site (and what you're selling), they must be able to locate you. Using a search engine is the most popular way to do this. Submitting your site to search engines is extremely helpful to increase your exposure. Start by going to the search engines that interest you and looking for a link or a help area inviting you to submit your site. Be sure to follow any specific instructions at this stage; some sites may limit the number of keywords and characters allowed in your description.

To submit your URL to search engines, you need to do a little work (nothing's easy, is it?). Write down twenty-five to fifty words or phrases that describe your Web site; these are your *keywords.* Now, using as many of the words you came up with as you can, write a site description. Make a list of the remaining words and short phrases, separating each one with a comma. You can use them to add *meta tags* to the header in your HTML document for your homepage. Meta tags are identifiers used by search engine *spiders,* robots that troll the Internet looking for new sites to classify on search engines. Meta tags are used like this:

```
<META NAME = "insert your keywords here separated by
        commas" CONTENT = "short description of your
        site">
```

If you have a problem coming up with keywords, check out Yahoo! GeoCities' handy meta tag generator, which you can use for free:

```
http://geocities.yahoo.com/v/res/meg.html
```

Submit It!

Submit It! (see Figure 8-5), part of Microsoft's Small Business Centre, automatically forwards your site submissions to hundreds of online search engines, saving you the trouble of going from site to site. For $49 USD a year, the service will submit as many as ten URLs as often as you'd like. Submit It! even sends you a regular report outlining your URL's progress. Free listing in the

Microsoft Small Business Directory is also included as part of your subscription — talk about money well spent! Get the full scoop on this great service at www.submit-it.com.

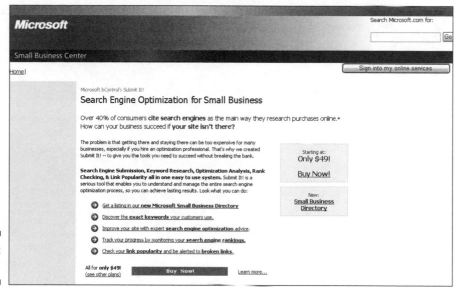

Figure 8-5:
Submit It!

Google

Google crawls the Internet regularly with its spider, Googlebot, looking for new sites to index on Google Search. If Googlebot has missed your site, go to the following and let Google know that your site is ready for listing:

```
www.google.com/addurl.html
```

Google doesn't guarantee that your site will be listed, but the process takes less than a minute. What could it hurt?

Yahoo!

Yahoo! is one of the more difficult sites to list with, although you *can* get a free listing if you're not in a hurry. Filling out all the forms correctly can be time-consuming, and then you must wait six to eight weeks to have them processed. Still, it may be worth it to save some money. Instructions for the free listing are at the following:

```
http://docs.yahoo.com/info/suggest/
```

Paying Yahoo! Express $299 USD gets your site listed immediately (funny how that works). For more information on this option, see:

```
http://smallbusiness.yahoo.com/marketing/directory.php
```

Yahoo! guarantees that, if you use this express service, your application will be reviewed in just seven business days.

Part III
Business Is Business — No Foolin' Around!

In this part . . .

Now it's time to delve into the dollars and sense of your eBay business. In this part, we discuss automating your business by using online and offline tools, jazzing up your auctions, setting up your home photo studio, and handling shipping (the bane of most businesses). We also give you the lowdown on two other important aspects of your business: working with customers and collecting payments.

Chapter 9

Software Built for Online Auctions

*N*ow that eBay has become a world marketplace, a single-page auction or item listing is becoming an increasingly valuable piece of real estate. Millions of people can view your sale — the more auctions and fixed-price items you can list, the better your chances are to make a good living. Time is money: You need to post your auctions quickly and accurately.

Auction posting, record keeping, inventory cataloguing, photo managing, and statistic gathering are all tasks that you can automate. The more your business grows, the more confusing things can become. Automated tools can help you keep it all straight. But remember: The more tools you use, the more expense you may be adding to your business. Always keep your bottom line in mind when evaluating whether to use fee-based software and services.

In this chapter, we discuss how to automate different tasks, the software available to help you, and Web sites offering services designed to make your daily chores considerably more bearable. After you read this chapter, you'll be well-equipped to decide whether or not you want to automate your business and how much.

Considering Tasks for Automation

No matter how few or how many auctions you're running, you'll have to perform certain office tasks. Depending on your personal business style, you may want to automate any or all of them. To automate the tasks we describe in this section, you can choose to use a single program or service, a manual method, or a combination of these options. For those who aren't ready to take the automated plunge, we also offer some alternatives. In this section, we also provide references guiding you to where in this book or on the Web you can find more information about the automated services we discuss.

Setting up images for automatic FTP upload

Several ways exist to store the display images in your auctions. If you're using an auction management service or software package (such as MarketWorks or Auction Wizard, both of which we discuss later in this chapter), an *uploader* is usually included. Many online services merely fetch the photos from your hard drive without the need for additional FTP software. To enable this, you use a screen similar to eBay's Sell Your Item Page, shown in Figure 9-1.

Figure 9-1: Uploading images from your hard drive.

With this format, you merely click the Browse button to access the Open File window, then find the location of the image on your hard drive. When you've located the images that you want to upload (one per line), click the Upload button and the images will be on their way to the service's servers.

If you choose to keep images on your own Web site (which makes the images available for your Web site, too), you'll have to use some sort of FTP software. You probably aren't even close to using the total space for your Web site that your hosting service has allotted to you, meaning you'll have plenty of room to store a separate folder of eBay images. ISPs also often give you several megabytes of storage space when you sign up for Internet service (see Chapter 8 for more information about this).

A straightforward, stand-alone FTP software program is important to include in your auction arsenal, even if you use a management service or other type of software (we like to have a backup method). Our personal favourite is CuteFTP from GlobalSCAPE, shown in Figure 9-2.

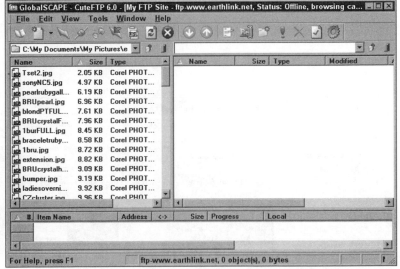

Figure 9-2:
CuteFTP
Home
Edition.

CuteFTP is so simple to use, you may never read the instructions. To send files to a site, type the location and your username and password. Click Connect, and CuteFTP automatically connects to the site. From this point, you merely drag and drop files from the screen on the left (your hard drive) to the screen on the right (your Web site). A 30-day free trial is downloadable from

```
www.globalscape.com/o/912
```

You can register the program for only $39.95 USD.

Setting up an auction photo gallery

Until you get your own eBay store, setting up a photo gallery is a great alternative. If your customers have a high-speed Internet connection, they're able to browse your auctions through photographs. Some auction management sites can host your gallery; some charge for this service, and others do not. The best part of setting up your own photo gallery is that you can produce it yourself without any fancy programs or auction management software, and at no additional cost to you.

To make your own gallery on eBay without installing fancy scripts in your listings, you need to do three things. First, you must include eBay gallery photos with each of your listings. (You're doing that anyway, right?) Next, you can test the following URL in your browser, substituting your own user ID where indicated in ***bold italic***:

```
http://search-desc.ebay.com/search/search.dll?
       MfcISAPICommand=GetResult&query=youreBayuserID&
       ht=1&srchdesc=y&SortProperty=MetaEndSort&st=1
```

Figure 9-3 shows you a sample of what you'll see.

Figure 9-3:
A home-made gallery linked page.

Now that you have seen a sample of your gallery, link it to your auction by inserting the following HTML into your auction:

```
<a href=" search-desc.ebay.com/search/search.dll?
       MfcISAPICommand=GetResult&query=youreBayuserID&
       ht=1&srchdesc=y&SortProperty=MetaEndSort&st=1">
       <B>Click <I>here</I> to view yourebayuserID
       Gallery</B> <img
       src="http://pics.ebay.com/aw/pics/ebay_my_butto
       n.gif" alt="My Gallery on eBay"></a >
```

As you can see in Figure 9-4, this HTML sniplet also inserts the custom eBay button.

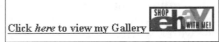

Sorting auction e-mail

A vital function of any auction software or system is the ability to customize
and send e-mails to your auction winners. Many sellers use the default letters
in these programs, which tend to sound a bit — no, incredibly — impersonal
and uncaring. (To see some examples of customer-friendly e-mails and tips
on drafting your own, head to Chapter 12.) Also, you must decide whether
you want your program to receive e-mail as well as send it.

Most computer-resident auction management programs have their own built-
in e-mail software. When you download your winner's information from eBay,
the program automatically generates invoices and congratulatory e-mails.

How to handle your auction-related e-mail is a personal choice. Although we
currently use eBay's Selling Manager to send it, we receive our auction e-mail
through Outlook using a separate folder titled "Auctions" with subfolders for
eBay Buying and eBay Selling.

Automating end-of-auction e-mail

If you want to set up e-mails to be sent automatically after an auction ends, you
must use a software application. Software is available that downloads your final
auction results, generates an e-mail, and lets you preview that e-mail before
sending it out. Many of the online sites that we discuss later in this chapter
(see the section "Online auction management sites") automatically send out
winner confirmation e-mails when an auction is over. Be sure that you set your
preferences to Preview the e-mail before sending if you want to use this option.

Keeping inventory

Many eBay PowerSellers depend on the old clipboard or notebook method,
crossing off items as they sell them, to keep track of their stock. If that works
for you, great. Others prefer to use an Excel spreadsheet to manage inventory.

Most of the auction management packages that we detail later in this chapter (see the section "Auction management software") handle inventory for you. Some automatically deduct an item from inventory when you launch an auction. You have your choice of handling inventory directly on your computer or keeping your inventory online with a service that's accessible from any computer, wherever you are.

We both handle inventory through QuickBooks. When buying merchandise to sell, we post the bill to QuickBooks, which automatically registers the merchandise as inventory. When, later, we input a sale, the program deducts the items sold from that inventory list. A status report can be printed whenever we need to see how much of an item is left in stock — or if we need to reorder stock.

Generating HTML

Fancy auctions are nice, but fanciness doesn't make an item sell any better. Competitive pricing and low shipping rates work in your favour — especially with eBay's Compare Items feature in the Search option. Also, a clean listing with as many photos as necessary goes a long way to sell your product. Some software and services offer a large selection of templates to gussy up your auctions. But you must think of your customers before deciding to use elaborate visuals to improve the look of your listings. Many Internet users still use dial-up connections to log on to the Internet, which are notoriously slow. While the use of simple HTML doesn't slow the loading of your pages, the addition of miscellaneous images (decorative backgrounds and animations, for example) makes viewing your auctions a chore for those dialing up. And forget the background music — it *really* slows things down!

Don't fret — you can make do without either boring or frustrating potential buyers by repeatedly incorporating two or three simple HTML templates into your auctions, cutting and pasting new text as necessary. Most auction management programs offer you the choice of several templates. Major companies "brand" themselves by giving a standard look to their advertising and identity; we recommend that you do the same by sticking with a couple of templates that are similar when designing your auctions. Your customers will get used to the look of your auctions and feel comfortable each time they view one.

Marsha uses CuteHTML to generate much of the code for her auction descriptions. An important line of code that everyone seems to forget is the one that inserts a picture into your auction description. On the Sell Your Item page, click the tab to view it in HTML mode. Then, insert the following line in your description just below where you'd like your image to appear:

```
<img src="http://www.yourserver.com/imagename.jpg">
```

Be sure to substitute your own server and image name. If you want to put one picture on top of another, just type <P> between the lines of code — then repeat the HTML line with a different name for each image that you want to display.

If you're in a rush and need a quick and easy HTML generator, go to Marsha's Web site at www.coolebaytools.com and click Tools. Also, her book *eBay Timesaving Techniques For Dummies* (Wiley) has sample HTML code for auction descriptions as well as a chart of all the code you'll ever need for an eBay auction.

One-click relisting and selling similar items

Using an auction software package or service speeds up the process of posting or relisting items. After you input your inventory into the software, posting or relisting your auctions is just a mouse click away. All the auction management software packages that we detail later in this chapter include this feature.

If you buy your items in bulk, you might want to take advantage of eBay's free relisting tool. By clicking the <u>Sell Similar</u> link (see Figure 9-5) on any successful listing, you can automatically relist your items. Sell Similar starts each listing as new, so if it doesn't sell, you can avail yourself of the Relist feature. This way, if the item sells the second time, your insertion fees for the first listing will be credited.

Figure 9-5: The <u>Relist</u> and <u>Sell Similar</u> links on a completed auction page.

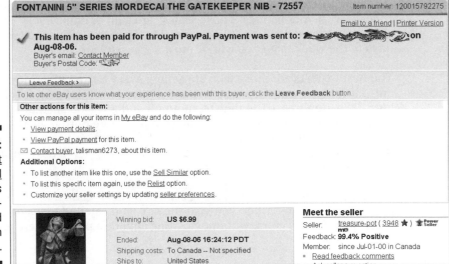

Although eBay says that Sell Similar is for relisting items, the feature is also useful when listing a duplicate of an item that has sold successfully. The only difference is that you aren't credited for the unsold auction listing fee.

One savvy seller we know about uses the eBay Sell Similar feature to post new auctions. She simply clicks the <u>Sell Similar</u> link and then cuts and pastes her new information into the existing HTML format. That's why her auctions all have the same feel and flavour.

Scheduling your listings for bulk upload

If you want to schedule the unattended launch of your auctions without incurring eBay's ten-cent fee, you must use an online management service (check out the "Online auction management sites" section later in this chapter). If you can be at your computer to send your auctions to eBay either individually or in bulk, you can use the Turbo Lister application that eBay offers at no charge. (For details, see the "Turbo Lister" section later in the chapter.)

Researching your statistics

So many questions arise when you're selling on eBay. What is the best time to end my auction? What day of the week is best to start my listing? Is it better to run a five-day or a seven-day auction? Now an online service can help you separate the rumours from the facts.

Lots of eBay *experts* out there will give you hard and fast rules to guarantee success with your listings. Those "rules" are a lot of bunk. Every category and every type of item has the potential to draw shoppers, and the times and days of the week that each will be most successful are varied.

The best experts are those who are selling every day on eBay, day in and day out. They are usually PowerSellers and do their own research for their listings. They don't have the time to spout off and give you secrets — they are too busy using their research to make money. We're both regular sellers on eBay (PowerSellers, too), and have seen distinct variations in sales patterns through the use of a fantastic online service called ViewTracker from Sellathon. It's really one-of-a-kind.

Sellathon tracks your listings using a small piece of code that you insert in your auctions. Later, when you visit the site, you can find loads of information about your visitors, without violating anyone's privacy. Here are some of the things you can find out:

✔ How many times has the user visited your auction?

✔ What date and time did the visitor arrive at your auction?

✔ Where is the visitor from (which city, province or state, and country)?

✔ How did the visitor find your auction: Did they search all of eBay, browse or search a category (Sellathon will specify which ones), or use eBay's Product Finder utility? Were they directed by the "See Seller's Other Items" link or a similar page?

✔ What search terms did the visitor use to find your item, if they were searching? Did they search Titles Only or Titles and Descriptions?

✔ Did the visitor elect to view Auctions Only, Buy It Now, or both?

✔ Was the item's reserve price met when the visitor arrived?

✔ How much time did the visitor actually spend viewing your item?

✔ Did the visitor choose to watch this listing in his or her My eBay page?

✔ How many bids have been placed on the item up to date? (Sellathon reports each bid as it comes in.)

All this information and more is available to you through Sellathon. You can get a free thirty-day trial by visiting www.sellathon.com. After that, the service costs $4.95 USD a month or $49 USD a year.

To end an old wives' tale about what days your auctions get the highest hits, view the chart from Marsha's Sellathon account in Figure 9-6. You can see how many visits twenty-six listings got each day. Verrrrry interesting.

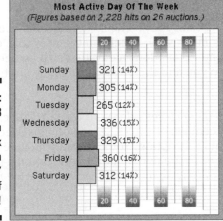

Most Active Day Of The Week
(Figures based on 2,228 hits on 26 auctions.)

Day	Hits	
Sunday	321	(14%)
Monday	305	(14%)
Tuesday	265	(12%)
Wednesday	336	(15%)
Thursday	329	(15%)
Friday	360	(16%)
Saturday	312	(14%)

Figure 9-6: That's 2,228 hits on twenty-six auctions in seven days' worth of listings!

Photo hosting

If all you need is photo hosting, and you've checked that your ISP doesn't give you any free Web space (please check Chapter 8 for a short list of ISPs and the amount of Web storage space they offer their customers), you can always rely on eBay's picture services. For fifteen cents an image, you can host an additional picture in each auction.

If you run more than forty auctions a month, a better alternative exists. Pair Networks offers a reasonably priced package called the FTP Account, which seems to be tailored for eBay sellers. For $5.95 USD a month plus an initial $20 setup charge you get 250MB of storage space to hold your eBay images and 20GB of transfer bandwidth. Also, the service gives you an e-mail address and unlimited e-mail forwarding from this account to your private address. For more information, visit

```
www.pair.com/services/web_hosting/ftp.html
```

Automating other tasks

That's not all! You can automate a few more tasks. Having so many options is like being in a candy store: You may want it all, but that might not be good for you. For example, if you use online postage, you may not want to print your labels because that would be doubling your work. Take a serious look at the options you're offered when deciding what tasks to automate and see whether they fit into your particular work style.

Checking out

When someone wins or buys an item, eBay's checkout indicates your preferred forms of payment, including PayPal, which it integrates with directly. If you're closing less than a hundred auctions a day, that's all you need. eBay and PayPal also send e-mails to you and the buyer at this time so that you can arrange for payment.

Some online auction management services offer your own private checkout area, which will cost you a percentage of your sale, so you must decide whether your business warrants this option. You can easily include a link to your PayPal payment area in the personalized notification e-mail that you will send your winner; doing so makes a checkout service unnecessary.

Printing shipping labels

Printing shipping labels without printing postage can be the beginning of a laborious two-step process. PayPal now allows you to print your labels and postage all in one step. Check out Chapter 17 for information on how this works.

Some services print your winner's address labels without postage, including eBay's Selling Manager and Selling Manager Pro. That works well if you don't mind carrying your packages to the post office for postage. (Why would you do that? A burning need to stand in line, I guess!)

Tracking buyer information

Keeping track of your winners isn't rocket science. You can do it in an Excel spreadsheet or a Word document, both of which are exportable to almost any program for follow-up mailings promoting future sales. If you choose to have an online management service do this for you, be sure that you can download the information to your computer (in case you and the online service part ways someday).

Generating customized reports

Sales reports, ledgers, and tax information are all documents that are important to have for your business. Online services and software supply different flavours of these reports.

PayPal allows you to download your sales data into a format compatible with QuickBooks, a popular and highly respected bookkeeping program. You can also choose to download your data as an Excel spreadsheet, which is also compatible with Microsoft Works. PayPal reports are chock full of intensely detailed information about your sales and deposits. Putting this information in a standard accounting software program on a regular basis makes your year-end calculations easier to bear. (In Chapter 16, we detail what else you might need for this task.)

Submitting feedback

If you're running a lot of auctions, leaving feedback can be a chore. One solution is to automate the submission of feedback with software or an online service. But be careful — timing the automation of this task can be tricky.

Don't leave feedback for an eBay transaction until after you've heard from the buyer that the purchase is satisfactory. Leaving positive feedback immediately after you've received payment from the buyer is too soon. After you receive an e-mail assuring you that the customer is satisfied, manually leaving feedback by going to the feedback forum (or the item page) can be just as easy — if not easier — as bulk-loading feedback.

Managing Your Business with Online Resources and Software

If you search the Internet for auction management services and software, you'll come up with a bunch. For simplicity's sake, in this chapter we've chosen to examine just a few examples of what's available. After speaking to many sellers, we've found online services that offer uptime reliability (this is important; you don't want the server that holds your photos going down or mislaunching your auctions) and software that's continually updated to match eBay changes.

Using a site or software to run your auctions takes practice, so we suggest you try any and all of the services you find appealing that offer free preview trials. We include a link with each of the applications we profile so that you can check them out further. Also, we compare the current costs of many auction management and online services in Table 9-1.

Table 9-1	Cost Comparisons for Auction Management Services and Software
Site Services or Software	*Cost*
AAASeller.com	$9.95/month*
Auction Wizard 2000 (auctionwizard2000.com)	$75.00 (first year), $50.00 renewal*
ChannelAdvisor.com	$29.95/month ($270.00/year)*
eBay's Selling Manager	$5.99/month
eBay's Selling Manager Pro	$19.99/month
InkFrog.com	$9.95/month*
MarketWorks.com	2% of sales ($0.20 minimum); $29.95/month (minimum)*
Meridian (www.noblespirit.com)	$9.95/month*
Shooting Star (www.foodogsoftware.com)	$60.00 flat fee*
Spoonfeeder.com	$49.95 + various monthly service plans*
Vendio (www.vendio.com)	$.12 per listing + 1.25% final value fee*
Zoovy.com	$49.95 ($399.95 setup fee) + 2% of sales*

* indicates amounts in USD

Some software and services work on a monthly fee, whereas others work on a one-time purchase fee. For a one-time-purchase software application to truly benefit you, it *must* have the reputation of updating its software each time eBay makes a change in its system. The programs that we discuss in this chapter have been upgraded continually to date.

Most services have a free trial period. Be sure not to waste your precious time inputting your entire inventory, only to discover you don't like the way the service works. Instead, give the service a whirl by inputting only a few items.

Online auction management sites

Auction management Web sites can handle almost everything, from inventory management to label printing. Some sellers prefer online (or hosted) management sites because you can access your information from any computer. You might use every feature a site offers, or you might choose a bit from column A and a bit from column B, then perform the more personalized tasks manually. Read on to determine what — and how much — service might best suit your needs.

Although quite a few excellent online services for automating sales are available, we have room here to show you only a few. Remember that by using an online service, your information resides on a server out there in cyberspace; if you're a control freak, that may be a bit much to bear. Many services are similar in format, so in the following sections we point out the highlights of a few representative systems.

When selecting a service, look for a logo or bit of text indicating that it is an eBay Certified Developer, Preferred Solution Provider, or API licensee. These people have first access to eBay's system changes and can implement them immediately. Other services may need a day or so lag time to update their software.

Following are some of the popular sites in the online auction management arena:

AAASeller (`www.aaaseller.com`)

ándale (`andale.com`)

Auctiva (`www.auctiva.com`)

Inkfrog (`www.inkfrog.com`)

Zoovy.com (`www.zoovy.com`)

ChannelAdvisor

ChannelAdvisor's founder Scot Wingo got into the auction business around the turn of the century. His first foray into the eBay world was AuctionRover, a site that had tools to perform an extensive eBay search, list auctions, and check pricing trends. The company's cute Rover logo was fashioned after Wingo's border collie, Mack.

Fast forward to today. ChannelAdvisor is a highly popular management service used by all levels of eBay sellers. This company supplies listing and management services to everyone from Fortune 1000 companies to the little old lady next door.

How? They offer three levels of software: Enterprise, for large businesses who want to outsource their online business; Merchant, for mid-sized businesses and higher-level PowerSellers; and Pro, for small businesses and individuals. These powerful software suites help eBay sellers successfully manage and automate the sale of their merchandise.

Starting at the entry level, you can get the Pro version of ChannelAdvisor for $29.95 USD a month. Here's what they offer the beginning level seller:

- **Listing design and launching:** Create your listings with ChannelAdvisor's standard templates or use your own HTML to design auction descriptions. List your items immediately or schedule a listing to be posted in the future. ChannelAdvisor will launch the auction when you tell them to.

- **Item and inventory management:** If you want to keep your inventory online, you can create a file for that on the ChannelAdvisor system. If you prefer to input your inventory offline, you can import it from their Excel template. You can also import open auctions or store listings to your ChannelAdvisor account for relisting or servicing.

- **Image hosting:** You get 250MB of space to host your images. You can upload them to the site four at a time, or use FTP to upload a large quantity.

- **Post-auction management:** This company merges your winning auction information and generates customized e-mail and invoices for your buyers. You can print mailing labels, too.

To tour the various offerings of ChannelAdvisor and find out about their free trial period, visit

www.channeladvisor.com

MarketWorks (previously AuctionWorks)

A group of collectors who saw the need for power tools for PowerSellers developed this highly graphical site (www.MarketWorks.com). We think they've succeeded. (This company was known in the eBay community as AuctionWorks, but changed its name in June 2004.) A high percentage of eBay PowerSellers use this site, collectively launching approximately two million listings on eBay every month. MarketWorks offers its registered users help links at every turn, a first-rate online tutorial, free toll-free support (both the phone call and the support are free), and free interactive training classes. The site integration is broad; here are just a few of their features:

- ✔ **Item and inventory management:** Features the ClickLaunch Single Step Launcher, which simultaneously launches individual items to auction while adding them to your inventory. (The site is also capable of bulk item launching.) LaunchBots provides automated launching of your listings. You can import existing auctions from eBay and import with their Bulk Inventory Upload form in Excel and MS Access.

- ✔ **Image hosting:** Enables you to bulk upload fifteen images at a time to their servers. The basic account allows 100MB of storage. If your images average 30K each, you should be able to upload almost 3,500 images into the 100MB image hosting space.

- ✔ **Auction reporting:** Generates accounts receivable, item history, and post-sales reports from the Reports area. MarketWorks has its own Traction System for sales and item tracking. The reporting feature offers customizable views of your sales data, item, and auction data, as well as accounts receivable!

- ✔ **Templates and listing:** MarketWorks uses their own trademarked Ballista template listing system. You can use their predefined colour templates or use their macros with your own predefined HTML template, substituting the macros for stock areas in your template. By using their custom ad template option and well-thought-out macros, you can take your own HTML template and make a MarketWorks template.

- ✔ **Post-auction management:** Sends out automated e-mail to your winners, linking them back to your own branded checkout page. If customers want to pay with PayPal or your own Merchant Account, they have to link from there. MarketWorks combines multiple wins (for a single buyer) for shipping and invoicing. Also, you may pre-set six different feedback comments that you can select from at the time of posting.

MarketWorks offers all their users a StoreFront with its own URL at no additional charge. If an item sells from your StoreFront, you pay MarketWorks the standard rate of 2 percent commission. When you load items into inventory, you have the choice of immediately listing them in your StoreFront. All your items are seamlessly integrated. To get current information about MarketWorks and sign up for a free trial, go to

www.MarketWorks.com

eBay's Selling Manager

Some time ago, eBay began to offer a powerful tool to simplify the All Selling page found in My eBay. Selling Manager displays a summary of your scheduled, current and closed transactions (see the figure). Many sellers (even many PowerSellers) rely on Selling Manager to handle their eBay management chores.

From Selling Manager, you can:

✔ **View listing status:** See which sales activities you've completed and what you have left to do.

✔ **Send custom e-mail and post feedback:** Customize your e-mail templates and set up stored feedback comments to help you run through the post-sales process quickly.

✔ **Relist in bulk:** Relist multiple sold and unsold listings at once.

✔ **Maintain sales records:** View individual sales records for every transaction, including a history of the transaction status.

✔ **Print invoices and shipping labels:** Print labels and invoices directly from your sales records.

✔ **Download your sales history:** Export your sales records to keep files on your computer.

✔ **Keep track of NPB and FVF:** File non-paying buyer alerts and Final Value Fee requests.

The fee to use Selling Manager is $5.99 CAD a month. They also offer a Pro version that incorporates inventory management and more for $19.99 CAD a month.

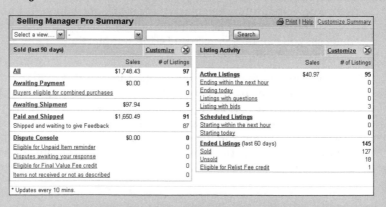

Meridian

Meridian Software was developed by eBay Shooting Star PowerSeller Joe Cortese. Through his own experience on eBay, he developed this service to fulfill all the needs of an eBay seller at a very reasonable entry level price. Users can currently access Meridian software for $9.95 USD a month (about $11 CAD).

As a high-volume eBay seller, Joe Cortese was looking for an easier way to handle his 3,000 unique auctions a month. You may not be listing as many items, but you can still take advantage of the features he enjoyed. Meridian features hands-free, enterprise-level listing and more, including:

- **Item and inventory management:** Provides automated auction scheduling (by the date and time), automated launching and relisting, the ability to import past or current auctions, and the ability to import auction data from a spreadsheet or database.

- **Image hosting:** Offers unlimited space for storing pictures. You can upload bulk images to Meridian's Web site or FTP your images directly.

- **Auction reporting:** Generates accounts receivable, item history, and post-sales reports from the Reports area. MarketWorks has its own Traction System for sales and item tracking. The reporting feature offers customizable views of your sales data, item and auction data, and accounts receivable.

- **Post-auction management:** Allows you to send a variety of customized e-mails to winners and non-paying bidders, either manually or automatically. Also, you can have your invoices linked directly to PayPal, create mailing labels for each sale, and send automatic feedback. (To avoid allowing Meridian to post feedback before you are ready, you may want to disable the automatic feedback feature.)

- **Consignment tools:** For consignment sellers (see information on eBay's Trading Assistants program in Chapter 6), Meridian offers complete tracking and inventory within their auction management system. Information is sorted by consignor.

For more information on Meridian and to learn about their free trial, go to

```
www.noblespirit.com
```

Auction management software

Many sellers prefer to run their auction businesses from their own computers. Some actually enjoy having the option to reference their old auctions through their backup files. Luckily, several valuable auction software programs are available to perform the same tasks available from online services.

For those who would rather use software at home, there are some solid choices available other than the ones we examine in the next section. You might also want to visit these other sites for their quality auction management software:

Auction Tamer (`auctiontamer.com`)

Shooting Star (`foodogsoftware.com`)

SpoonFeeder (`www.spoonfeeder.com`)

You can accomplish almost all the same tasks on your own computer as you can with online services — except online auction checkout. You can always use eBay's checkout as your final stop or include a link to the checkout in your end-of-auction e-mails. Or, if you want, you can set up a checkout page on your own Web site that gathers your auction information.

Most software packages for auction management will do the following:

- ✔ Maintain inventory
- ✔ Prepare and list auctions
- ✔ Manage e-mail
- ✔ Automate feedback
- ✔ Provide HTML templates
- ✔ Track income and expenses

Auction Wizard 2000

Way back in 1999, Standing Wave Software developed a product that would handle large inventories and meet the needs of the growing eBay population. Enter Auction Wizard. In 2000, the company introduced a more robust version called (not surprisingly) Auction Wizard 2000 to meet the challenges presented by changes on eBay.

This software is a tour de force of auction management that combines a number of impressive features into one program. Aside from the basic processes just described, you can also

- ✔ **Handle consignment sales:** Keep track of consignment sales by consignees, including all fees.
- ✔ **Edit your images before uploading:** The software allows you to import your images, and crop, rotate, or resize them for your auctions.
- ✔ **Upload your pictures with built-in FTP software:** Allows uploading while you're working on your auctions and eliminates the need for another piece of auction business software.

Auction Wizard 2000's interface is straightforward. If, like us, you often plunge into new programs without reading the instructions, you'll like this one — Auction Wizard 2000 is easy to use right off the bat. It takes an effort to learn the ins and outs, but that's probably because it has so many features that it requires some time to study them all.

To begin using the software, simply download your current eBay auctions directly into the program. When your auctions close, manage all your end-of-auction business, including sending customized e-mails (the program fills in the auction information). Some sellers use TurboLister (see the "Turbo Lister" section at the end of this chapter) to launch their auctions, then call on Auction Wizard 2000 to retrieve them and handle the end-of-auction management. For a 60-day free trial, go to their site at

```
www.auctionwizard2000.com
```

eBay Blackthorne Basic and Pro

Formerly called Seller's Assistant Basic and Seller's Assistant Pro, these two pieces of software were recently totally revamped and renamed; now the family of products is called eBay Blackthorne. Of the two versions, Basic and Pro, your eBay business will benefit most if you use the professional version.

Because Blackthorne products are so tightly integrated with eBay, they are always among the first to be updated with that company's latest changes.

Like other management programs, both versions take awhile to set up. Also, both allow you to use eBay Picture Services for your photos if your Web site goes down for any reason.

Blackthorne Basic is a solid listing program, offering a variety of templates. It automatically inputs your auction messages and standard shipping information into your auctions so you don't have to continuously retype them. The program helps you customize your e-mail correspondence, and will generate the appropriate e-mail messages after retrieving your completed auction information from the eBay site. Blackthorne Basic is available as a monthly subscription, with fees charged to your regular eBay bill.

The Blackthorne Pro version takes things up a notch, supporting multiple user IDs, handling your auction listings, automating bulk listing, and managing end-of-auction business. The Pro version will also

- ✔ Spell check your auction listings
- ✔ Schedule your auction launches to be posted later (see the following tip)
- ✔ Keep track of your inventory

- ✔ Launch items directly from stock at hand
- ✔ Automate bulk feedback posting
- ✔ Print shipping labels
- ✔ Create sales reports

The template studio in Blackthorne Pro can be a bit of a challenge until you're used to it. The program comes with a gaggle (yes, a gaggle) of themes for you to choose from. One benefit of using a theme is that you can put your picture anywhere you want in the description. A drawback is that you have no control over how the lines of text are spaced. Luckily, you can edit the themes to customize a look for your auctions. Refer to the beginning of the chapter for more about creating a "brand."

One of the finer points of the Pro edition is that, when you have a group of items to be listed, it lets you space out your auctions to begin at set intervals within a certain time period. This is valuable because so many people bid during the last few minutes of each auction, when the highest bidding takes place. Spacing the listings so that they end a few minutes apart (instead of them all ending at the same time) allows buyers time to move from one listing to the next to bid up your auctions and — hopefully — make multiple purchases from you.

Currently eBay will add $9.99 USD a month to your bill for Blackthorne Basic and $24.99 USD a month for the Pro version.

To compare the two versions of Blackthorne's software more closely and take advantage of free trial offers, visit

```
pages.ebay.com/sell/tools/allinone/
```

Turbo Lister

An all-new version of the popular Turbo Lister program was released in 2006. We like Turbo Lister because the program is simple and easy to use. It has a built-in WYSIWYG (what you see is what you get) HTML editor and makes preparing your listings offline easy — when you are ready, you just click a button, and they're all listed at once. While the program itself is free to use, eBay will charge you a small fee, if you want to use one of the program features that allows you to stagger listings or schedule them for a later date.

Using Turbo Lister is as simple and straightforward as listing your merchandise on eBay's Sell Your Item page. One of the program's benefits is that it allows you to prepare auctions offline and then group them for launching on eBay all at once. Getting started with Turbo Lister is a two-step process. First, you download the application from eBay at

```
pages.ebay.com/turbo_lister/
```

Next, you can install Turbo Lister on your computer. Now you are ready to list your auctions on the easy-to-use form shown in Figure 9-7. When you have done that, send them all to eBay in a group. You can also save your listings in Turbo Lister for relisting in the future. What could be simpler?

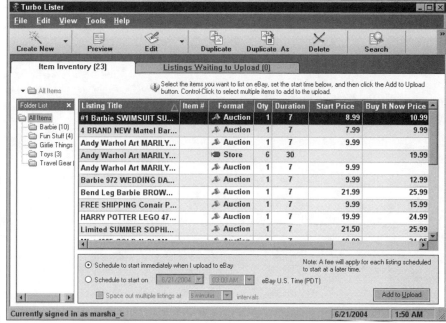

Figure 9-7:
The Turbo
Lister
program,
ready to go
on your
home
computer.

Chapter 10

Dollars and Sense: Budgeting and Marketing Your Auctions

In This Chapter

▶ Marketing your listings by choosing the right category

▶ Using promotional options to your advantage

▶ Paying eBay: The lowdown on basic fees

*Y*our entire online business is just that: a business. In every business, decisions are made regarding how much money is spent for each division of the company. Because you're the head of your company, you must make these decisions. Even if you're running auctions on a part-time basis, you still have to consider budget concerns. The one area you don't have to set money aside for is shipping and fulfillment; in the eBay model, the buyer pays your shipping and handling costs. (See Chapter 14 for more information on shipping.)

When you list an item for sale on eBay, you must consider what the item will sell for, what category to list it in, and whether to supplement the posting with any eBay listing options. Establish a minimum percentage that you assign as your profit so that you can determine how much to spend on your advertising budget. If your item has a considerable amount of competition in its category, you may want to add some of the options eBay offers to make folks notice it and want to buy it. The cost of these options needs to fit into your established advertising budget for the particular item.

In this chapter, we give you a preview of the various options eBay offers its users, highlighting the cost of each option along the way. We also detail the basic eBay fees. When you've finished reading this chapter, you'll have a handle on marketing your items and will be well on your way to establishing a working budget.

Listing Your Items

With tens of thousands of categories to choose from on eBay, finding the right place for your item can be daunting. (For more on eBay categories, see Chapter 2.) You need to apply some marketing techniques when deciding where to place your auctions. Also, think about your budget when you do this; you can list an item in two separate categories, but your costs will be doubled. Can you afford it?

To find out where other sellers have listed items similar to yours, perform a search of completed listings on the Advanced Search page. In the Search box, type your item keywords, click the option to search Completed Listings Only, and indicate that you want your results sorted by highest prices first. Figure 10-1 illustrates the results of this kind of search.

Figure 10-1:
Results of an item search by category, showing the categories where the item is listed on the left.

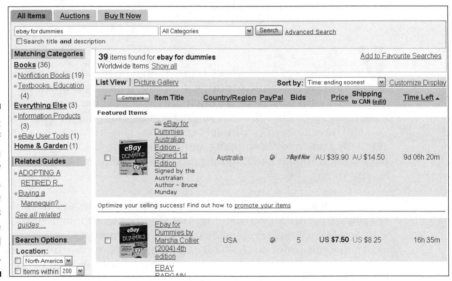

After you have your results, click the completed listings with the highest-priced bids. At the top of auction page, you'll see the listed category. You may find that your item is listed successfully in more than one category.

Check the active listings; are lots of people selling your item? If you see that you're one of forty or fifty trying to sell the same product, you need to get creative about where to list your item. Evaluate the item and its potential buyers. In what categories would someone shopping for your item search?

Suppose you've found two perfect categories in which to list your item. eBay allows you to list your item in both, if you wish (see Figure 10-2), but is doing so the best marketing decision for your auction? That depends. When you list an item in two categories, you must pay two listing fees. Depending on the time, the season, the availability of your item, and how much you paid for it, you may or may not have the money in your budget for listing an item twice. In addition, many eBay buyers are quite savvy when using the search engine. If they search for specific items more often than browse the eBay categories, listing the item in two categories might be a needless expense.

You can change your category mid-auction, starting your item in one category and ending it in another. Also, if your item doesn't sell initially, you can use the relisting feature to auction it again in another category.

Figure 10-2:
Listing your
item in two
categories
on the Sell
Your Item
form.

Second category	
Listing in two categories has been shown to **increase final price on average by 18%.** Learn more	**Enter item keywords to find a second category**
Insertion and most listing upgrade fees will be doubled. Final value fees will not be doubled.	[ ] Find Tips

Select a Previously Used Category
Click to select

Browse categories   ☐ Minimize second category selection area next time I list

Click a category in each box until the last box turns gray   Category #[   ]

Antiques -->
Art -->
Books -->
Business & Industrial -->
Cameras & Photo -->
Clothing, Shoes & Accessories -->
Coins -->
Collectibles -->
Computers & Networking

eBay's Optional Listing Features

When you come to the point in listing your item where you are shown eBay's optional listing features, you see the headline, "Get more bids with these optional features! Make your item stand out from the crowd!" Sounds pretty good, doesn't it? But getting carried away by these options is easy and can lead to spending all of your expected profits before you earn them.

Many experienced eBay sellers can quote success rates for many of the optional listing features but in the real life of your business, success varies from auction to auction and category to category. If you use the boldface option and then your auction appears in a category full of boldface auction titles, the bold just doesn't have the punch you paid for. Your auction would stand out more without the bold option. The same problem can arise with highlighting. Certain categories are loaded with sellers that go overboard using the highlighting feature — all the auction titles appear in a big, lavender blur.

You must weigh the pros and cons in terms of how these options affect your eBay business. Will spending a little extra money enhance your item enough to justify the cost? Will you be able to make the money back in auction profits? To use the listing options effectively, you must have a good understanding of what they are and when and how you can use them to their fullest advantage.

In every auction you run, an insertion fee for listing your auction and a Final Value Fee are paid to eBay. (We discuss these two fees in the section "Paying the Bills: eBay's Cut of the Action," later in this chapter.) If you accept credit card payments, you will also owe the payment service a fee. Estimate your expenses based on these fees before you consider spending money for advertising. (See Chapter 9 for information on software that calculates fees and can help you make up your auction budgets.)

Homepage-featured auctions

A user who goes to www.eBay.com arrives at the eBay homepage first. In the middle of the homepage a Featured Items area appears, and below this area are links to six featured auctions. When you click the <u>all featured items</u> link (see Figure 10-3), the homepage-featured items page appears (see Figure 10-4). Most of these "items" are actually fixed-price listings including hundreds of items at a time. Many also feature merchandise that lists for more than $1,000 USD.

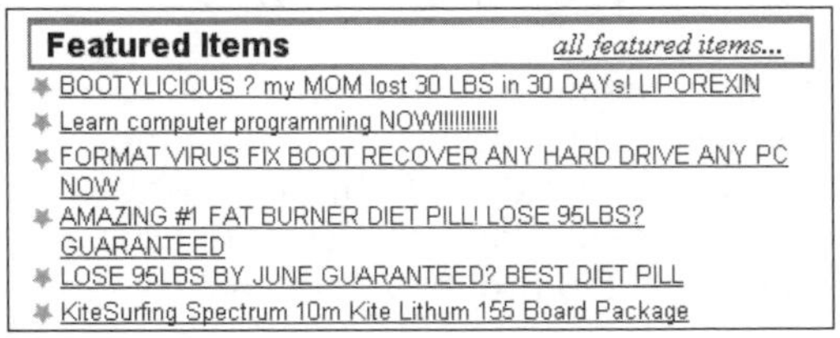

Figure 10-3: The <u>all featured items</u> link on the eBay homepage.

Featured Items	*all featured items...*
✦ <u>BOOTYLICIOUS ? my MOM lost 30 LBS in 30 DAYs! LIPOREXIN</u>	
✦ <u>Learn computer programming NOW!!!!!!!!!!</u>	
✦ <u>FORMAT VIRUS FIX BOOT RECOVER ANY HARD DRIVE ANY PC NOW</u>	
✦ <u>AMAZING #1 FAT BURNER DIET PILL! LOSE 95LBS? GUARANTEED</u>	
✦ <u>LOSE 95LBS BY JUNE GUARANTEED? BEST DIET PILL</u>	
✦ <u>KiteSurfing Spectrum 10m Kite Lithum 155 Board Package</u>	

List View | Picture Gallery   Sort by: [Time: ending soonest ▾]   Customize Display

Item Title	Price	Bids	Time Left ▲
Featured Items			
UNIQUE 16" ARABIAN ARAB WESTERN SHOW SADDLE NEW ⌐⌐ GORGEOUS UNIQUE STYLING, WITH A HARD TO FIND ARAB FIT!	$152.50 $699.99 ⁼Buy It Now	8	12m
AMAZING #1 CARB BLOCKER DIET PILL! LOSE 95LBS + 4 GIFTS ⌐⌐ FOR ATKINS DIETERS. 60 CAPSULES +4 FREE GIFTS	$2.25	4	27m
Learn to program computers NOW!!!!!!!!!!! ⌐⌐ Make more money by learning to write computer software!	$0.10	1	28m
$153 DIET PILL? my MOM LOST 12LBS IN 3 DAYS! InteliSLIM ⌐⌐	$14.49	5	34m
CARTIER TANK FRANCAISE WATCH $1 no reserve ⌐⌐ Awesome Real Cartier at a Great Price	$1,575.00	51	37m
WONDERFUL VERY BIG VIENNA REG. "3 wt 1860"	$1,225.00	11	47m
#1 ITALIAN MASSAGE SHOWER PANEL NEW BESTPRICE ⌐	$249.00 ⁼Buy It Now		1h 12m

Figure 10-4:
The homepage featured items page.

To feature your auction on the eBay homepage will set you back $39.95 USD for a single item. If you have two or several hundred widgets to sell, it'll cost $79.95 USD. For big-ticket items, you've found the perfect location to draw an audience that may easily earn back your money. People who are new to eBay come in through the front page — this is prime real estate. The six auctions featured on the homepage rotate randomly throughout the day. No guarantee can be provided that ensures your item will be featured as one of the six homepage links — but it will appear in the Featured category, linked from the homepage.

Another benefit of having your auction featured is that, if someone searches your keywords or browses through your category, your featured auction will appear at the top of the page. (Featured Plus auctions, which we describe next, are also displayed there.) Still, you must keep in mind how much money this option is costing you. Unless your auction will bring you more than a few hundred dollars, this marketing tool probably isn't worth the additional cost.

Just a heads-up: The Home Page Featured Item option is offered on the US site only. If you want to sell your valuable widget with the greatest exposure, list your item on eBay.com.

Featured Plus

Featured Plus is an option we've used with much success. Using Featured Plus, your auction is listed at the top of the page when a shopper searches for keywords or browses category listings. Although your auction doesn't appear on the eBay.com homepage (refer to the previous section), it will appear at the top of the homepage of your selected category (see Figure 10-5).

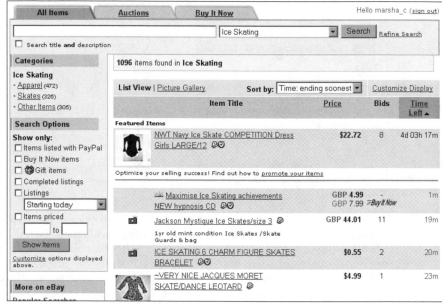

Figure 10-5: A category page showing the position reserved for Featured Plus auctions.

For just $23.50 CAD, the Featured Plus option buys you more exposure, but you must still consider your auction budget. How much do you expect your item to sell for? Will the fee paid benefit your auction enough to justify the expenditure? Be sure that your item will bring you more than a few hundred dollars before choosing this option.

Subtitle

You may use fifty-five characters for your item's title. Searching by title is the de facto method of searching on eBay. If the statistics from our own auctions are any indication, 90 percent of searches are made for title only, versus title and description. But how can you make your item stand out when it shows up with hundreds of other products that look and are titled the same? Use the subtitle option!

When your item has something special about it or could use some extra description, the subtitle option gives you more space to provide the browsing shopper with vital information. Take a look at the examples of subtitles in Figure 10-6.

Figure 10-6: eBay seller aunt*patti makes good use of the subtitle option by adding additional pertinent information.

Highlight option

We were excited when eBay announced the highlight option. We're both big fans of highlighting books, reports, and the like. In fact, ever since college, Marsha just can't read a book without her trusty neon-yellow highlighter. Highlighting makes anything stand out on a white page of text. This works just as well on eBay as it does on paper, except that eBay uses a lavender-coloured highlighter — ick!

Unfortunately, as with most things in life, less is more. If you choose to list your auction in a category where all the sellers are using the highlight option, only the listings that *aren't* highlighted will stand out.

The highlight feature will set you back just $5.90 CAD. Does your budget allow for that? To give your auction title a punch for an even smaller amount of money, consider the bold option, described later in this section.

Listing Designer

eBay comes up with options to fill the needs (or wants, in this case) of its users. Sellers enjoy putting colourful graphics around their descriptions. It will also help you design your description, placing pictures in different places on the page. But if you already have a good description (creatively rendered with HTML colour and emphasis, of course) plus a good picture (inserted with the HTML code we gave you), you may not need this option — as it is, your item will draw bids just as well as if you spend an extra twelve cents CAD per listing to use the Listing Designer.

If you want to surround your descriptions with graphics, make sure the visuals aren't too intensive. Otherwise, the pages will load too slowly for dial-up users. Developing your own template is another alternative to using the Listing Designer; or, you can buy one from a savvy eBay graphics guru (refer to Chapter 9).

You can use a graphics template to "brand" your listings on eBay, giving them a uniform look. If you want to use a template, decide on one and make it your trademark. (Refer to Chapter 9 for more about branding.)

Boldface option

The boldface option is one of our favourites, and is probably the most used option in the eBay stable. An auction title in bold type stands out in a crowd, unless . . . you got it, unless it's in a category loaded with auction titles in boldface. If the $1.20 CAD that eBay charges for this benefit is in your auction budget, odds are good that it will get you a great deal more views than if you didn't use it. Boldface is an exceptional buy; we suggest going for it whenever you can.

To recap your title option costs, see the "Insertion (listing) fees" section later in this chapter.

View counter

Counters have become a popular option in the online world. Placed on your auction, by an outside service at your request, a numeric view counter ticks up each time someone loads your page from eBay. Eventually, the numbers displayed are large enough to impress bidders (who are convinced they're viewing a hot deal) or impress other sellers to run out and sell the identical item on eBay.

A counter is a terrific tool for marketing your auctions — sometimes. If you have an auction with no bids and a counter displaying a high number, newbie bidders may be dissuaded from bidding on your auction. Their thinking may be that if so many people looked at the auction and didn't bid, something must be wrong with the item. They'll tend to doubt their own instincts about what is and isn't a good deal. What might actually be going on in the above situation is that savvy bidders are just watching the auction and are waiting to bid at the last minute.

A *private counter* shields the number of hits to your auction from the eyes of casual lookie-loos. The figures are available to only you on a password-protected login page.

Private counters come in different flavours. Some of the most helpful private counters are smart counters that offer an hour-by-hour breakdown of visitors' habits. This type of counter is available from several online vendors (see Figure 10-7). eBay offers you a free counter, but it's not a smart counter.

Figure 10-7:
A Manage-
Auctions.
com private
counter.

Auction Site: eBay.com; Seller ID: marsha_c; Item #: 580920588
NWT $220 Diane Von Furstenberg Silk Dress 8

Day\Hour	00	01	02	03	04	05	06	07	08	09	10	11	12	13	14	15	16	17	18	19	20	21	22	23
04/18/2001										2		3	2	3	1	3	4	4	2	1	1	2		
04/19/2001					1				3	2		1	2		1	2			2		2	1		
04/20/2001					1	1	2	1		1	3	1	3	1	2	3	1	2	2		3	1		
04/21/2001	1					1	2		1	3	1	1			2		1			3				
04/22/2001	1			1				1		3	1			1	4	4	1	2	2					
04/23/2001	2		2			1	1	3		4	6	2	1	1		2	2	2	2	2	1	2	1	
04/24/2001	4		2		3	1	6	2	1	3	3	10	7	10	9		1		1		1			

The gallery

eBay bills the gallery as its "miniature picture showcase," and, indeed, that's what it is. Adding a gallery photo causes a thumbnail image of your item (96×96 pixels in size) to appear next to your listing when a user browses the category view or search results. Using gallery photos can reap you many benefits. When someone runs an auction search, eBay defaults to show all items that relate to the search term; including gallery previews. See the examples in Figure 10-8.

If you don't use a gallery image but still have a picture in your description, your listing features only a lowly camera icon when searched. This makes choosing the forty-one-cent CAD gallery option a worthwhile expenditure. On the other hand, if your item will sell for less than $10, we recommend that you reconsider the extra charge.

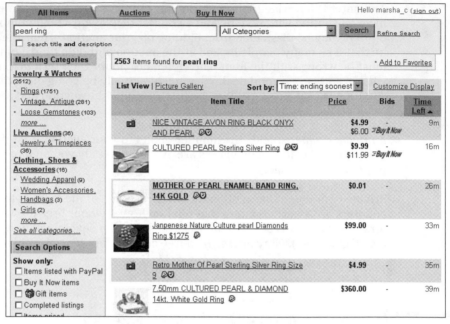

Figure 10-8:
Note how
the gallery
photos draw
your
attention.

Nothing draws the eye better than a gallery photo in a search with hundreds of results. Which auction would you check out? The one with the tiny camera icon, or the one with the crisp, clear gallery picture tempting you to open the listing? Pictures are the key to all quality advertising. Don't miss the opportunity to add an extra little "billboard" to your listings.

Don't get carried away by the idea that a large percentage of bidders are going to view their search results in the picture gallery option, which results in pages featuring only gallery photos and titles. Those who know what they're doing — and who are searching for a deal — aren't going to dismiss auctions without gallery photos. The newbies — or anyone for that matter — with dial-up connections may not have the patience to wade through pages of images.

eBay also offers to feature your gallery photo at the top of gallery-only pages for $23.50 CAD. These photos run three across the top of the page (see Figure 10-9), rather than five across, as the regular gallery pictures do. These featured pictures are also larger (140 × 140 pixels) than the regular pictures in the gallery.

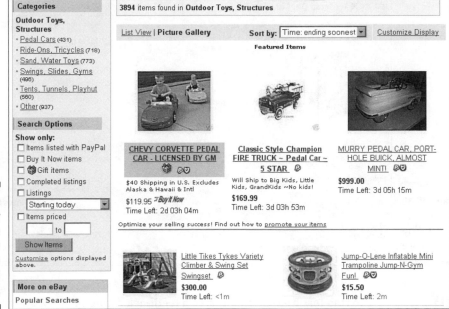

Figure 10-9:
The eBay picture gallery page with featured photos.

When you take advantage of the gallery, be sure to crop your photo tight to the subject to take full advantage of the 96 × 96 pixel allowance. If your advertising budget for an item doesn't allow for the highlighting feature, you can also draw attention to your auction by placing a brightly coloured border around the image to be used as your gallery photo. Doing this is a great way to stand out in search results from all the other gallery images without the extra expense. For more help with your images, see Chapter 11.

Buy It Now

The Buy It Now feature, shown in Figure 10-10, has a few significant benefits. If you have a target price for the item you're listing, make that your Buy It Now price. You can also use this option during frenzied holiday shopping times or with very hot items. Try posting a slightly higher than normal price and perhaps you'll get a bite, er, sale.

The Buy It Now feature disappears when someone bids on the item or, if you've placed a reserve on the auction, when a bidder meets your reserve price. You can't use Buy It Now in a Dutch auction.

Figure 10-10:
The Buy
It Now
feature.

To use this feature, you must have a feedback rating of at least ten.

Buy It Now adds $0.06 to $0.29 CAD to a regular eBay auction and $1.20 CAD to an eBay Motors auction. If your item will sell for a low price, remember our golden rule: Before paying for a feature, ask yourself whether it's in your listing budget.

Paying the Bills: eBay's Cut of the Action

Becoming complacent and blithely ignoring your eBay costs as you list items for sale is easy to do. As a person in business for yourself, you must always take into account outgoing costs as well as incoming profits. The cost of your initial listing is just the beginning of your advertising budget for that item; you have to factor in the cost of all the options and features you use as well. Then, when the item sells, you pay eBay a Final Value Fee. (For fees regarding your eBay store, check out Chapter 5.) In this section, we review the costs involved in posting an auction and the costs of a fixed-price listing on eBay.

The fees we detail here aren't the end of your fees. If you use a credit card payment service, they will also charge you a fee. In Chapter 13, we examine the costs of the most popular credit card payment services.

Insertion (listing) fees

Your insertion fee is based on the highest dollar amount of two things: your minimum opening bid or the dollar amount of your reserve price. If you start your auction at $0.99 and have no reserve, the listing fee is $0.23 CAD. But if you start your auction at $0.99 and set an undisclosed reserve price of $60.00 CAD, your auction costs $5.20 CAD to post. When you place a reserve on your item, you're charged an insertion fee based on the amount of the reserve — plus the reserve auction charge. So for a $60.00 reserve price eBay charges you an insertion fee of $2.80 CAD plus the Reserve Auction fee of $2.40 CAD. If your item does sell for the reserve price or greater, eBay will refund the Reserve Auction fee to your account.

The reserve auction charge is automatically refunded if the reserve price is met.

For a summary of eBay insertion fees, see Table 10-1. (The fees for eBay Motors are in Chapter 2.)

Table 10-1	eBay Listing Fees for Fixed-Price Single Items or Auctions (all figures in CAD)
Opening Bid or Reserve Price	*Insertion Fee*
$0.01 to $0.99	$0.23
$1.00 to $11.99	$0.41
$12.00 to $29.99	$0.71
$30.00 to $59.99	$1.40
$60.00 to $239.99	$2.80
$240.00 to $599.00	$4.20
$600.00 and more	$5.60

If your item doesn't sell, don't think you can get your insertion fees back. They are non-refundable. You do have the option of relisting your unsuccessful auction without being charged a second listing fee, but *only* if your item sells with the second listing. If it doesn't sell the second time, you *will* be charged again. Writing a better title, starting with a lower opening bid, or adding a snappier description will help sell the item. You might consider changing the category as well.

Whether you're listing one item with a starting bid of $1,000 or 100 items for $5.00 each in a Dutch auction, your insertion cost per auction is never more than $6.75.

The costs of the various eBay listing options are recapped in Table 10-2.

Table 10-2	Fees for eBay Listing Options
Option	*Listing Fee*
Home Page featured	$39.95 (single item); $79.95 (multiple items)*
Featured Plus	$23.50
Highlight	$5.90
Subtitle	$0.59
Bold	$1.20
Listing Designer	$0.12**
Gallery	$0.41
Gallery featured	$23.50
Buy It Now	$0.06–$0.29
Scheduled listing	$0.12
List in two categories	Double insertion fee
Ten-day auction	$0.47

*Feature available on eBay.com only and is shown in USD
**eBay waives the Listing Designer fees for Selling Manager Pro subscribers

Final Value Fees

eBay's version of the Hollywood back-end deal is the Final Value Fee. Big stars get a bonus when their movies do well at the box office; eBay gets a cut when your auction sells. After your auction ends, eBay charges the Final Value Fee to your account in a matter of minutes.

An auction in the Real Estate category is *not* charged a Final Value Fee. On the other hand, successful auctions in the eBay Motors category are charged a flat Final Value Fee. (See Chapter 2 for more information about fees in these categories.)

Even a rocket scientist would have trouble figuring out exactly how much eBay receives at the end of your auction. To help you calculate how much you'll owe eBay, see Table 10-3.

Table 10-3	Final Value Fees
If Your Item Sells For	*You Pay a Final Value Fee Of*
$0.01 to $30.00	5.25% of the selling price
$30.01 to $1,200.00	5.25% on the first $30.00, plus 3% of the remainder of the selling price from $30.01 to $1,200.00
$1,200.01 and up	5.25% on the first $30.00, plus 3% of the next $1,170.00, plus 1.5% of the remainder on selling prices over $1200.01

Here are some sample prices and commissions:

Closing bid	*What you owe eBay*
$10.00	5.25% of $10.00 = $0.53
$256.00	5.25% of $30.00, plus 3% of $226.00 = $8.36
$1,684.00	5.25% of $30.00, plus 3% of $1,170.00, plus 1.5% of $484.00 = $43.94
$1,000,000.00	5.25% of $30, plus 3% of $1,170.00, plus 1.5% of $998,800.00 = $15,018.68

To save yourself from brain-drain, use an eBay fee calculator to check your fees before you set prices. See Chapter 9 for software that will do this for you.

Chapter 11

Jazzing Up Your Auctions

● ●

In This Chapter

▶ Writing a great description

▶ Setting up a photo studio

▶ Shooting great pics

▶ Scanning your items

▶ Kicking it up with imaging software

▶ Hosting your pics

▶ Finding HTML templates

● ●

*R*ule #1: A good photograph and a concisely written description should be the goal for all your auctions. Years of advertising and marketing experience have repeatedly proved the value of this to us in almost every type of media. If you're trying to fetch the highest possible bid for an item, keep your auction listings simple and professional: no dancing clowns (unless you're selling clowns), no overdone graphics, and no difficult-to-read typefaces. Less is more.

In this chapter, you find out how to write eye-catching descriptions and improve the visual elements of your auction listings. From there, you can make decisions regarding what you want to do and how to best accomplish your goals.

Writing Winning Text

When you write descriptions for your auctions, be sure that you describe your items clearly and completely. Mention everything about the article, including any flaws or damage. When you're honest about your items up front, you'll have a happy bidder. Remember to include your terms of sale in the description and specify what types of payment and which credit cards you accept. Be sure to include your shipping charges, too. Following is a checklist of things to mention:

- ✔ Any damage to the item
- ✔ Condition (new, new with tags, used, gently used, well-worn)
- ✔ Fabric or material (if important)
- ✔ Manufacturer's name
- ✔ Size, style, colour (for garments, measurements are also valuable because sizes aren't always universal)
- ✔ Special features
- ✔ That you've stored it in a clean, dry place (if you have)
- ✔ Year of manufacture (if important)

After you list all the facts, get excited and add a little bit of flowery text to your description. Think infomercial! Think Home Shopping Network! Whoopee! Those TV services make things sound so good that you feel you *must* have whatever item they're selling. You can do the same, if you take the time. In Chapter 12, we give you some more pointers on writing the best auction descriptions possible.

Your eBay Photo Studio

Taking pictures? No problem! You have a digital camera, and you know how to use it. Just snap away and upload that picture, right? Sorry, but no. There's a good way and a bad way to take photos for eBay and, believe it or not, the professional way isn't necessarily the most expensive way.

We recommend that you set up a mini photo studio for taking your eBay auction pictures. That way, you won't have to clean off your kitchen counter every time you want to take pictures.

If you must use the kitchen counter or a desktop, be sure to use an inexpensive photo stage, which you can find on — where else — eBay.

You need several basic things in your photo studio; the extras you should have are based on the type of merchandise you're selling. If you're an eBay *generalist* — someone who will sell almost anything online — having quite a few extras is especially important for taking quality photos. Check out a portion of Marsha's home photo studio in Figure 11-1.

eBay Seller's Photo Lighting Kit

Tired of your auctions having fuzzy pictures? The answer is to use this professional photo light kit, designed for online images. It consists of two 10" reflectors with zinc die-cast stand adapters. Each reflector has an integrated ceramic socket for bulbs as high as 250 watts, with wood handling knobs. Two 6 foot all metal adjustable stands complete the kit. The kit comes with a short image tutorial by the author of "eBay for Dummies".

Bid with confidence and win this set at close to wholesale price as it is selling with NO RESERVE! Winning bidder to pay shipping & handling of $9, and must submit payment within a week of winning the auction. Credit cards are accepted through Billpoint and PayPal. Good luck!

*GOOD LUCK,
HAPPY BIDDING!*

Click below to...
View my other auctions – Win more than one and $AVE on shipping!

Figure 11-1:
Marsha's eBay photo setup, which she's featuring here in an eBay auction.

What you find in this section might be more than you thought you'd need to take good pictures. But your photographs can help sell your merchandise, so you need to take this part of your business seriously. Of course, if you sell only one type of item, you won't need such a varied selection of stuff, but having the basic photo setup is still important. Go into it slowly, spending only as much on photography equipment as is prudent at the time. Also, check Marsha's Web site (www.coolebaytools.com) for more ideas.

Digital camera

Digital cameras are mysterious things. You may read about *mega pixels* (a million pixels) and think that more is supposed to be better, but that doesn't apply to eBay applications or to Web images. Mega pixels measure the image resolution that the camera is capable of recording. For online use, all you need from a camera is 640×480 pixels (or, at most, 800×600) because computer monitors are incapable of taking advantage of any more. If you use a higher-resolution picture, all you'll do is produce a pixel-bloated image that takes a looooong time to load online.

You don't need a million pixels, but you do need the following:

- **Quality lens:** Anyone who has worn glasses can tell the difference between a good lens and a cheap one. Really cheap cameras have plastic lenses, and the quality of the resulting pictures is accordingly lousy. Your camera will be your workhorse, so be sure to buy one from a company known for making quality products.

- **Removable media:** Some people find that taking the camera to your computer and using cables and extra software to download pictures to your hard drive is annoying. Removable media eliminates this annoyance. The most popular types are Smart Media cards (black wafer-thin cards), Compact Flash cards (in a plastic shell), and Sony Media Sticks; all are no larger than a matchbook. Insert these cards into your computer, if your computer has ports for them, or you can get an adapter that connects to your computer through a USB or parallel port. You can get either device on eBay for less than $30.

  Some older cameras (such as the Sony Mavica FD series) use a regular 3½-inch floppy disc as a convenient storage method. These cameras are hugely popular with eBay sellers for just that reason.

- **Tripod and tripod mount:** Have you ever had a camera hanging around your neck while you're trying to repackage some eBay merchandise that you've just photographed? Or perhaps you've set down the camera for a minute and then can't find it? Avoid this hassle by using a tripod to hold your camera. Tripods also help you avoid blurry pictures from shaking hands. To use a tripod, you need a tripod mount, the little screw hole that you see in the bottom of some cameras. In the following section, we give you some tips on finding the right tripod.

- **Macro setting capability or threading for a lens adapter:** If you're ever going to photograph coins, jewellery, or small, detailed items, these tools will come in handy. A camera's macro setting enables you to get in really close to items while keeping them in focus. A threaded lens mount enables you to add different types of lenses to the camera for super macro focus or other uses.

- **Autofocus and zoom:** These options just make life easier when you want to take pictures. The ability to zoom in and keep things in focus should be standard features.

The bottom line here is to buy a brand-name camera. Marsha uses a Sony Mavica FD92. It's outdated, but it's also loaded with all the bells and whistles she needs for eBay photos. The camera stores images on a Sony memory stick or on a floppy disk, either of which she just pops out and inserts into her computer. The camera's floppy disk convenience makes the Mavica FD series one of the favourites of eBay sellers.

Bill, on the other hand, uses a Sony Cybershot DSC$^{F_{928}}$ that he connects to his computer quickly using a USB cable. With Windows XP, the camera media is recognized as a mini hard drive, and a popup allows him to quickly access his photos and move them over to his computer. The camera has great zooming ability and a very high quality lens. The picture quality is what made this the camera choice for him.

We bet you could find a camera that fits your immediate needs right now on eBay for less than $150. Remember that many digital camera users buy the newest camera available and sell their older, low-megapixel cameras on eBay for a pittance. Many professional camera stores also sell used equipment.

Other studio equipment

Certain endeavors seem to be open pits that you throw money into. We promise that your eBay photo studio will not be one of these pits — now or later.

Tripod

A tripod is an extendable aluminum stand that holds your camera. Look for one that has a quick release so that if you want to take the camera off the tripod for a close-up, you don't have to unscrew it from the base and then screw it back on for the next picture.

Ideally, the legs of your tripod can extend to your desired height, lock in place with clamp-type locks, and have a crank-style geared center column so that you can raise your camera up and down for different shots. Most tripods also have a panning head for shooting from different angles. You can purchase a tripod on eBay or from a camera store for as low as $30.

Power supplies

If you've ever used a digital camera, you know that they can blast through batteries faster than sugar through a five-year-old. A reliable power supply is a must. You can accomplish this in a couple of ways:

- **Rechargeable batteries:** Many specialists on eBay sell rechargeable batteries and chargers. Pick up quality Ni–MH (nickel metal hydride) batteries because this kind, unlike Ni–Cad (nickel cadmium) batteries, has no memory effect. That means you don't have to totally discharge them.

- **CR–V3 lithium ion batteries:** This is a new kind of battery that takes the place of two standard AA batteries. Lithium batteries are the longest lasting and lightest batteries available, but they're also expensive. Recently, some smart guy figured out a way to put two batteries into one unit; considerably cutting the price. This new battery can average 650 photos before you have to change it. The CR–V3 is also available in a rechargeable form, thereby extending its life even further — and reducing your battery budget significantly.

If you plan to shop on eBay for rechargeable or lithium ion batteries, consider buying original manufacturer brand names. Many of the low-cost generic batteries can be of suspect quality and are subject to leaking or even exploding! Saving a few dollars on your batteries is pointless if you damage your camera as a result.

If your eBay photo studio includes a camera on a tripod (and it should), you can use a good old-fashioned AC adapter (you know, the kind that plugs into the wall).

Lighting

Trying to take good pictures of your merchandise can be frustrating. If you don't have enough light and use the camera's flash, the image might be washed out. If you take the item outside, the sun might cast a shadow.

We've seen some eBay sellers simultaneously use a flash and instruct their children to shine a flashlight on an item as they photograph it from different angles — all the while hoping that the colour isn't wiped out. The autofocus feature on most digital cameras doesn't work well in low light.

After consulting specialists in the photo business to solve the digital camera lighting problem, Marsha put together an inexpensive studio lighting set for online auction photography. Please check her Web site (www.coolebaytools. com) for information on how to obtain this package. This is the same one that she successfully uses in her home photo studio (refer to Figure 11-1).

Professional studio lights can be expensive, but you might also be able to find a set for around $150 USD. (You need at least two lights, one for either side of the item, to eliminate shadows.) Search eBay for used studio lighting; we're sure you'll find a good deal.

Cloud Dome

If you're going to attempt to photograph a lot of jewellery, collectible coins, or other metallic items, you may become frustrated at the quality of your pictures. Metallic objects seem to pick up random colour from any kind of light you shine on them when taking pictures. Gold jewellery will photograph with a silver tone, and silver will look goldish!

According to lots of eBay photo gurus, the secret of getting crisp, clear, close-up pictures is to use a Cloud Dome. It stabilizes your camera (just as if you were using a tripod) and filters out all unwanted colour tones, leaving only the colours that are actually in your item.

The Cloud Dome is a large plastic bowl that you mount your camera on. You take pictures through the dome. The translucent white plastic diffuses the light so that your item is lit evenly from all sides, eliminating glare and bad shadows. Check out the manufacturer's Web site at www.clouddome.com to see some amazing before and after pictures.

The Cloud Dome also helps you to get the best images of gems. You can actually capture the light in the gems' facets! Pearls, too, will show their lustre. Several eBay members (including Marsha) sell the Cloud Dome; she highly recommends it!

Props

To take good photos, you need some props. Although you may find it strange having a line item in your accounting program that reads "Props," they do qualify as a business expense. (Okay, you can record them as a photography expense; *props* just sounds so Hollywood!)

How often have you seen some clothing on eBay from a quality manufacturer, but you just couldn't bring yourself to bid more than $10 for it because it appeared to have been dragged behind a car and then hung on a hanger before it was photographed? Could you see how the fabric would hang on a body? Of course not. Take a look at Figure 11-2; that dress looks simply fantastic, darling!

Figure 11-2: Midge the mannequin modeling one of Marsha's eBay successes.

Mannequin

We hate to even say it, but if you're selling clothing, you'd better photograph it on a mannequin. If you don't want to dive right in and buy a mannequin, at least get a body form to wear the outfit. Just search eBay for *mannequin* to find hundreds of hollow forms selling for less than $20 USD. If you sell children's clothing, get a child's mannequin form as well. The same goes for men's clothes. If worse comes to worst, find a friend to model the clothes. No excuse is valid for hanger-displayed merchandise in your auctions.

Marsha got her mannequin (Midge) at a department store liquidation sale in Los Angeles. She paid $25 for her. Her face is a little creepy, so she often crops her head out of the photos. She has a great body, and everything she wears sells at a profit. Many stores upgrade their mannequins every few years or so. If you know someone who works at a retail store, ask when they plan to sell their old mannequins; you may be able to pick one up at a reasonable price.

Steamer

Clothing is fairly crumpled when it comes out of a shipping box. It may also get crumpled lying around, waiting for you to photograph and then sell it on eBay. If the clothing isn't new but is clean, run it through your dryer with Dryel (the home dry cleaning product) to take out any musty smells. Nothing will sour a potentially happy customer like old, musty-smelling clothes.

The clothes you want to sell may be wrinkled, but ironing is a bear and may damage the fabric; instead, do what the retail professionals do: Use steamers to take the wrinkles out of freshly unpacked clothing. Get the type of steamer that you use while the article of clothing is hanging up so you can just run the steamer up and down the piece to get the wrinkles out. The gold standard of steamers is the Jiffy Steamer. It holds a large bottle of water (distilled only), rolls on the floor, and steams from a hose wand. Some models sell on eBay for under $100 USD. Until you're ready to make an investment that large, at least get a small hand-held version that removes wrinkles; search eBay for *(garment, clothes) steamer* to find some deals.

Display stands, risers, and more

Jewellery does not photograph well on most people's hands; it actually looks a lot better when you display it on a stand (see Figure 11-3) or a velvet pad. If you're selling a necklace, display it on a necklace stand, not on a person. Display stands are available from manufacturers but you may have to wait several months to receive them. Apparently, this type of quality display stand is made to order, so we recommend searching for one on eBay (you'll get them sooner).

Risers can be almost anything that you use to prop up your item to make it more attractive in a picture. Put riser pieces that aren't attractive under the cloth that you use as a background. (You can find risers on eBay.)

You wouldn't believe what the back of some professional photo setups look like. Photographers and photo stylists think resourcefully when it comes to making merchandise look good — from the front of the picture, anyway! In many years of working with professional photographers, we've seen the most creative things used to prop up items for photography:

✔ **Bottles of mercury:** Mercury is a heavy liquid metal. Some photographers use little bottles of this stuff to prop up small boxes and other items in a picture. But mercury is a poison, so we suggest you use small bottles filled with sand (prescription bottles work well) for the same effect.

✔ **Beeswax and clay:** To set up photos for catalogues, we've seen photographers prop up fine jewellery and collectible porcelain with clay or beeswax (the kind you can get from the orthodontist works great). Beeswax is a neutral colour and doesn't usually show up in the photo. However, you must dispose of beeswax often because it picks up dirt from your hands and fuzz from fabric.

✔ **Museum Gel and Quake Hold:** These two products are invaluable when you want to hold a small object at an unnatural angle for a photograph. (They're like beeswax and clay, but cleaner.) Marsha discovered these two products after losing everything breakable in her home during the Northridge, California earthquake. Museums use these putty-like products to securely keep breakables in one place — even during an earthquake!

✔ **un-du:** Un-du is a clear liquid that will get sticky residue off of almost anything. If your item has sticker residue on it, it's bound to show up in the picture. Squirt on a little un-du and use its patented scraper to remove the goo and bring back the shine.

✔ **Metal or plastic clamps and duct tape:** These multipurpose items are used in some of the strangest places during many photo shoots. Your mannequin may be a few sizes too small for the dress you want to photograph. How do you fix that? Don't pad the mannequin; simply fold over the dress in the back and clamp the excess material with a metal clamp, or use a small piece of duct tape to hold the fabric taut.

Keep a collection of risers, propping materials, adhesives, pinning materials and the like in your photo area so they're always close at hand.

Figure 11-3:
An eBay listing featuring a professional jewellery display.

Ralph Lauren Signed Silver 16' Necklace

This stunning, brand new designer necklace is just the right length, 16" - and adjustable for smaller necks. Signed on reverse of stirrup goldtone plate *(see photo below)*, also signed on the silver toggle. Your chance to get this retail $48 necklace for a fraction of the cost! The perfect gift for you or a friend.

Bid with confidence and bid whatever you feel this item is worth to you, as it is selling with *NO RESERVE!* I pack all my items carefully. Winning bidder to pay shipping & handling of $3, and must submit payment within a week of winning the auction. I will accept credit cards through BillPoint and PayPal - Good Luck, Happy Bidding!

Backgrounds for your images

Backgrounds come in many shapes and sizes. You can use paper, fabric, or one of the portable photo stages for smallish items.

In professional photo-talk, *seamless* is a large roll of 3-foot (and wider) paper that comes in various colours. Photographers suspend and drape the paper behind their models and over the floor. (Ever wonder why you never see the floor and wall come together in professional photos?) Photographers also drape the seamless over tabletops in some shots. Some people use fabrics such as muslin instead of seamless.

A good choice is to keep satin and velvet on hand when setting up shots; both are reliable backgrounds. (Be sure to clean black velvet with sticky tape before you use it for a photo — lint appears huge in pictures.) We recommend using neutral-coloured fabrics (such as white, light grey, natural, and black) for photographing your merchandise so that the colour of the fabric doesn't clash with or distract from your items.

The Cloud Dome people have also invented a cool photo stage. Many people like it because it's portable and easy to store, unbreakable, simple to clean, and inexpensive. The Cloud Dome's photo stage is sold on eBay and is pictured in Figure 11-4.

Figure 11-4: Cloud Dome's photo stage (seltzer bottle not included).

Taking Good Pictures

If you have a small home photo studio setup (see the preceding section) that includes a quality camera, a tripod, props, and lights, you're well on your way to taking some quality shots for your auctions. A few things to remember:

✔ **Get as close as you can to your item:** Don't leave an expanse of extraneous background in your pictures. If you can't get close enough to your item, you can always use the camera zoom to allow you to get a closer shot. Crop extra background in your photo-editing program (see the "Image-Editing Software" section a bit later in this chapter) before you upload the images to your image hosting service.

✔ **Watch out for distracting backgrounds:** If you don't have a tabletop in your studio, or if the item is something that won't fit on a table, try to make the background of the photo as simple as possible. If you're shooting the picture outside, shoot away from chairs, tables, hoses — you get the idea. If you're shooting in your home, move the laundry basket out of the picture.

One of our favourite eBay display photos featured a piece of fine silver; the photo was taken by the husband of the lady selling the piece on eBay. Silver and reflective items are hard to photograph because they pick up everything in the room in their reflection. In her item description, the seller explained that the man reflected in the silver coffee pot was her husband, and not part of the final deal. She handled that very well!

✔ **Be sure your items are clean:** Cellophane on boxes can get nasty-looking, clothing can get linty, and all merchandise can get dirt smudges. Not only will your items photograph better if they're clean, they'll sell better, too.

Clean plastic or cellophane with WD-40 (no kidding); it will take off any sticker residue and icky smudges. Un-du is the best adhesive remover for paper, cardboard, clothing, and more, plus it comes with a handy plastic scraper. You can also keep a kneaded rubber art eraser around to clean off small dirt smudges on paper items. Any cleaning solution helps your items (even a little Fantastik or Formula 409), but use these chemicals with care so that you don't destroy the item while cleaning it.

✔ **Check the camera's focus:** Just because a camera has an autofocus feature doesn't mean that pictures automatically come out crisp and clear. Low light, high moisture, and other things can contribute to a blurred image. Double-check the picture before you use it.

Scanning Your Images

Scanners have come a long way in the past few years. A once-expensive item, they can now be purchased new for a little more than a hundred dollars. If you sell books, autographs, stamps, or documents, a scanner may be all you need to shoot your images for eBay.

When shopping for a scanner, don't pay too much attention to the resolution. As with digital cameras, images for the Internet (JPEGs) needn't be any higher than 72 ppi (pixels per inch). Any quality scanner can get that resolution these days. Quality in the manufacture of the scanner does make a difference, so stick with brand names when you are purchasing one.

Use a *flatbed* scanner on which you lay out your items and scan away. Marsha replaced her old scanner with an HP OfficeJet, which is not only a scanner but a printer and a reducing/enlarging colour copier — some models like hers even come with a fax! These nifty flatbed units are available brand new on eBay. I've seen the HP models, new and in the original box, sell for as low as $100 USD.

A few tips on scanning images for eBay:

- ✔ If you're taking traditionally processed photographs and scanning them on a scanner, have them printed on glossy paper because they'll scan much better than those with a matte finish.

- ✔ You can scan 3-D items, such as a doll, on your flatbed scanner and get some respectable-looking images. To eliminate harsh shadows, lay a black or white t-shirt over the doll or her box so that it completely covers the scanner's glass. This way, you'll have a clean background and you'll get good reflection from the scanner's light.

- ✔ If you want to scan an item that's too big for your scanner's glass, simply scan the item in pieces and then reassemble it to a single image in your photo-editing program (see the following section for more tips on how to do this).

- ✔ Boxed items are a natural for a flatbed scanner. Just set them on top of the glass and scan away. You can crop the shadowed background with your photo-editing software (see the following section).

Image-Editing Software

Lose the idea that the software that comes with your scanner is good enough. It may be just fine for some uses, but the kind of control that you need is only available in *real* image-editing software, not a mere e-mail picture generator.

Many people are happy using Photoshop to edit their pictures, but it's a large and expensive program. It's also a bit of overkill for eBay images. For much of the bang but far fewer bucks, you can look for Adobe's Photoshop Elements. It has much of the feel of the full-blown Photoshop program but isn't laden with some of the less frequently used features and filters (we think that's why they call it *Elements*). Older versions of Adobe Photoshop Elements sell on eBay for as little as $20 USD, which won't break the bank.

Marsha uses Paint Shop Pro by Jasc software. It's a robust, professional program that costs a fraction of the price of Photoshop. It's also one of the easiest-to-learn programs on the market. We've seen new packages of Paint Shop Pro 8.1 sell for as low as $50 USD on eBay (if you're a good shopper, we know you *can* find these deals). Hint: Look for sellers putting *Paint Shop* as one word (*Paintshop*) in the title.

Paint Shop Pro offers features that enable you to make a good picture out of a bad one. It also has an awesome export-to-Web feature that compresses the images so that they hold their quality while becoming smaller. Images compressed in this fashion download a lot faster for dial-up customers. You can also touch up your family photos in this easy-to-use (okay, low learning curve) program.

And don't forget that you'll be working with images not only for eBay items but also for your Web site. (Check out Chapter 8 for more about putting together a Web site.) The manufacturer of Paint Shop Pro, Jasc Software, runs an eBay store where they sell their software at a discount. You can also go to the manufacturer's Web site www.jasc.com to download a free trial.

A Home for Your Images

You need a professional and safe place to store your pictures for eBay. If your images don't appear when someone clicks your auction, or if your images take too long to load, a user might click off your auction and go to the next one. If you have more than one option for where to store your images, test each one with a few pictures to make sure you find one that's reliable.

If you use auction management software, you may not need an FTP program to upload your images. Most complete management programs integrate their own FTP program as part of the package and may also include image storage space on their server. Check out Chapter 9 for more about auction management software packages.

Always put your eBay images in a separate directory — not in an active part of your Web site. You may think that using your business Web site is a good idea for storing your images, but that's not true. If you want to keep track of your site statistics, such as the number of visitors, hits, and the like, hosting your own images will ruin the data. A call for one of your eBay images counts as a hit on your site, meaning you'll never get accurate Web site stats if your photos are on the site.

Free ISP space

Most ISPs (Internet Service Providers) give you at least 5MB of storage space for your personal homepage. Although this space isn't appropriate for your final business site, it's a perfect place to host your pictures. Everyone has an ISP, and all ISPs give you space. You may have to use an FTP program to upload to your Web space, or your ISP may supply its own uploader. Go to the homepage of your ISP (the member area) and check out what it offers. Visit Chapter 8 for more information on ISP space.

AOL will try to get you to build some kind of hometown page, but here's what to do instead: Go to the top of the AOL page frame and click the Internet tab. Then click FTP. When another screen appears, click the <u>Go to FTP</u> link. (Whew, you're almost there.) Now click the `members.aol.com` FTP site, and you'll be taken to your FTP area. From there, you can upload all your files, up to a maximum of 2MB per screen name. Remember which photos are stored in each screen name FTP space because the URL locator for each screen name is different.

Auction management sites

If you're using one of the auction management Web sites that we discuss in Chapter 9, you're covered for most of your back office tasks. These Web sites supply enough Web space to hold all your eBay images. They also have a convenient one-click upload from your hard drive.

If you find that you truly have no place to host your images, take a look at some of the less expensive auction management sites. As of this writing, you can get image hosting *and* other auction utilities for around $10 USD a month at

```
AAASeller.com, AuctionHawk.com, Inkfrog.com,
       manageauctions.com, and nucite.com
```

eBay Picture Services

You can also use eBay Picture Services to host your photos for eBay, but the quality of your photos is better if you host them directly from a site. Really clear pictures on Picture Services are few and far between. Picture Services converts your image into a jpeg file (if it isn't one already), reformats your photo to fit in a layout 400 pixels wide by 300 pixels tall, and then compresses the file for quick viewing. This process can destroy the quality of your carefully photographed images if you haven't saved them in a compatible size. You're running a business, so be businesslike and use the method that presents your photos in their best light.

To get the free top-of-page image that you see on many auctions, you must use eBay Picture Services. I suggest that you use eBay Picture Services for your primary image and also use secondary images of your items hosted elsewhere. If one of the picture servers goes down, at least your listing will have pictures. The first picture is free; all you have to do is click the box on the Sell Your Item page's Picture Services area, next to Add picture. This picture will also be the default picture for use as your all-important gallery image. (See Chapter 10 for more on using the gallery.)

eBay offers two versions of Picture Services. The basic version (see Figure 11-5) allows you to upload eBay-ready images as they appear on your computer.

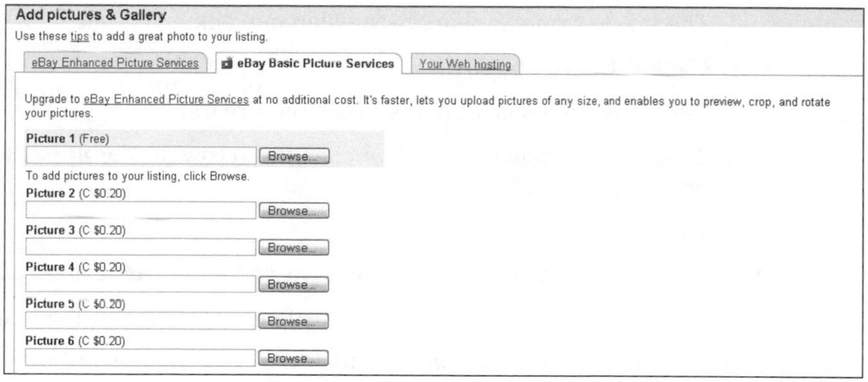

Figure 11-5:
The basic
Picture
Services
photo-
hosting
page.

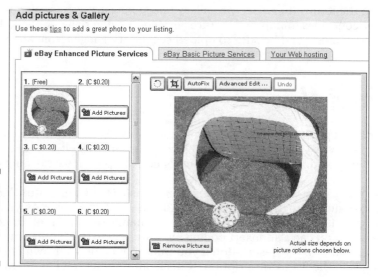

If you want to rotate or crop the picture, you need the advanced picture service. Click the Upgrade link, and a screen similar to Figure 11-6 appears.

Figure 11-6:
eBay's
advanced
Picture
Services.

To upload your pictures using the advanced version, follow these steps:

1. **Click the Add Picture button that appears in the picture frame.**

   A browsing window appears.

2. **Locate the directory that holds your eBay images on your computer.**

3. **Click the image in the browsing window.**

   The image name appears in the filename box.

4. **Click the Open box.**

   The selected image appears in the picture frame.

5. **To rotate the image, click the circular arrow (at the upper left of the main image box).**

6. **To crop the image:**

   a. **Click the crop box in the right corner of the larger image.**

      Two squares appear at opposite corners of your main image.

   b. **Click the frame on the outside of your image and move the bar until the offensive area is cropped out.**

      You can do this from the sides, top, and bottom of the picture.

Sometimes Picture Services will shrink your image to a too-small size, but you can't do much about it. Just be sure to reload the image any time you relist the item; otherwise, the gallery image may just get smaller and smaller. eBay continues to improve Picture Services, so don't give up on it. Use it for the free image, and be sure to upload secondary images from an outside site.

HTML and You

Our small grasp of HTML gets us only so far. We both frequently use a program such as CuteHTML to produce code for our Web sites or eBay listings. Luckily, you don't have to know a lot of code to produce eBay auctions.

The Sell Your Item form has an excellent, basic HTML generator that has a toolbar similar to the type you can find in a word processor. As you can see in Figure 11-7, you can use the toolbar to change the size, font, or colour of the text. You can also insert coding by switching to the "Enter your own HTML" view of the description if you want to include your own hosted images in the listing description. (Check out Chapter 9 for some sample coding to use in your own listings.)

For a quick and easy HTML fix, go to Marsha's Web site at

```
www.coolebaytools.com
```

Describe your items features, benefits, and condition. Get tips on writing a great item description.

| Standard | Enter your own HTML |

Verdana ▾ 12 ▾ Red ▾ **B** *I* U | ≡ ≡ ≡ | ≔ ≔ ≔ ≔

• Spell Check

> *Black and white photo of*
> ## The Beatles and Cassius Clay
> (Mohammad Ali)
>
> Up for auction is a print of a photo that I took long, long ago when I skipped school to see The Beatles do a publicity shoot with then Cassius Clay at the 5th Street Gym on Miami Beach. The image quality is kind of fuzzy and is taken from a scan of the original. I snapped it with my old Kodak camera and I was excited beyond belief. (Holding the camera steady was not an option).
>
> • Picture is 4" x 5"
> • Printed on HP Photo glossy paper
> • Comes with a two page description of the event

You can add pictures and themes on the next page.

Figure 11-7:
eBay's
HTML code
generator.

In the Tools area of the site, click <u>Cool free ad tool</u>. You'll get a quick HTML generator; feel free to use it as often as you like, at no charge. With the tool, you can select border colours and include an image in your description area — nothing fancy, mind you, just nice, clean, HTML. You type your information as indicated and also select colours, as shown in Figure 11-8. When you're finished, click the View Ad button. On the next page, you'll see HTML code for your auction description that you can cut and paste into the auction description area of the Sell Your Item page.

Tools

COOL FREE AD TOOL

Title:	
Description:	
Photo URL:	(Must start with http://)
Shipping Terms:	
Your Email Address:	
Border Color:	navy ▾
Background Color:	navy ▾
Navigation Font Color:	white ▾
Navigation Font Size:	+1

View Ad

Figure 11-8:
The Cool
Free Ad
Tool page.

Chapter 12

Providing Excellent Customer Service

*B*usiness, bah! eBay's supposed to be fun! But business is business, and if you're in business, you must remember that your customers are number one. Businesses become successful by providing fantastic customer service and selling quality merchandise; you have to move in the same direction. The image that you project through your e-mails and ads identifies you to the bidders as a good guy or a bad guy — no kidding. Your e-mails must be polite and professional. Don't let your ads make prospective buyers feel like you're hustling them, sneaking in hidden fees, or being pushy with too many rules for bidding.

You don't have to have the most beautiful auctions on eBay to succeed. You need products that sell, and you need to take the time to build good customer relations! In this chapter, we cover some ways — from writing effective auction descriptions to sending cordial e-mails — to let your customers know that they're number one in your book.

Meeting Your Customers

eBay is a person-to-person marketplace. Although many sellers are businesses (like you), the perception is that sellers on eBay are individuals (versus large companies) working to earn a living. The homespun personal approach goes a long way to being successful when selling on eBay. One of the reasons many buyers come to eBay is that they want to support those individuals who had the gumption to start their own small enterprise on the site.

After you've written a brilliant title for your auction, prospective buyers click your listing and scroll down to your description. Do they have to dodge through pointless verbiage, losing interest along the way? Or do you get right down to business and state the facts about your item?

Telling your story

Being honest and forthright encourages customers to consider your offerings on eBay. If you go the extra mile and give some bonus information, the customer will feel more at ease.

An excellent example comes from John Rickmon, also known as e.vehicles. This PowerSeller throws in a few special touches to his descriptions to draw in customers. As you may gather from his user ID, John sells vehicles on eBay — and does very well at it!

When you participate in eBay Motors, the prospective buyer has the option of ordering a CarFax report on the vehicle's history from the listing page. This costs the buyer a special eBay price of $19.99 USD just to view the report. John orders the CarFax report himself, and includes a link right in the auction description to a PDF version. Saving the buyer $19.99 USD doesn't seem like much, but doing so is one of those simple touches that makes the customer feel comfortable.

John also posts his business philosophy at the end of his auctions. Here's part of it:

"My dealership is entirely focused on the sale of vehicles via the eBay format. I make all purchasing and sales decisions and am 100 % responsible for the content of my auctions, including all text and photography. I personally answer every email and conduct all business regarding the sale of this vehicle.

I buy and list approximately 10-15 units per month. I look at hundreds of vehicles each week that do not make the cut . . .

This is my living. *I do this full-time. I do not have a "car lot." eBay has been my dealership for years, and all operations are focused towards bringing you the best vehicle possible at the best price you will find. I am committed to this format and take your vehicle purchase very seriously. You are dealing with a secure seller."*

Wow — don't you just want to buy a car from this guy?

Here are a few things to do when writing your auction description:

- ✔ **Choose a reasonable typeface size.** Many users are still looking at eBay on an 800 × 600 display. If you design your auctions at 1024 × 768, your typefaces may be way too large for the average user. Forcing a user to scroll and scroll to find the details only leads to frustrated customers.

- ✔ **Describe the item factually.** Do you carefully describe the item, stating every fact you know about it? Are you clear in your description and careful not to use any jargon? Finally, does your description answer almost any question a potential buyer might ask? If not, do some revising.

- ✔ **Include some friendly banter.** You want to make the customer feel comfortable shopping with you. Don't be afraid to let your personality show!

- ✔ **Limit the number of auction rules (or terms of sale).** Some sellers include a list of rules that's longer than the item's description. Nothing will turn off a prospective buyer like paragraph after paragraph of rules and regulations. If you really *must* put in a litany of rules, use the following bit of HTML to make the size of the text smaller: `<font size=-1>`

✔ **Quote a shipping amount.** Many bidders pass up auctions that don't disclose the shipping charges. Include fair shipping and handling costs in the listing so that buyers feel confident in knowing what their actual cost will be. If many others are selling the same item you're selling, quoting reasonable shipping costs will help you reel in customers.

✔ **Update your My eBay page.** Let people know a little about you and who they're dealing with. When customers have to decide between two sellers selling the same item and all else is equal, they will place their bid with the seller who makes them feel secure.

Overcharging on shipping is just bad taste. eBay buyers expect that you'll add up to a dollar to the price of your item for packing and shipping costs, but adding more than that can make you look like you're trying to squeeze every penny out of your bidder . . . Not a good feeling when you're on the other end!

✔ **Keep photos a practical size.** Many users still connect with a dial-up Internet connection, and if they have to wait for your large pictures to load, they may go elsewhere for the item. If your listing doesn't fully open within a few seconds, the person will back out and go on to another listing.

Communicating with Your Customers

Perhaps English class wasn't your favourite, but when it comes to being a professional, incorporating good grammar, proper spelling, and punctuation in your communications portrays you as a pro. Before writing this book, even we hooked up with some grammar and punctuation sites to brush up on our writing skills. (Okay, we also have brilliant editors covering up our transgressions. . . .)

Throughout the rest of this section, we provide some examples of effective e-mails. Study these and also check out a few books about writing business letters — *Writing Business Letters For Dummies* by Sheryl Lindsell-Roberts (Wiley) is a good one. And don't forget good manners. You don't want to be too formal, but you do want to be personable and polite.

The initial inquiry

The first written communication you have with a prospective buyer is an inquiry e-mail. A bidder can ask you a question about your item by clicking the Ask seller a question link on the auction or sale page, which automatically generates an e-mail addressed to you. Often these questions are brief.

At least 20 percent of the time that we send an inquiry to a seller, we don't get a response — guaranteeing that we won't be buying that product. Neither of us is interested in buying from someone who doesn't even care to respond to a question. Frequently, when we do get responses, they amount to nothing more than a terse, brusquely written note. Many people choose not to use punctuation or capitalization in their e-mails. How professional looking is that? Not very. Sellers who take the time to write a short, considerate reply that includes a greeting and a thank you for writing get my money.

Respond quickly, clearly, and politely — and with a sales pitch. Remind the soon-to-be bidder that you can combine several wins to save on shipping costs. And by all means, use this opportunity to point out other auctions you have that may also interest the writer. Now that's customer service.

The letter can be brief and straightforward. For example, Marsha wrote the following note in response to a question regarding the condition of a Christmas tree in one of her auctions:

Hello,

Yes, the aluminum Christmas tree in my auction is in excellent condition. The 58 branches are full and lush and will look great for the holidays. Please write again if you have any more questions or concerns.

Don't forget to check my other auctions for a colour wheel and a revolving tree turner. They would look great with this tree, and I can combine them for shipping.

Thank you for writing,

Marsha
`www.coolebaytools.com`

Isn't that nice? The note addresses the question in a respectful and person-able manner. Writing a note like this doesn't take long. Be sure to do it.

Also, putting your Web site or eBay store URL in your signature is a great way to get new customers to view your other merchandise.

The winner's notification letter

Have you ever received a bulk-generated, boilerplate winner's confirmation letter? The seller hasn't bothered to fill in half the blanks, and you're almost insulted just by reading it? Receiving a note like this after you've requested that the seller combine purchases (when the letter pays no attention to your request) is especially annoying. E-mails can cross paths in cyber space, but a personal approach goes a long way with customers.

We're not saying you shouldn't automate your eBay business. We're merely suggesting — well, strongly recommending — that you take the time to personalize even your canned e-mail responses. If you decide to send automated responses, choose a program that allows you to combine multiple wins in one letter and to apply the correct shipping costs the first time.

Here's the tried-and-true winner's notice that Marsha sends out:

Congratulations!

Yours was the winning bid on eBay item #122342911 for the Emilio Pucci book. You got a great deal! I am looking forward to a pleasant transaction and positive feedback for both of us.

Please include a copy of this e-mail with your name and shipping address along with your payment:

Winning Bid Amount	*$14.95*
Shipping and Handling	*$ 2.50*
TOTAL Amount Due	*$17.45*

You may pay by money order, with a personal check, or with a credit card through PayPal. If you are not set up with them, just e-mail me and I'll send you a PayPal invoice.

A money order or online payment assures immediate shipping upon receipt of payment! If you pay by check, I will ship your item after a 14-day clearing period; be sure to include the item name and your e-mail address with payment. Please send your payment to the address shown below:

Marsha Collier
1234 Anywhere Street
Los Angeles, CA 91352

Your payment is expected on or before Saturday, April 2, 2006. I look forward to receiving it. I will ship on receipt of payment in full, via U.S. priority mail with delivery confirmation.

Thank you for your Winning Bid! I am delighted to be dealing with you and know you will enjoy your purchase.

Marsha_cs
Marsha Collier
`www.coolebaytools.com`

At the end of a winner's notice letter, offer your winner some special discounts or other offers from your Web site. Include a few items this particular winner may be interested in (based on the current win) and a link to your site. Also remind the winner that you can combine shipping for multiple purchases and that you look forward to a response.

The payment reminder

Writing a payment reminder can get sticky. You don't want to aggravate the buyer, but time is wasting, and you could spend this time reposting your item. When writing a payment reminder you need to be firm but pleasant. Real problems can come up in people's lives. Family members get sick, and people just plain forget. Perhaps your payment fell between the seat of the winner's car on the way to the post office. (That's the excuse Bill uses when he forgets to mail a payment — feel free to use it.)

When you honestly forget to send a payment, nothing is more humiliating than someone debasing you through e-mail. So remember that people do make mistakes, and check the winner's feedback before you send the letter. If you can garner from the feedback that this winner has a habit of not following through on bids, you can definitely be a bit firmer in your wording. Always set a clear deadline for receiving payment, as shown in the following letter:

Hello,

You won an auction of mine on eBay last week for the Emilio Pucci book. Your payment was due yesterday and it still has not arrived. Perhaps sending payment has slipped your mind considering your busy schedule. I know it can easily happen.

Please e-mail back within 48 hours and let me know whether you want to go through with our transaction. I'd like to put the item back up for sale if you don't want it.

Thank you for your bid,

Marsha Collier

How firm you choose to get with a non-paying bidder is up to you. We've dealt with many non-paying bidders on eBay, but have left relatively few negative feedback comments. Some people who tend to overbid are indeed violating the contract to buy, but legitimate reasons might explain why someone hasn't followed through on an auction. You must decide which method to take when dealing with a non-paying bidder and how far you want to stretch your karma — remember, what goes around comes around. Assess each case individually, and don't be hasty in leaving negative feedback until you know the whole story.

Leaving feedback for buyers

After you leave feedback, you can't take it back, and you can't repost to correct an erroneous evaluation of another user. We know that it's easier to leave feedback after you receive payment, but waiting to see how the transaction evolves afterwards is prudent — especially if the package gets lost in the mail, turning a previously kind and sweet buyer into a screaming nutcase. Same thing if the item is damaged. Evaluate a buyer based on more than whether the person pays for an item. (Buyers are supposed to do that — you have a contract, remember?) When leaving feedback for buyers, consider the following:

✔ Did they return your communications quickly?

✔ Did they pay in a timely manner?

✔ If a problem occurred with the item or in shipping, did they handle it in a decent manner or did they try to make your life a living hell?

Remember that sellers are judged on communication, shipping time, the quality of packaging, and friendliness. As a seller, you have a duty to leave quality feedback that sets guidelines for all sellers to use for rating buyers.

The payment received and shipping notice

We know that you probably aren't going to send out a payment received letter for every transaction, but it would surely be nice if you did. Staying in constant communication with your buyers will make them feel more secure with you and with buying on eBay. You want them to come back, don't you?

When you receive payment and are ready to ship, sending a short note like the following helps to instill loyalty in your customers:

Hi there (insert name of winner*),*

Your payment was received, and your item will ship tomorrow. Please e-mail me when it arrives so that I can hear how pleased you are with your purchase.

When the transaction is over, I hope you will leave positive feedback for me because building a good reputation on eBay is very important. I'd really appreciate it, and I'll be glad to do the same for you.

Thank you for bidding and winning,

Marsha Collier
Marsha_c
`www.coolebaytools.com`

If you haven't heard from the buyer within a week, send another note.

The "Your item is on the way" e-mail

We always send out an e-mail to let our buyers know that their package has been shipped — you should too. We also recommend sending your buyers tracking information and an approximate date of delivery. eBay and PayPal can send out automated e-mails for you, but these e-mails aren't very personalized. A good idea is to follow up with another, more personal note similar to this one:

Subject: Your book is on the way!

*Hi (*insert buyer's name*)!*

I shipped your package today and you can expect to receive it in the next five to eight business days. You will be receiving another e-mail shortly with the package's delivery confirmation number and information on the mode of shipment.

Thank you for buying my item. If you have any questions when the package arrives, PLEASE e-mail me immediately. Your satisfaction is my goal, and I'm sure any problem can be easily taken care of. Please let me know when the package arrives so that we can exchange some very positive feedback!

Marsha Collier
www.coolebaytools.com

Good customer service will get you many repeat customers and buckets of positive feedback. Good communication will head off problems before they start. If your customers have received communication from you throughout your transactions, they'll be more likely to discuss a glitch with you rather than make a knee-jerk reaction and leave negative feedback.

Chapter 13

When the Money Comes Rolling In

• •

In This Chapter

▶ Finding the payment method that suits your needs

▶ Discovering the ins and outs of payment services

▶ Exploring merchant accounts

• •

*T*he hours you spend selecting your items, photographing them, touching up the pictures, and writing brilliant auction copy all come down to one thing: getting paid. At first thought, you might be happy to take any form of negotiable paper, bonds, and stocks (okay, no dot-com stock). As you become more experienced and collect money for more auctions, however, you'll decide which payment methods you prefer and which are more heartache than they're worth.

Receiving and processing payments takes time and patience. The more forms of payment that you accept, the more you have to keep track of. Throughout this chapter, we detail the various payment options (including how to handle payment from international buyers) and how each affects your business.

For Old-Fashioned Buyers: Money Orders & Cashier's Cheques

We begin our discussion of payments with money orders and cashier's cheques because you will occasionally encounter a customer who still prefers to pay in a non-electronic manner. PayPal (which we talk about later in this chapter) has become such a dominant and convenient form of pay-ment on eBay that, for Bill, receiving more than three or four alternative methods over the course of a month is extremely unusual. All the same, for some of your U.S. buyers in particular, money orders and cashier's cheques can be fast, cheap, and readily negotiable — just like cash. Canadian money orders are considerably more expensive.

A cashier's cheque or bank draft can be purchased at a bank and is generally debited immediately from the buyer's chequing account. For some unknown reason, many banks take it upon themselves to charge a minimum of $5 to issue a cashier's cheque. This is a pretty steep charge to the buyer, and is why we usually suggest money orders as an alternative to our customers who insist on mailing their payments.

In the U.S., where most will likely be sent from, money orders are available almost anywhere and usually cost less than $1.00. Still, prices can vary; in Marsha's neighborhood, many stores charge from as little as $0.99 for a money order up to $500. In this section, we detail three of the main outlets that offer money order services. Table 13-1 shows a cost comparison of these vendors.

Table 13-1	Money Order Cost Comparison	
Vendor	*$25 Money Order*	*$500 Money Order*
7-Eleven (U.S. only)	$1.00 USD	$1.00 USD
United States Postal Service (international)*	$3.45 USD	$3.45 USD
Canada Post (Canadian Currency)	$3.95 CAD	$3.95 CAD
Canada Post (U.S. Currency)	$4.95 CAD	$4.95 CAD

* USPS issues two types of money orders — one for domestic use and one for international use. Remind your U.S. winning bidders that the domestic use money order available from USPS cannot be cashed outside of the U.S. and that they are required to send the international version — this is important.

If you do want to accept money orders, familiarize yourself with the various charges so that you can recommend the service with the most reasonable cost to your winners. Saving your customers money (especially when it's not going to you) is a sign of good customer service, and asking buyers to pay a large additional fee is unfair. For the most part, you may want to avoid accepting money orders from countries other than Canada and the U.S. In Bill's experience, many bank tellers are completely confused by money orders from foreign sources. If you decide to accept money orders from other countries, insist that buyers obtain the payment through an issuer like American Express, which has offices in most countries and is internationally recognized. When purchasing a money order, international buyers deal in the currency of their own countries; when the payment reaches you, you're paid with cash in your own currency.

In the U.S. — 7-Eleven (and other convenience stores)

More than 21,000 7-Eleven stores are open around the world. We bet one exists within driving distance of your house. For your American customers, the best part about 7-Eleven is that most of their stores have an ATM that draws cash from credit cards; that cash can then be used to purchase a money order. At only $1.00 USD, money orders from 7-Eleven are a bargain! If your American customer doesn't know where the closest 7-Eleven is, send them to the following:

```
www.7-eleven.com/storelocator/PrxInput.aspx
```

Your customers in the U.S. can also buy money orders from several other convenience store chains, such as Circle K, Dairy Mart, Piggly Wiggly, and AM/PM. Even their local Wal-Mart store generally has money orders readily available.

Canada Post

Canada Post is one of the most convenient places to purchase a money order — even if they're also one of the most expensive. Postal outlets now adorn many retail operations that vary from large department stores like Zellers to small business havens like Staples. You'll also find them in many drug and convenience stores. These postal outlets readily offer money orders in both Canadian and U.S. denominations, which makes it easy for your Canadian customers to pay you in the currency of your choice.

United States Postal Service

Most sellers especially love USPS money orders. Besides having all the benefits of a regular money order, Canada Post outlets will cash these for you with proper identification. (Canada Post and USPS have an agreement to accept each other's money orders.) Postal money orders are acceptable most everywhere, including your local bank, and they are safe, too: USPS goes to great pains to ensure the authenticity of their money orders by including a Benjamin Franklin watermark, a metal security thread, and a double imprint of the dollar amount on each one. (No more need to fear that you've received a colour copy instead of legitimate currency.)

Both domestic and international money orders are available at U.S. post offices, which does occasionally pose a problem. Domestic money orders from USPS cannot be used outside the boundaries of the U.S. and its possessions (Guam, Puerto Rico, and the U.S. Virgin Islands). Still, many buyers miss the bold red warning on the money order and mail it to you anyway, blissfully unaware. Of course, when you receive one, you have the problem of contacting the buyer to explain that it is not a valid form of payment in Canada. Despite taking measures to caution buyers during his eBay auctions and in his e-mails to winning bidders, Bill must frequently send polite e-mails to buyers informing them of this problem and asking for an acceptable replacement payment. After receiving a replacement payment, the easiest way to resolve the problem is to enclose it (the original domestic version) with the shipped item so that the sender can return it to USPS for a refund.

Buyers like the security of using money orders because they know that if the money order is lost or stolen (in eBay-speak, that may mean the buyer hasn't sent it to you yet), they can have it traced by presenting their receipt to USPS. For a small fee, buyers can also get a copy of a paid money order for up to two years after the date it was purchased.

Many sellers bring their money orders to Canada Post outlets when they ship their packages and cash them to keep in their petty cash fund — or to pay for outgoing postage.

Pay Me When You Get This: Cash On Delivery

We can't say enough to discourage you from using Cash on Delivery (COD) as a payment method — but we're gonna try! When using COD, you give your package to Canada Post, UPS, or FedEx, which collects the payment after delivering the package. Sounds straightforward and easy, right? What happens when the carrier tries to deliver the package and the recipient isn't home? In this situation, your items can sit in a warehouse for a week or two, during which time the buyer may decide that they don't want to pick up the items from the shipper. If you're lucky, you'll get your items back in two to three weeks.

Cash on Delivery service is also expensive. In addition to postage, Canada Post charges $6.00 for COD service and only offers it within Canada. If the buyer decides not to claim the item or refuses it for any reason, you, the seller, will also be asked to pay the return shipping cost. You might get your item back, but that will seem little consolation if you are out of pocket for shipping the item both ways and the COD charges.

Accepting cash payments

If you have been selling on eBay for any length of time, we're sure you've received cash from some of your winners. We don't like cash as an eBay payment option. In fact, eBay's new *Acceptable Payments Policy* will not even allow sellers to offer cash as a payment method. Dealing in cash can cause many problems. If the buyer doesn't send the exact amount due, you have to call them, at which time they may claim that the correct amount of money is there. Mail can also be stolen; people steal envelopes right out of mailboxes more frequently than you might expect. All of a sudden, the buyer can imply that *you* must have lost the difference — and you have no recourse with cash.

Postal inspectors are constantly battling the problem, but you won't know your mail is being stolen until you've lost quite a few envelopes — usually bills and outgoing cheques. Explaining to a buyer that their money never arrived is difficult. The thief has the cash, while your reputation may be shot. You can e-mail and phone the buyer to talk and discuss the mishap, but the bottom line is that you haven't received your money and they insist you have it.

Another bad part of COD? You might wait a month to receive payment, even when the addressee is home the first time and accepts delivery. Do yourself a favour and don't offer it as a payment option — if you do, you're only asking for trouble. You're not a bank, and you're not in the finance business. Get your money up front.

The Cheque's in the Mail: Personal Cheques

Personal cheques are the easiest way for buyers to make payments. They can just dash off a cheque, put it in the mail, and bam, you're paid. But this type of transaction is not always as easy for the seller. You have to deposit the cheque into your bank account and wait for the cheque to clear. Believe it or not, in these days of electronic transfers, wiring funds, and international money transfers, you still might wait well over two weeks for a cheque to be approved.

Paper cheques

After you deposit a cheque, your bank sends it to a central clearinghouse, which then sends it to the clearinghouse of the signatory (buyer)'s bank. Then, the signatory's bank decides whether the cheque can be paid. You may think you've found a way around the system by calling the bank to see whether the account has sufficient money in it. This is not the answer; while the account may have sufficient funds when you call, the depositor can withdraw money before the cheque gets through the system — and then the cheque bounces. And don't forget the twenty-four-hour turnaround rule: Even if there is money in the account and you're standing there with the cheque, the bank can deny payment within twenty-four hours of its deposit, leaving you with a bad cheque.

Even though everything seems to be electronic these days, the paper routing of old-fashioned cheques can take two weeks or longer. Marsha has received only one bad cheque as an eBay payment. She deposited the cheque, waited ten business days, and then shipped the item. On the eleventh business day, the bank sent her the bounced cheque. The buyer clearly knew that the cheque had bounced but didn't notify her. Luckily, the buyer made good on the cheque by sending her another one.

Another issue for Canadian sellers is that the Canadian and U.S. banking systems just don't seem to communicate well. According to Bill's bank, it can take up to six months for a cheque drawn from a U.S. bank to completely clear in his Canadian account. Bill has never accepted personal cheques as a form of payment for his eBay auctions.

 If you find yourself with a cheque that's bouncing higher than a Super Ball and an uncooperative buyer, remember that passing bad cheques is against the law. An exhaustive search of the Web for a similar Canadian site led nowhere, but to see a list of penalties in the U.S., state by state, visit their National Check Fraud Center at the following address:

```
www.ckfraud.org/penalties.html#civil
```

In Canada, it can be very difficult to prosecute someone for passing a bad cheque; you must be able to show that they knowingly attempted to defraud you, and are not merely bad accountants. In many U.S. states, if someone passes a bad cheque, you are legally able to collect three times the amount of the bad cheque! Collecting the money is another matter, especially if the buyer is in the U.S. and only for a small amount.

The bottom line? Marsha warns all her winners that, if they intend to pay by cheque, she may hold the item for more than two weeks before she ships. She makes exceptions for buyers who have an excellent feedback rating or who she has successfully done business with before. Dealing with personal cheques isn't worth the potential grief they can cause. Try to get an e-cheque, an instant transfer through PayPal (see the following section), or have your winners pay with credit cards through a payment service. For more on payment services, see the "I Take Plastic: Credit Cards and Credit Card Payment Services" section later in this chapter.

Bank debits (e-cheques and instant transfers)

Despite the attached fees and a *short* waiting period, accepting a PayPal e-cheque or an instant transfer is a nice, clean transaction because it puts immediate cash in your account. After indicating that they want to pay with an e-cheque, buyers must register their bank account with PayPal by giving them the required information shown in Figure 13-1.

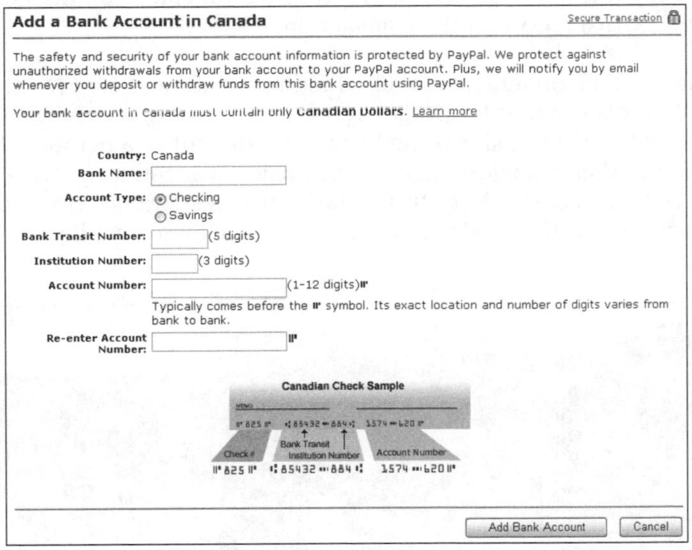

Figure 13-1: The information required to register your bank account with PayPal.

Add a Bank Account in Canada   Secure Transaction

The safety and security of your bank account information is protected by PayPal. We protect against unauthorized withdrawals from your bank account to your PayPal account. Plus, we will notify you by email whenever you deposit or withdraw funds from this bank account using PayPal.

Your bank account in Canada must contain only **Canadian Dollars.** Learn more

Country: Canada
Bank Name:
Account Type: ⦿ Checking
　　　　　　　　○ Savings
Bank Transit Number: (5 digits)
Institution Number: (3 digits)
Account Number: (1-12 digits)⊩
Typically comes before the ⊩ symbol. Its exact location and number of digits varies from bank to bank.
Re-enter Account Number: ⊩

Canadian Check Sample

⊩⁞ 825 ⁞⊩ ⊰85432 ⊰884⊰ 1574 ⊾620 ⊩
Check #　　Bank Transit　Account Number
　　　　Institution Number
⊩⁞ 825 ⁞⊩ ⊰85432 ⊰884⊰ 1574 ⊾620 ⊩

[Add Bank Account] [Cancel]

When a buyer pays with an electronic cheque, it will take as many as four days to clear. An instant transfer, on the other hand, credits your account immediately, as long as the buyer has a credit card (or bank debit card) as a backup funding source — the bank uses this if your instant transfer fails. PayPal allows you to accept e-cheques for up to $10,000, but will charge you the same fees as those for a credit card.

Interac Email Money Transfers

Formerly called CertaPay, Canada's five big banks jointly provide the Interac Email Money Transfer service, touted as the first of its kind in the world (see Figure 13-2). If both you and your Canadian customer bank at BMO (Bank of Montreal), CIBC (Canadian Imperial Bank of Commerce), RBC (Royal Bank), Scotiabank, or TD Canada Trust, this great service provides a fast, inexpensive, and secure payment option. For sellers, the service is free, and the buyer bears a small charge that varies from bank to bank.

The process is a very simple one — the buyer logs on to his or her bank account and chooses the option to make an e-mail money transfer. After entering the recipient's e-mail address (that's yours, as the seller), entering the amount and providing a security question and answer (these are discussed before beginning the process) you are sent an e-mail from your bank advising that you have funds awaiting and providing a URL link. After entering the URL into your web browser, you answer the security question, and the funds are deposited into your account — no problem! The sender's bank account is debited the amount of the transfer when it's completed, leaving the buyer with a record of the transaction.

The one small inconvenience of conducting an Interac Email Money Transfer is that it is really meant for person-to-person transfers — when Bill uses the service for his eBay business, he has the funds sent to a personal bank account and then transfers them to his business account. A little extra work is involved when using these transfers for business transactions, but the speed with which the funds are received makes it worthwhile.

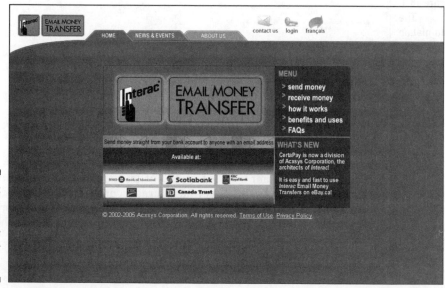

Figure 13-2:
The Interac
Email
Money
Transfer
home page.

You can get all the details about using the Interac Email Money Transfer service at

```
www.certapay.com
```

I Take Plastic: Credit Cards and Credit Card Payment Services

As people become more comfortable using credit cards on the Internet, credit cards become more popular for eBay payments. Plus, major credit card payment services have insured eBay payments to registered users, making credit cards safe for the buyer and easy for you. Credit card transactions are instantaneous; unlike payments by cheque or money order, you don't have to wait for a piece of paper to travel cross-country.

For all this instant convenience, however, you pay a price. Whether you have your own *merchant account* (a credit card acceptance account in the name of your business) or take credit cards through a payment service (more on this in a minute), you pay a fee. Your fees can range from 2 percent to 7 percent of the payment amount, depending on how you plan to accept cards and which ones you accept. Unfortunately, throughout most of North America, adding a credit card surcharge is illegal. You have to write off the expense of accepting credit cards as part of your business budget.

The fees brick and mortar stores pay for accepting credit cards are much less than those paid for online, mail, or phone orders. In most promotional material from credit card companies, the vendor usually quotes the "swiped card" rates. Because you won't have the buyer's card in hand to swipe, be sure to inquire with your provider for the internet transaction rate before signing any papers.

We have to explain the downside of accepting credit cards for your online sales. To protect yourself, please be sure to check the feedback — both feedback they've received and feedback they've left — of all bidders before accepting any form of credit card payment for a high-ticket item. Some buyers are chronic complainers and are rarely pleased with their purchases. They may not be satisfied with your item after it ships. In that case, they can simply call their credit card company and get credit for the payment; you'll be charged back (your account will be debited) the amount of the sale. (See the "Forget the buyer: Seller beware!" sidebar in this chapter.)

Forget the buyer: Seller beware!

When buyers dispute a sale, they can simply call PayPal or their credit card company and refuse to pay for the item. You lose the sale and possibly won't be able to retrieve your merchandise. A payment service or merchant account will then revoke the buyer's payment (banks call this a *chargeback*) from your account without contacting you and without negotiating. Technically, the buyer has made the purchase from the payment service — not from you — and the payment service won't defend you. We've heard of chargebacks occurring as much as six months after the transaction, although eBay says they can occur no later than sixty days after they sent you the first bill on which the transaction or error appeared. No one is forcing the buyer to ship the merchandise back to you. Just like eBay Fraud Protection (see Chapter 3), the credit card companies skew the rules to defend the consumer. As the seller, you have to fend for yourself. See Chapter 4 on how to report fraudulent buyers. Unfortunately, you usually have no way to verify that the shipping address is the one the credit card bills to. So, to add to your problems, the card may actually be stolen.

PayPal confirms through AVS (Address Verification Service) that the buyer's credit card billing address matches the shipping address provided and gives you the option not to accept payments from buyers whose addresses don't match. PayPal offers seller protection against spurious chargebacks under the following circumstances:

- Fraudulent card use
- False claims of non-delivery

See the section on PayPal for more details on how to be covered by seller protection.

If the bank that has issued the credit card resolves a chargeback in the buyer's favour, PayPal charges you $10 if you're decidedly at fault but will waive the fee if you meet all of the requirements of the PayPal Seller Protection policy.

Here's some good news: Major credit card companies are trying to curb online fraud for their merchant accounts. Visa has the new Verified by Visa acceptance, which takes buyers to a Visa screen (through software installed on the merchant's server) and verifies their identity through a Visa-only password. MasterCard uses SET (Secure Electronic Transactions), a similar encrypted transaction verification scheme. These systems are expected to substantially reduce fraud and chargebacks.

Credit card payment services

Person-to-person payment systems, such as eBay's PayPal, allow buyers to authorize payments from their credit cards or chequing accounts directly to the seller. These services make money by charging percentages and fees for each transaction. It all happens electronically through an automated clearinghouse — no fuss, no muss. The payment service releases to the seller only the buyer's shipping information; all personal credit card information is kept private. This speeds up the time it takes the buyer to get merchandise because sellers are free to ship as soon as the service lets them know that the buyer has made payment and the payment has been processed.

From the seller's point of view, person-to-person payment service transaction fees are frequently lower than the 2.5 to 3.5 percent (per transaction) that traditional credit card companies charge for merchant accounts. (Get the details in the "Your very own merchant account" section, coming up.) Even traditional retailers may switch their online business to these services to save money. In this section, we limit our discussion to PayPal because it's the payment method of choice by buyers on eBay. In Bill's case, more than 95 percent of his eBay sales are paid by PayPal. Other services exist but none have the confidence of so many eBay buyers. Before committing to a payment service other than PayPal, be sure to review eBay's Accepted Payment Policy to see if it's allowed on the site. You can learn more at

```
pages.ebay.ca/help/policies/accepted-payments-policy.html
```

When you pay the fee to your payment service, realize that the total amount of your transaction — including shipping fees, handling charges, and any sales tax that you charge — is incorporated into that fee. The payment service charges a percentage based on the total dollar amount that's run through its system.

PayPal

PayPal is the largest of the online person-to-person payment services. After several years of trying to compete against PayPal with an in-house service called BillPoint, eBay decided to acquire PayPal. If you can't beat 'em — buy 'em! PayPal has now become the de facto standard for eBay payments.

PayPal (see Figure 13-3) allows buyers to safely click and pay from their PayPal balance with a credit card or e-cheque after they've won an auction or made a purchase. PayPal is conveniently integrated into all eBay transactions; if your auction uses the Buy It Now feature or is a fixed-price listing, buyers can pay for their purchases immediately with PayPal payments.

To accept credit card payments, you must have a premier or business-level account with PayPal. Buyers may either join when they win their first auction and want to pay with PayPal, or they can go to www.PayPal.com and sign up before ever making a purchase. The story's slightly different for sellers: you need to set up your PayPal account *before* you choose to accept it in your auctions or sales.

Here are more than a few particulars about PayPal accounts:

- Auction payments are deposited into your PayPal account. Choose one of several ways to get your money:
  - Have the money transferred directly into your registered chequing account.

- Keep the money in your PayPal account for making payments to other sellers.

- Withdraw the cash from an ATM with a PayPal debit card and get back 1.5 percent of the money spent on purchases.

- Shop online with a virtual MasterCard that carries your balance to any Web site that accepts MasterCard.

✔ PayPal has its own feedback system, the Buyer Community Participation Number. The number after a user's name reflects the number of PayPal Verified users with whom this user has done business. The higher the number, the more likely the user is experienced and trustworthy. Clicking the number produces a report like the one shown in Figure 13-4.

✔ As a seller with a premier or business account, you can choose to accept or deny a payment without a confirmed address. A confirmed address means that the shipping address indicated by the buyer is the same as the billing address on the credit card the buyer chose to register with PayPal. On the accept or deny page, information about the buyer is shown, including verification status, account creation date, and participation number.

To specify whether you want to accept a credit card payment from a buyer without a confirmed address, log on, go to your account, and then click the Profile tab. Next, scroll down Selling Preferences and click Payment Receiving Preferences. If you accept payment from a non-confirmed address, that transaction will not be covered by the PayPal Seller Protection policy.

Figure 13-3:
The PayPal.com home page.

Getting more for your U.S. dollars

If you want to reduce the money you lose on exchange when transferring U.S. dollars from your PayPal account to your bank account in Canada, consider opening a bank account in the U.S. that has direct links to your Canadian bank. Many sellers that transfer funds from PayPal to their Canadian account find that the PayPal exchange rate allowed is substantially below the going rate offered elsewhere. For that reason, Bill has an account in the U.S. with TD USA Bank. He transfers U.S. funds from his PayPal account to that account on a frequent basis. When he's ready, he simply makes a call using the bank's toll-free number to arrange a transfer of the funds — converted into Canadian dollars — to his TD Canada Trust account. The funds are always transferred the same day and he generally saves a minimum of 1.5 percent on the exchange rate offered by PayPal. Although that might not seem like much on the surface, calculate it over the course of a year, and it can be a very substantial amount of money. Business owners will need to go to the extra trouble of transferring the funds to a personal account and then again to their business account because TD USA Bank will not transfer to business accounts.

Check with your bank to learn if they have an associated bank in the U.S. — the extra savings will make it worth your while.

Figure 13-4: Marsha's PayPal Member information box.

✔ PayPal charges your account $10 for any chargeback. The fee is waived if you've fulfilled the requirements in the PayPal Seller Protection policy (see the next point for more about this).

✔ The PayPal Seller Protection policy protects you against chargebacks, unauthorized card use, and non-shipments. To comply with this policy, you must do the following:

- **Be a verified member of PayPal:** Allow PayPal to confirm with your bank that your chequing account and address is your own.

- **Ship only to a confirmed address:** PayPal confirms that the buyer's shipping address coincides with the address to which the credit company sends monthly bills. Fraudulent shoppers often ask you to ship to another address — don't do it.

- **Keep proof of shipping that can be tracked online:** Here's where those delivery confirmation things come in handy. See Chapter 14 to learn more.

- **Ship tangible goods:** PayPal doesn't cover goods that are transmitted electronically.

- **Accept only single payments from a single account:** Don't let a buyer try to pay portions of a purchase from different e-mail addresses. Someone who's trying to pay using several accounts may be attempting to defraud you.

- **Ship PayPal purchases only to Canadian and U.S. buyers at confirmed addresses:** Seller protection isn't extended to international shipments beyond the U.S.

In June 2004, PayPal changed the tier system of its seller's fees. Seller's fee brackets are now adjusted based on the prior month's volume of transactions. Look at Table 13-2 for the updated PayPal fee tiers.

Table 13-2	PayPal (CAD) Fees		
Standard Rate	*Merchant Account Tiers*		
$0.00 – $3,000.00	*$3,000.01 – $12,000.00*	*$12,000.01 – $125,000.00*	*> $125,001.00*
2.9% + $0.55	2.5% + $0.55	2.2% + $0.55	1.9% + $0.55

A brilliant feature of PayPal is the ability to download your sales and deposit history to your computer. Although PayPal also offers files that integrate with QuickBooks (more on QuickBooks in Chapter 16), the standard downloads are feature-rich. Rather than importing just sales figures, with PayPal, you see each and every detail of your transaction — dates, names, addresses, phone numbers, amounts, and more. Even fees and taxes (if you charge sales tax) are broken down separately, making bookkeeping a breeze. The download imports into Microsoft Works and Excel. Downloading your history will help you calculate income taxes and sales taxes, reconcile your accounts, predict sales trends, calculate total revenues, and perform other financial reporting tasks. Doing so will also give you an excellent customer database.

Downloading a record of your deposits will give you detailed information for all the money that you receive for your eBay business: payments, PayPal transaction and deposit fees, refunds, rebates, and any adjustments made to your account.

Follow these steps to download your sales and deposit histories:

1. **Click the History tab on your PayPal Main Overview page.**

2. **Click the <u>Download My History</u> link on the right side of the page.**

3. **Enter the time span and the file format of the information you want to view.**

4. **Click the Download History button.**

   The information you have requested now appears on the screen. Alternatively, if the servers are busy, you'll receive an e-mail when the reports are ready (usually this takes a minute or two).

5. **Save the file in a directory that you can conveniently access for book-keeping.**

Just double-click the file to open it in Excel or Works. You now have all the information you may possibly need to apply to your bookkeeping program.

Registering with PayPal

If you aren't registered with PayPal yet (what's holding you up?), use the con-venient <u>Selling</u> link on the All Selling page, which you reach from your My eBay page. To get more information, just click the <u>PayPal</u> link to arrive at the PayPal Seller Overview page (see Figure 13-5), and then click the Sign Up button to begin registration. The registration form in Figure 13-6 appears. Tell them what country you're from, fill in the basic required information, and you're in.

The convenience of PayPal's integration into the eBay site shines when your item is purchased. Winners just click a Pay Now button that pops up on your auction page immediately after the listing closes. When you list auctions, you pre-set the shipping and handling charges that appear in the shipping box at the bottom of the page. When winners click the Pay Now button (see Figure 13-7), they're taken directly to a payment page set up with your infor-mation. The process is as easy as purchasing something through Buy It Now.

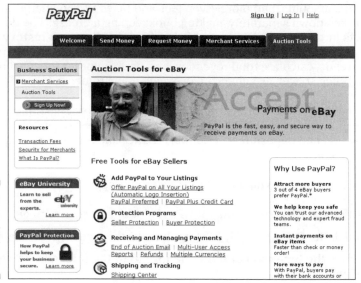

Figure 13-5:
The PayPal Seller Overview page.

Figure 13-6:
The new seller registration page.

When a purchase is made and the payment is deposited in your PayPal account, the system holds the money until you choose how you want to withdraw it.

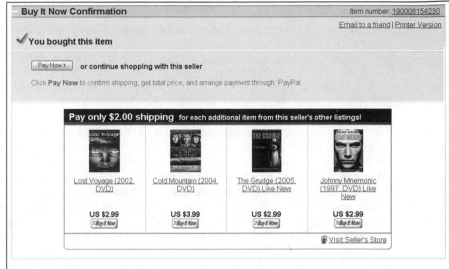

Figure 13-7:
The Pay
Now button
appears
when the
buyer wins.

PayPal accepts payments from fifty-five countries. For a current list of countries from which PayPal accepts payments, sign on to your PayPal account and go to

```
www.paypal.com/us/cgi-bin/webscr?cmd=_display-approved-
                signup-countries
```

Because credit card and identity theft is so prevalent on the Internet — and an expensive burden to e-commerce — PayPal uses the extra security measure provided by Visa and MasterCard called CVV2. Most credit cards have three additional numbers listed on the back, immediately following the regular sixteen-digit number. Merchants use these numbers for security or verification but aren't allowed to store them, so they're presumably protected from hackers. In the unlikely event your credit card doesn't have these numbers yet, PayPal still allows you to use your card by verifying it through a procedure known as *random charge*. PayPal charges about $1 or so to your card and asks you to disclose the pin number printed on your statement. Then PayPal knows that you control the card and didn't steal it.

Withdraw the funds from your PayPal account on a regular basis; you need that money to operate your business. Don't let your PayPal account become a temporary savings account — unless you choose the PayPal interest-bearing account (check out www.PayPal.com for more details). Also, any money you leave in your account can be extricated for a chargeback — and chargebacks can be applied as many as sixty days after a transaction. For more about chargebacks, refer to the "Forget the buyer: Seller beware!" sidebar earlier in this chapter.

Dealing with PayPal and Canadian sales taxes

One of the few frustrations Canadian eBay sellers have with PayPal is the company's inability to program in and collect Canadian sales taxes. Try as they might, and despite frequent lip service to try to get it right, PayPal just can't seem to understand that Canadian businesses are required to charge multiple levels of tax — GST (Goods and Services Tax), applicable PST (Provincial Sales Tax), or HST (Harmonized Sales Tax).

PayPal does allow you to set the amount of tax you charge to Canadian buyers but does not allow this amount to fluctuate by the buyer's home province. For example, Bill can set his tax preferences to collect 14 percent (8 percent PST for Ontario, plus 6 percent GST; coincidentally, this is also the HST for Newfoundland & Labrador, Nova Scotia and New Brunswick), but that's unfair to buyers in the remaining six provinces and three territories (especially to lucky Albertans who still don't pay a provincial sales tax). The solution for many Canadian sellers is to set their preferences to add 6 percent GST only. This allows them to collect some of the tax due but forces them to dip into their own pockets to pay PST or the balance of HST where applicable. Rather than set up the tax rate in their preferences, some sellers we know of will ask Canadian buyers to add the applicable tax on the insurance line when making their PayPal payment. This is a bit of a messy workaround — it's far from a great solution because it depends on buyers to conscientiously calculate and enter the correct amount. If a buyer fails to add the applicable tax in this manner, the seller is forced to refund the entire payment and ask the buyer to make a second corrected payment.

The real solution will come when PayPal puts their programming gurus to the task of allowing the system to add applicable sales taxes based on the buyer's province or territory of residence. eBay and PayPal have announced that August 2006 will see the introduction of PayPal Canada and the transferring of all Canadian accounts to the new company from the U.S. parent company. Hopefully this issue will be high on the priority list for the endeavour.

Your very own merchant account

If your eBay business is bringing in more than $20,000 a month, a credit card merchant account may be for you. At that level of sales, discounts kick in and your credit card processing becomes a savings to your business rather than an expense. But before you set up a merchant account, we recommend that you look at the costs carefully. We frequently get e-mails begging us to set up our own merchant accounts, and each one offers lower fees than the last. But charges buried in the small print make fees hard to calculate and even harder to compare. Even those who advertise low fees often don't deliver. Be sure to look at the entire picture before you sign a contract.

The best place to begin looking for a merchant account may be your own bank, where they know you, your credit history, and your business reputation and have a stake in the success of your business. If your credit isn't up to snuff, we recommend building good credit before pursuing a merchant account because your credit rating is your feedback to the offline world.

If your bank doesn't offer merchant accounts for Internet-based businesses, find a broker to evaluate your credit history and hook you up with a bank that fits your needs and business style (or join Costco as a last resort; see the following section). These brokers make their money from your application fee, from a finder's fee obtained from the bank that you finally choose, or both.

Canadian banks are now recognizing that e-commerce is here to stay and have rolled out a variety of products to meet the demands of small businesses that sell exclusively on the Web. Once you have decided on a bank, you need to decide how you want to process your online credit card transactions. Assuming that you have already developed your Web site (or that you have a site devoted to processing your eBay sales) and that you are now looking to add e-commerce capabilities with online authorization and credit card processing, most banks now offer payment services tailored to fit your needs. Generally, they allow you to choose from the following options:

- ✔ Payment services without a shopping cart
- ✔ Payment services with a shopping cart
- ✔ Payment services with an online storefront
- ✔ Web terminal only

If you opt for payment services with a shopping cart, the banks require that you have a separate cart for each currency accepted. In Table 13-3, we highlight various possible costs associated with setting up and maintaining a merchant account.

Table 13-3	Possible Internet Merchant Account Fees	
Fee	_For Cdn. Currency_	_For U.S. Currency_
Setup fee	$99.00 – $345.00 CAD	$71.00 – $247.00 USD
Monthly processing fee to bank	$35.00 – $95.00 CAD	$21.00 – $68.00 USD
Fee per transaction	$0.15 – $0.35 CAD	$0.11 – $0.25 USD
Internet discount rate	2.95% – 3%	2.95% – 3%
Monthly minimum processing fee	$10.00 CAD	$10.00 CAD
Chargeback fee	$10.00 CAD	$10.00 CAD

Remember that some merchant accounts will charge you with this type of fee scale and schedule while others may have a bunch of little snipes at your wallet. In the following list, I define some of the fees in Table 13-3:

- ✔ **Setup fee:** A one-time cost that you pay to either your bank or to your broker.

- ✔ **Discount rate:** A percentage of the transaction amount (a discount from your earnings) that is taken off the top along with the transaction fee before the money is deposited into your account.

- ✔ **Transaction fee:** A fee per transaction that's paid to the bank or to your gateway for the network.

- ✔ **Monthly minimum processing fee:** If your bank's cut of your purchases doesn't add up to this amount, the bank takes it anyway. For example, if your bank charges a minimum monthly fee of $20 and you don't hit $20 in fees because your sales aren't high enough, the bank charges you the difference.

If you're comfortable with all the information in the preceding list and Table 13-3, you may be ready to look for a broker. Heed our advice and read everything a broker offers carefully. Be sure you aren't missing any hidden costs.

Costco members' credit card processing

Here's some true discount credit card processing: a one-stop merchant account and gateway! Not only can you buy tuna fish in bulk with a Costco membership — you can also obtain a reasonably priced way to handle a merchant account (check out Table 13-4) through the NOVA Network. Costco got together with Nova Information Systems, one of the world's largest processors of credit card transactions, to offer Costco Executive Members a discounted Internet credit card processing service. Costco Executive Membership brings the cost of a Costco membership up from $45 to $100, but you get the benefit of receiving 2 percent back for most purchases (not including tobacco, gas, food, and some other purchases).

Table 13-4	Fees (CAD) for Costco Executive Member Internet Credit Card Processing*
Fee	*Amount*
Discount rate per transaction to NOVA	2.81%
Debit card transaction fee	$0.08
Monthly fees minimum	$10.00

Fee	Amount
Equipment rental	$25.00 per month (or purchase outright for $995.00)
Application Fee	$25.00 (waived for Executive Members)
Monthly Statement Fee	$5.00

* You also need a gateway, in the form of software (such as PC Transact It) or a relationship with a gateway service.

To get any Internet commerce account, the following details of your business must already be in place:

- An active customer service phone number
- A privacy policy stating that you will not share your customers' information with any other entity
- A registered domain in your name or the name of your business
- A return and refund policy
- A secure order page with https and lock
- Posted delivery methods and shipment time
- Products and pricing

To begin the application process, go to

www.costcocanada.novainfo.com

Figure 13-8: The Costco merchant credit card processing service.

Completing the online form will help to speed up the process of applying for credit card processing through Nova. After sending your form, you'll receive the full application package in the mail; also, a Costco representative will contact you by telephone. For further information or to apply by phone, call Costco Member Services at 866-325-3281 and refer to priority code 83630.

The VeriSign Payflow link service

If you have fewer than 1000 transactions a month through eBay and your Web site, you may want to check out some of the services offered by VeriSign, a publicly traded company and the world's largest Internet trust service. A respected world-class company and the leader in its field, VeriSign offers gateway services at a reasonable price.

To participate, you must first sign up for a merchant account from your bank, from Costco, or by applying through the Payflow preferred Merchant Account providers. The VeriSign Payflow service picks it up from there. You can integrate the Payflow service directly into your Web site. When you send out your winner's congratulatory letter, include a link to the page on your site that links to VeriSign. When your orders are submitted to VeriSign for processing, both you and your customer receive a transaction receipt through e-mail that acknowledges when the transaction has been processed. VeriSign processes your transactions while you're online.

VeriSign charges a $179 USD setup fee as well as $19.95 USD a month for up to 500 transactions. Additional transactions cost $0.10 USD each. For more information, go to the following:

```
www.verisign.com/products-services/payment-processing/
                online-payment/payflow-link
```

Chapter 14

Getting It from Your Place to Theirs

. . . .

In This Chapter

▶ Examining shipping options and costs

. . . .

*W*e think the best part of eBay is making the sale and receiving payment. After that comes the depressing and tedious process of fulfilling your orders. Don't feel bad if this part makes you take pause and sigh. Order fulfillment is one of the biggest problems (and yuckiest chores) for any mail order or online enterprise. The onerous task of packing and mailing merchandise is the bane of almost all businesses.

But as an eBay businessperson, you *must* attend to these tasks, however much you'd rather not. See Chapter 17 for tips on what you need for packing (boxes, bubble pack, and so on) and some options for purchasing online postage. In this chapter, we explain just how your items will get to their destinations, exploring your shipping options, costs, and insurance coverage along the way.

Finding the Perfect Shipping Carrier: The Big Three

When you're considering shipping options, you must first determine what types of packages you'll generally be sending (small packages that weigh less than two pounds or large and bulky packages). Then, decide how you'll send your items. Planning these details before listing your items is a good idea.

Choosing your carrier can be the most important decision in your eBay business. You need to decide which service is most convenient for you — which one is closest to your home base? Which provides pickup service? Which gives superior customer service? Also decide which service is the most economical:

which one leverages your bottom line? Most eBay sellers send packages using ground service rather than airmail or overnight, but a shipper who can give you both options may be offering you a good deal because you don't have to communicate with more than one vendor.

Settling on one main shipper to meet most of your needs is important because that way all your records will be on one statement or in one area. You might also need a secondary shipper for special types of packages. One shipper can't be everything to every business, so having an account with more than one can be to your advantage. Also, shippers may not sign up new accounts as readily in the middle of a competitor's strike or work slowdown.

In this section, we give you the lowdown on the three major carriers — FedEx Ground, UPS, and Canada Post — so you can see who fits your requirements. For a summary of shipping costs from these three carriers, see Table 14-1. Note that FedEx and UPS include tracking numbers for delivery confirmation. Canada Post offers free delivery confirmation for most services but not all.

Delivery confirmation and tracking aren't the same thing — delivery confirmation will only tell you when a successful delivery has been made to the customer, whereas tracking will usually show a package's progress in transit. Check out Chapter 17 for more information on shipping by mail.

Table 14-1	Shipping Costs (CAD) from Canada to the U.S. (Ontario to California with Residence Delivery)			
Delivery Service	*1 kg*	*3 kg*	*5 kg*	*10 kg*
FedEx Residential (2–7 days)*	$15.24	$19.77	$25.72	$40.32
UPS Residential (2 days)*	$22.99	$32.05	$33.52	$49.34
Canada Post Expedited U.S.A. (6–12 days)*	$15.52	$20.28	$21.57	$33.89
Canada Post Xpresspost U.S.A. (5–6 days)*	$31.92	$31.92	$33.11	$51.89
Canada Post Surface Small Packet (6–12 days)**	$9.90	N/A	N/A	N/A

* Based upon package dimensions of 12″ x 12″ x 12″

** Size restrictions apply

You can now prepare many Canada Post shipping documents online through PayPal. See Chapter 17 for the ins and outs (and pros and cons) of shipping through PayPal.

When you start shipping a few dozen packages a week, you might want to check out another of Marsha's books, *eBay Timesaving Techniques For Dummies* (Wiley), for an in-depth analysis of the big three and their variable shipping rates.

Federal Express

Federal Express (FedEx) is world-famous for its reliable service. In fact, FedEx is the number one choice for all major companies who "Absolutely, positively have to get it there on time." FedEx also has a reputation for some of the highest costs in the business — but only to the untrained eye. FedEx acquired Roadway Package Service (RPS) and formed FedEx Ground, which is their most economical service for delivery to residential addresses. For the services FedEx provides, you'll be happy to pay what you do. Read on.

FedEx Ground

FedEx Ground offers low rates and high-quality service. They're one of the few shippers that offer a money-back guarantee on deliveries within Canada. Unfortunately, FedEx Ground does not offer a residential pickup service, so if you ship from your home, they will require that your packaged and labelled items be delivered to one of their drop centres.

You must have an account that is guaranteed by a credit card to ship by FedEx Ground. To open an account, visit the FedEx Web site, shown in Figure 14-1, at

```
https://www.fedex.com/ca_english/OADR/index.html
```

Figure 14-1: FedEx allows you to open an account online.

Shipping the BIG stuff!

When it comes to shipping heavy or big stuff, you have a couple of options. Because we like using FedEx, we call FedEx Freight first. Marsha's husband once purchased four large heavy equipment tires on eBay, and there was no way they could be shipped by a regular small parcel carrier. She told the seller to place the tires on a pallet and secure them; then she called FedEx Freight, who picked them up. The cost of shipping was reasonable — the only caveat was that the shipment had to be delivered to a place of business, not a residential location.

You can also call local freight forwarders who specialize in LTL (Less than Truck Load) shipments. Many of these carriers will require that the shipment be prepared and delivered to them; few are willing to pick up or deliver in residential neighbourhoods. Some also offer motorized-lift tailgate services, but for an additional charge.

Even if you have a current Federal Express account, you need to sign on to add the Ground service. Registering for Ground service is even easier than registering on eBay, so give it a shot.

Marsha opened her FedEx Home Delivery account through a link on the main FedEx home page and, in the meantime, got the skinny on how to use the service. The online calculator will allow you to view all potential services and rates, so you don't even have to look up alternative rates and charts. And just as other shippers do, FedEx Home Delivery gives you a service schedule to let you know how long it will take your package to arrive at its destination (see Figure 14-2).

Figure 14-2:
The FedEx rate calculator for a shipment from Kitchener to California.

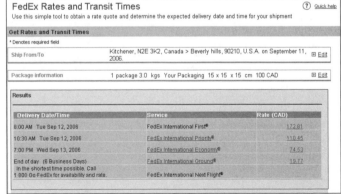

Here are a few fast facts about FedEx Ground:

- ✔ Deliveries by FedEx occur Monday through Friday during normal business hours.

- ✔ Dropping off packages at Federal Express counters incurs no additional charge.

- ✔ Each shipment is covered for $100 CAD in declared value. Additional insurance is 90 cents per $100 or a fraction thereof.

- ✔ FedEx allows you to print out labels and barcodes for your packages at home and track your packages online.

- ✔ FedEx works on a zone system based on your postal code and how far the package is going. Refer to the FedEx zone charts or find the cost of your shipment using the online calculator.

- ✔ If you plan to use FedEx to ship internationally (especially to the U.S.) you will need to establish an account with a customs broker to ensure proper documentation is supplied for clearance. FedEx has their own brokerage business, but a separate account is needed if you plan to use them. You can arrange for a FedEx Trade Networks account by calling 1-800-463-3339.

- ✔ Residential deliveries are limited to packages of 150 pounds or more.

If FedEx Ground shipping charges seem to be a great deal, they are! You can get an even better deal if you charge your FedEx shipping to an American Express Corporate Business card (one that gives you access to the American Express Open Network). You save an additional 10 percent on all FedEx Ground shipments within Canada and an amazing 20 percent on international shipments when you use online shipping and place your orders online. If you have such a card, be sure it is officially linked to FedEx so you get the discount. Call the FedEx/Open Network desk at 1-800-463-3339.

FedEx Online

FedEx has one of the most intuitive online applications for shipping. The FedEx Ship Manager interface will turn your computer into a one-person shipping shop. You can generate labels for all forms of FedEx services in one place. Also, the site allows you to search for rate quotes and track packages; it even includes a shipping notification option so you can send tracking information e-mail to your recipients.

Larger businesses can get FedEx's Ship Manager workstation, complete with PC and printers. The workstation has the unique ability to choose from other carriers. Aside from FedEx Express and FedEx Ground, you can also access UPS shipping services, which allow you to rate, track, report, and ship using multiple carriers on one system.

United Parcel Service

Everyone's familiar with the big brown trucks that tool around town delivering packages hither and yon. Those trucks belong to the United Parcel Service, or UPS, whose homepage is shown in Figure 14-3.

Figure 14-3:
The UPS
Canada hub.

UPS offers three levels of service based on your shipping needs:

- ✔ **Internet account:** Print your own bar-coded labels so that you can drop off packages at the UPS counter (you can also do that without an account) or give packages to a UPS driver.

- ✔ **Occasional shipper account:** Use UPS for the rare large box or heavy shipment you have to send. As an occasional shipper, you can call UPS for same-day pickup, provided you call before the local cut-off time (you'll need to call UPS to find out what that is). No additional charge is added for pickup.

- ✔ **Pickup account:** When you hit the big time, you can negotiate with UPS to get substantially lower rates and arrange for a driver to make daily stops to pick up your packages, whether you have packages to ship or not. Fees for pickup accounts generally run from $6.75 CAD to $15.50 CAD per week (based on the weekly number of packages you ship), plus the regular shipping costs for your packages.

For big shippers, UPS offers its Application Program Interface (API), which can be integrated into a company's home servers.

To register for UPS online, go to

```
https://www.ups.com/account/ca/start?loc=en_CA
```

After typing your personal or business information and answering a few basic questions, UPS will decide what type of account is right for you. By registering, you can also track packages and ship online.

Here are some quick facts about UPS:

✔ Shipping with UPS requires that you pay a different rate for different zones within Canada or internationally. The cost of your package is based on its dimensional weight, your postal code (where the package ships from), and the addressee's location (where the package is going). To figure out your cost, use the handy UPS cost calculator shown in Figure 14-4.

✔ Delivery of UPS packages occurs Monday through Friday.

✔ Each package has a tracking number that you can input online to verify location and time of delivery.

✔ Insurance ($100 CAD) is included with every shipment. For valuations over this amount, insurance costs an additional 90 cents per $100 CAD.

✔ Like FedEx, UPS requires that all shipments be cleared through a customs broker. UPS does offer this service but it can be rather expensive.

✔ No surcharge exists for delivery to a residential address.

✔ UPS offers a chart that defines the shipping time for your ground shipments.

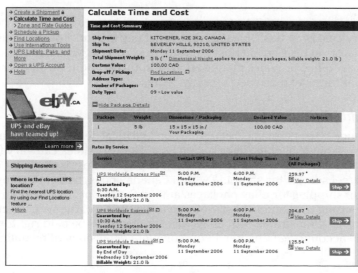

Figure 14-4:
The UPS cost calculator.

Canada Post

Whether you call it snail mail, pops (plain old postal service), or whatever nickname you like, Canada Post has been the staple for eBay shipping by Canadians from the beginning. This service is the only one that can promise to deliver every piece of mail in their possession to any part of our country. Check out its Web site in Figure 14-5.

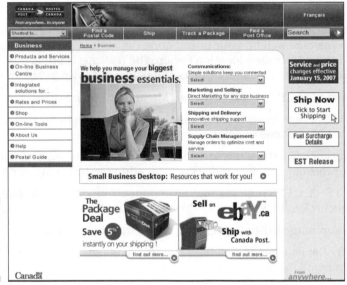

Figure 14-5:
The Canada
Post
Web site.

Canada Post is available to everyone; you don't have to set up an account to use its services. For a basic idea of what you'll pay to send a package, use the rate calculator on the Canada Post Web site (`http://www.canadapost.ca/`). The post office provides many services; in this section, we go over the most popular forms of mail used by eBay sellers.

Expedited

The huge size of Canada creates certain logistical delivery problems — even for a well-oiled machine like Canada Post. Delivery times can vary from one to fifteen days within our own country. Expedited Post is the most economical parcel service for shipping within Canada and is, by far, the most popular form of shipping for eBay packages among Canadians. Postage can be printed online using the Canada Post Web site or PayPal — of the two, we much prefer PayPal, as it integrates with eBay. Also, postage can be paid right from your PayPal account. See Chapter 17 for complete details regarding online postage.

Expedited Post is perfect for smaller packages, but the rates can vary wildly from city to city. Canada Post now also assesses a fuel surcharge for all domestic packages; this additional fee can greatly inflate your cost.

Delivery confirmation and the first $100 CAD of insurance are included in the cost of Expedited Post at no additional charge. Remember, delivery confirmation tells you only *if* the package was delivered; it doesn't trace the package along its route.

Expedited Parcel USA

Expedited Parcel USA is the shipping method of choice to the U.S. for packages that exceed 1 kilogram in weight. According to Canada Post, delivery times can vary from six to twelve business days but, in reality, there are no guarantees; packages can frequently take more than fifteen to twenty days to reach some U.S. destinations — especially Alaska, Hawaii, and Puerto Rico.

Delivery confirmation and the first $100 of insurance are included in the cost of Expedited U.S.A. This method of shipping qualifies for PayPal's Seller Protection Policy.

Small Packet

Small Packet is a service that Canada Post offers only for international shipping. There are different Small Packet services that apply to the U.S. and to the rest of the world. Small Packet services are for packages that weigh less than 1 kilogram to the U.S. and less than 2 kilograms when being sent elsewhere. There are also Small Packet Surface and Small Packet Air distinctions. All this can seem confusing, so we will point out only the major advantages and disadvantages of each type.

Small Packet is a flat rate service — no distinction is made between two packages of the same size and weight going to Hawaii and Florida for the U.S. rates or Scotland and Australia for the international rates. Neither tracking nor delivery confirmation is available for this service, so PayPal does not consider it an acceptable method of shipping to qualify for its Seller Protection Policy. Surface Small Packet shipping is also considerably slower than Expedited U.S.A service because packages shipped this way are only given space available in trucks after all Expedited U.S.A mail is loaded. No guarantee of service is offered but, through experience, delivery times to the U.S. appear to vary between eight to twenty days, whereas Surface Small Packet service to destinations other than the U.S. routinely takes months. Small Packet Air shipments to the U.S. or elsewhere in the world are given a considerably higher priority than surface shipments, improving delivery times dramatically.

Canada Post offers a maximum of $100 CAD in insurance for Small Packet shipments at no additional charge.

Small Packet services are best used when mailing inexpensive items and when delivery confirmation and delivery time are not of highest importance.

Light Packet — USA

Light Packet is a relatively new service introduced by Canada Post to ensure that Canadian shippers are meeting the requirements of U.S. Customs.

In the past, many eBay sellers frequently shipped small, lightweight items — such as CDs or DVDs — by regular letter mail and without a customs declaration. To ensure that non-paper items are properly declared to U.S. Customs; the United States requires that a Customs form (CN 22) be attached to all packages sent by letter mail. The maximum allowable weight is 500 grams and there are size restrictions. At this time, Light Packet — USA postage can only be purchased at retail postal outlets.

Xpresspost

A faster level of service is available from Canada Post, but at a substantially higher cost. Normal delivery times when using Xpresspost vary from the next day to six days when sending items within Canada or the U.S. Delivery confirmation and the first $100 CAD of insurance are included in the price. One of the benefits of paying for this level of service is that Canada Post will generally guarantee delivery within a specified amount of time or refund the postage. But keep in mind that there are exceptions — for instance, peak rush periods near Christmas — where the guarantee will not apply.

Canada Post's Electronic Shipping Tools (EST)

If you want to print your own postage, you can use PayPal or you can use Canada Post's Electronic Shipping Tools for most services (see Figure 14-6). Using the online tools eliminates standing in line at a retail postal outlet; you can purchase and print your postage right from your home office. An added advantage of using the Electronic Shipping Tools is that you will save 3 percent on postage for most services and an additional 5 percent if you join Canada Post's VentureOne program for small business.

Once you register to use the EST you can choose to print your postage online — one package at a time — or download their software and print all your postage for the day at once. Payment for postage is charged to the credit card number you provide at the time of registration. The label pouches you need for shipping can be ordered directly from Canada Post on a no-charge basis.

Figure 14-6:
The Canada
Post
Electronic
Shipping
Tools page.

One of the advantages of using the Canada Post EST is that the postage you pay is solely between you and Canada Post; it is never revealed to your customer. This can be important, as many buyers do not fully understand that shipping and handling charges are not to be equated with postage. Charges for shipping and handling will often include packaging, labels, and invoicing costs. By not revealing the postage on the package, you can avoid many lengthy (and sometimes hostile) e-mail discussions with your buyers about why you charged $2 more than the actual postage.

Part IV
Your eBay Back Office

The 5th Wave   By Rich Tennant

"I think we ought to check first to see if eBay has a category for 'Fertility gods. Ancient.'"

In this part . . .

Setting up your eBay business as a real business entity involves some unpleasant paperwork, including applying for licences, record-keeping, and various types of organizing. Even though you should discuss your issues with a professional, we fill in the blanks and get you started on the right track. We also provide a handy checklist of the items you need to run your business online, such as your legal status, bookkeeping requirements, and software to automate shipping.

Chapter 15

Going Legit

In This Chapter

▶ Deciding your business format

▶ Covering the legalities

*B*usiness format? You ask, "What's a business format?" We hate to be the ones to tell you — you can't just say, "I'm in business," and be in business. When you started selling on eBay, maybe you were happy just adding a few dollars to your income. Now that the money is coming in faster, you have a few more details to attend to. Depending how far you're going to take your business, you have to worry about taxes, bookkeeping, and possible ramifications down the line.

We want to remind you that we're *not* lawyers or accountants. The facts we give you in this chapter are from what we've learned over the years. When you begin a formal business, it's best to involve a lawyer and a chartered accountant. At the very least, pay a visit to this great Web site, which offers some excellent business start-up advice and forms.

www.canadaone.com/tools/startingabusiness.html

One of the first rules in the eBay User Agreement reads ". . . your eBay account (including feedback) and User ID may not be transferred or sold to another party." This means if you begin your business on eBay with another person, you'd better have some kind of agreement up front about who gets the user ID in case of a sale. And if you sell your business, the person with the original ID had better be involved actively with the new company — as the rules say, your feedback can never be transferred or sold. A new owner would have to start a new account on eBay with a new name — unless the principal from the old company was contractually involved and was the actual eBay seller.

To our knowledge, no one has tested this rule in court, and we'll bet you don't want to be the first to face eBay's top-notch lawyers. Know that this is the rule and plan for it.

Types of Businesses

Businesses come in several forms, from a sole proprietorship all the way to a corporation. A corporation designation isn't as scary as it sounds. Yes, Microsoft, IBM, and eBay are corporations, but so are many individuals running businesses. Each form of business has its plusses and minuses — and its costs. We go over some of the fees involved in incorporating your business later in this chapter. For now, we detail the most common types of businesses, which we encourage you to weigh carefully.

Before embarking on any new business format, be sure to consult with professionals in the legal and financial fields. We also encourage you to check out the *Canadian Small Business Kit For Dummies* by Margaret Kerr and JoAnn Kurtz (Wiley). It's packed with valuable information that will help make the start-up of your business venture less of a mystery.

Sole proprietorship

If you're running your business by yourself part-time or full-time, your business is a *sole proprietorship*. Yep, doesn't that sound official? A sole proprietorship is the simplest form of business — nothing is easier or cheaper. Most people use this form of business when they're starting out. Many then graduate to a more formal type of business as things get bigger.

If a husband and wife file a joint tax return, they *can* run a business as a sole proprietorship (but only one of you can be the proprietor). However, if both you and your spouse work equally in the business, running it as a partnership — with a written partnership agreement — is a much better idea. (See the next section, "Partnership," for more information.) A partnership protects you in case of your partner's death. In a sole proprietorship, the business ends with the death of the proprietor. If the business has been a sole proprietorship in your late spouse's name, you may be left out in the cold.

Being in business adds a few expenses, but you can deduct many of those business expenses from your taxes. A sole proprietorship *can* be run out of your personal chequing account (although we don't advise it). The profits of your business are taxed directly as part of your own income tax, and the profits and expenses are reported on your tax return. As a sole proprietor, you're personally at risk for your business's liabilities. All outstanding debts are yours, and you could lose personal assets if you default.

Also, you must consider the liability of the products you sell on eBay. If you sell foodstuff, vitamins, or neutraceuticals (new age food supplements) that make someone ill, you may be personally liable for any court-awarded damages. If someone is hurt by something you sell, you may also be personally liable as the seller of the product.

Partnership

When two or more people are involved in a business, it can be a *partnership*. A general partnership can be formed by a verbal agreement. Each person in the partnership contributes capital or services and both share in the partnership's profits and losses. The income of a partnership is taxed to both partners, based on the percentage of the business that they own or upon the terms of a written agreement.

You'd better be sure that you can have a good working relationship with your partner; this type of business relationship has broken up many a friendship. Writing up a formal agreement when forming your eBay business partnership is an excellent idea. This agreement is useful in solving any disputes that may occur over time.

In your agreement, be sure to outline things such as

- Compensation to each of you
- Duties and responsibilities of each partner
- How disputes will be settled
- How to divide the company's profits and losses
- Restrictions of authority and spending
- What happens if the partnership dissolves
- What happens to the partnership in the case of death or disability

One more important thing to remember: As a partner, you're jointly and severally responsible for the business liabilities and actions of the other person or people in your partnership — as well as your own. Again, this is a personal liability arrangement. When you enter into this kind of arrangement, you and your partner are both personally open to any lawsuits that come your way through the business.

Financial information from the partnership is combined with the personal income of each of the partners to determine each person's overall tax liability. Any partnerships with more than five partners will also have to comply with the Canada Revenue Agency (CRA)'s reporting requirements.

LLC (limited liability company)

A *limited liability company,* or LLC, is similar to a partnership but also has many of the characteristics of a corporation. An LLC differs from a partnership mainly in that the liabilities of the company are not passed on to the members (owners). Unless you sign a personal guarantee for debt incurred, you and any other members are responsible only to the total amount you have invested into the company. Unfortunately, all members *do* have liability for the company's taxes.

You'll need to put together an operating agreement, similar to the partnership agreement, when setting up an LLC. Doing so will also help establish which members own what percentage of the company for tax purposes. Most provinces will require you to file Articles of Incorporation forms to start this type of business.

An LLC is taxed like a sole proprietorship, with the profits and losses passed on to each member's personal tax return. An LLC may opt to pay taxes like a corporation and keep some of the profits in the company, thereby reducing the tax burden to the individual members. Although members pay the LLC's taxes, the company must still file a T2 return with the CRA at the end of the year. This gives the CRA extra data to be sure that the individual members properly report their income.

Corporation

A *corporation* has a life of its own: its own name, its own bank account, and its own tax return. A corporation is a legal entity created for the sole purpose of doing business. One of the main problems a sole proprietor faces when incorporating is realizing that he or she can't help themselves to the assets of their business. Yes, a corporation can have only one owner: the shareholder (or shareholders as a unit). If not writing yourself cheques from your business (unless they are for your salary or reimbursement of legitimate expenses) is something you understand and can handle, you may be ready for the responsibility of running your own corporation.

Generally, the province in which you run your business sets up the rules for corporations operating within its borders. A corporation can also be registered federally, which means that you deal with the folks in Ottawa. In most cases you can find the forms required to incorporate your business on either provincial or federal Web sites, and they are relatively simple to fill out. Don't let that fool you — you may still want a professional to help you with this step, as mistakes made when registering a corporation can be very difficult and expensive to correct after the fact.

Once the forms are completed and the fees paid, the government to which the application has been made will issue a Certificate of Incorporation or, in Prince Edward Island or Quebec, a Charter by Letters Patent. Combined federal and provincial taxes for corporations range from approximately 31 to 39 percent at present, and they're generally based on your profits.

The federal government's small business deduction can reduce the federal tax rate to between 13 and 22 percent on the first $400,000 of business income. Provinces are also making an effort to lighten the burden on small business owners by reducing the taxes owed by small businesses to between 24 and 28 percent (depending on the province).

Often employee owners of corporations will use the company to shelter income from tax by dividing that income between their personal and corporate tax returns. This is frequently called *income splitting* and involves setting salaries and bonuses so that any remaining profits at the end of the company's tax year will be taxed at a lower percentage rate. Seeing how much the big guys pay in taxes compared to how much you'll pay if you leave profits in a corporation is kind of fun, so check out Table 15-1 for the rates for federal taxes only.

Table 15-1   Federal Tax Rates for Corporations (January 1, 2007)

Taxable Income	Tax Rate
$0–$400,000	13.1%
Above $400,000	22.1%
Corporate Investments	35.8%

Often in small corporations, most of the profits are paid out in tax-deductible salaries and benefits. The most important perk of having your business registered as a corporation is that any liabilities belong to that corporation. Your personal assets remain your own, because they have no part in the business.

Getting your legal documents prepared online

You just *knew* legal services would go online eventually, didn't you? If you're thinking of setting up one of the business formats described in this chapter, you might be interested in putting things together online. Real paralegals are there to help you on an ever-growing number of Web sites. Because most of these online services specialize in registering companies within specific provinces, shop carefully.

Additionally, you may want to have a consultation (at least over the phone) with a lawyer in your area, perhaps one who is a member of the local Chamber of Commerce. Most provinces also have a small business development office whose principle function is to help new ventures find their way through the red tape of government. Check your local Yellow Pages for an office near you.

Taking Care of Regulatory Details

Let us give you one important tip to make your life easier in the long run: Don't ignore municipal, provincial, or federal regulatory details. Doing so may simplify your life at the get-go, but if your business is successful, one day your casual attitude will catch up with you. Ignorance is no excuse. To do business in this great country, you must comply with all the rules and regulations that are set up for your protection and benefit.

Corporate Name Information Form

If you plan on running your business under a name different from your own, you may have to file a *Corporate Name Information Form,* regardless of the legal format of your business. In Canada, every person who regularly transacts business for profit under a fictitious business name (not their own name) must register. Depending on your plans for incorporation, you generally file this form either federally or with the province where the business is being established.

Before you try to register your corporate name, you will want to ensure that a thorough Newly Automated Name Search (NUANS) has been performed. Many online companies offer discounted NUANS searches; alternatively, you can visit the Industry Canada NUANS search page for federal incorporations only. You can find the page at:

```
www.nuans.com/nuansinfo_en/home-accueil_en.htm
```

Master Business Licence

Most provinces require the registration of a company name be granted with a Master Business Licence. This document enables you to open a business bank account and apply for Retail Sales Tax and Goods and Services Tax licences. It also provides the province with general information regarding the ownership and contact information of the company.

Goods & Services Tax Registration (GST)

In Canada, the GST applies to almost all goods or services sold. Unlike Retail Sales Tax, which is only paid by the final consumer (except in Quebec), GST is added at every step along the production and sale chain. Although everyone in this chain is charged the tax, the federal government only wants to keep the tax that is owed by the final consumer. All others can claim a refund of the tax paid (called an *input tax credit*).

You're required to register for the GST if your annual revenues are $30,000 CAD or greater. Even if your sales fall short of this amount, you may still choose to register, because doing so brings some distinct advantages. As most of your sales will likely be shipped to the U.S., and because you're not able to charge GST to American residents, registering for the program allows you to claw back all GST paid for products shipped to the U.S. You will also be able to claim credit for GST paid on many items that are used in the day-to-day running of your business. All of these factors could result in a substantial refund of GST paid. In fact, many sellers we know have yet to actually submit a payment of GST — they routinely claim a substantial refund.

Retail Sales Tax (RST) licence

Retail Sales Tax licences are the official-looking pieces of paper you see behind the register at local stores. Every retail business must have one, and it is in your best interest to obtain one, too. Yes, even if you're running a business out of your home and have no one coming to do business on-site, you may still need this. All provincial governments (except lucky Alberta) require that sales tax be charged to the consumer on most categories of merchandise. In Newfoundland and Labrador, Nova Scotia, and New Brunswick, the Provincial Sales Tax has been *"harmonized"* with the Goods and Services Tax (GST) collected by the federal government. In the other provinces that still administer their own sales tax programs you are required to collect sales tax from residents of the province in which you are licensed. If you don't, the authorities may charge you a bunch of penalties if they ever find out. Avoiding the step of getting a proper licence isn't worth the risk.

Your provincial government will require that you collect and remit RST on a regular basis (usually monthly or quarterly). You'll also be required to keep accurate records of tax charged, because you are subject to audit by the provincial watchdogs.

Securing an RST (Retail Sales Tax) licence does offer an advantage: having it will open many doors for you that will otherwise be closed. Most manufacturers and distributors will not consider selling their products to you unless you have this licence. Without it, you will also wind up paying the provincial tax for items that you plan to resell, a cost you would otherwise be exempt from.

Payroll taxes

Aye, caramba! We swear it feels like the rules and regulations are never going to end, but if you have regular employees, you need to collect income tax and money for Employment Insurance (EI) and the Canada Pension Plan (CPP) on behalf of your employees. You're also expected to remit those tax dollars, along with your business's contributions to EI and the CPP, to the CRA (Canada Revenue Agency). Many enterprises go down because the owners just can't seem to keep their fingers out of withheld taxes, which means the money isn't available to turn in when the taxes are due. (Another reason why having a separate bank account for your business is a good idea!)

Other business taxes

Just when you think the taxman has taken all he can, he makes several more grabs for your hard-earned cash.

Here are some of the additional taxes that you might expect to eventually pay:

- ✔ Municipalities also levy taxes on businesses. If your company owns real estate you will be required to pay property taxes. In some municipalities, even businesses that rent instead of own are required to pay taxes. These taxes can frequently be based on the annual rental value of the property, the square footage of the premises, or the value of the business's stock-in-trade.

- ✔ Some provinces add a tax on the *paid-up capital* of corporations. Paid-up capital is the total amount paid to the corporation for all of the shares that have been issued to shareholders.

- ✔ The federal government levies a large corporation tax on corporations with over $10 million CAD of taxable capital. But hey, if your sales have exceeded $10 million, you can probably afford it.

An accountant can tell you much more about these matters. You can also visit the federal, provincial, or municipal Web sites that deal with taxation for more information.

Chapter 16

Practising Safe and Smart Record-Keeping

● ●

In This Chapter

▶ Understanding first things first: Bookkeeping basics

▶ Saving your records to save your bacon

▶ Finding bookkeeping software

▶ Using QuickBooks for your bookkeeping needs

● ●

*B*ookkeeping, *bah!* You'll get no argument from us that bookkeeping can be the most boring and time-consuming part of your job. You may feel that you just need to add your product costs, add your gross sales, and bada-bing, you know where your business is. Sorry, not true. Did you add that roll of tape you picked up at the supermarket today? Although it cost only $1.29, it's a business expense. How about the mileage driving back and forth from garage sales and flea markets? Those are expenses, too. We suspect that you're also not counting quite a few other "small" items just like these in your expense column.

Once you get into the task, you may find that you actually enjoy posting your expenses and sales. Doing so gives you the opportunity to know exactly where your business is at any given moment. Of course, it's easier if you are not using a pencil-entered ledger system; consider using a software program that's easy and fun. In this chapter, we give you the lowdown on the basics of bookkeeping, emphasize the importance of keeping records in case the taxman comes calling, and explain why using QuickBooks is the smart software choice. Keep reading: This chapter is *required*.

Keeping the Books: Basics That Get You Started

Although posting bookkeeping can be boring, clicking a button to generate your tax information is a lot easier than manually going over pages of sales information on a pad of paper. That's why we like to use a software program, particularly QuickBooks (more about that in the section titled "QuickBooks: Making Bookkeeping Uncomplicated").

We suppose that you *could* use plain ol' paper and a pencil to keep your books; if that works for you, great. But even though that might work for you now, it definitely won't in the future. Entering all your information into a software program now — while your books may still be fairly simple to handle — can save you a lot of time and frustration in the future, when your eBay business has grown beyond your wildest dreams and no amount of paper can keep it all straight and organized. We discuss alternative methods of bookkeeping in the "Bookkeeping Software" section. For now, we focus on the basics of bookkeeping.

To effectively manage your business, you must keep track of *all* your expenses — down to the last roll of tape. You need to keep track of your inventory, how much you paid for the items, how much you paid in shipping, and how much you profited from your sales. If you use a van or the family car to pick up or deliver merchandise to the post office, keep track of the mileage used as well. When you're running a business, it's important to account for every penny that goes in and out.

Bookkeeping has irrefutable standards called GAAP (Generally Accepted Accounting Procedures) that are set by the country's Accounting Standards Board. (It sounds scary to us, too.) *Assets*, *liabilities*, *owner's equity*, *income*, and *expenses* are standard terms used in all forms of accounting to define profit, loss, and the fiscal health of your business.

Every time you process a transaction, two things happen: One account is credited while another receives a debit — kind of like yin and yang. (We've included a couple of features in this book to help you get more familiar with these terms and others, including those in the following list, that are used in bookkeeping. See the charts of accounts later in this chapter [in Table 16-2] and in Appendix A, a mini glossary we've included for your convenience.) Depending on the type of account, your account's balance either increases or decreases when you punch numbers into your program or ledger. One account that increases while another decreases is called *double-entry accounting*:

- ✔ When you post an expense, the debit *increases* your expenses and *decreases* your bank account.

- ✔ When you purchase furniture or other assets, it *increases* your asset account and *decreases* your bank account.

- ✔ When you make a sale and make the deposit, it *increases* your bank account and *decreases* your accounts receivable.

- ✔ When you purchase inventory, it *increases* your inventory and *decreases* your bank account.

- ✔ When a portion of a sale includes sales tax, it *decreases* your sales and *increases* your sales tax account.

Manually performing double-entry accounting can be a bit taxing (no pun intended). A software program automatically adjusts the accounts when you input a transaction.

As a business owner, even if you're a sole proprietor (refer to Chapter 15 for information on business types), it's a very good idea to keep your business books separate from your personal expenses. (We recommend using a program such as Quicken to keep track of your *personal* expenses for tax time.) By isolating your business records from your personal records, you can get a snapshot of which areas of your sales are doing well and which ones aren't carrying their weight. But that isn't the only reason keeping accurate records is smart; there's the CRA (Canada Revenue Agency) to think about, too. In the next section, we explain the taxman's interest in your books.

Hiring a professional to do your year-end taxes

When we say that you must hire a professional to prepare your taxes, we mean a chartered accountant (CA) if your business format is a corporation, or a licensed professional who specializes solely in taxation and current tax laws if your business is a sole proprietorship or partnership. Unlike a CA or an attorney, tax professionals don't charge an arm and a leg. They're a valuable addition to your business arsenal.

Although the folks at your local "We Do Your Taxes in a Hurry" store may be well-meaning and pleasant, the people doing your taxes may have only gone through a six-week course in the current tax laws. This does not make them tax professionals. When business taxes are at stake, a professional with whom you have a standing relationship is the best choice. If you don't know one, ask around or call your local Chamber of Commerce.

Posting bookkeeping can be boring. At the end of the year, if you have a professional do your taxes, you'll be a lot happier — and your tax preparation will cost you less — if you've posted your information clearly and in the proper order. That's why using QuickBooks (see the "QuickBooks: Making Bookkeeping Uncomplicated" section) is essential to running your business.

Records the Taxman May Want to See

One of the reasons we can have a great business environment in Canada is because we all have a partner, the CRA (Canada Revenue Agency). Our government regulates business and sets the rules for us to transact our operations. To help you get started with your business, the CRA maintains a small-business Web site (shown in Figure 16-1) at the following address:

```
www.cra-arc.gc.ca/tax/business/smallbus-e.html
```

In this section, we highlight what information you need to keep and how long to keep it (just in case you're chosen for an audit).

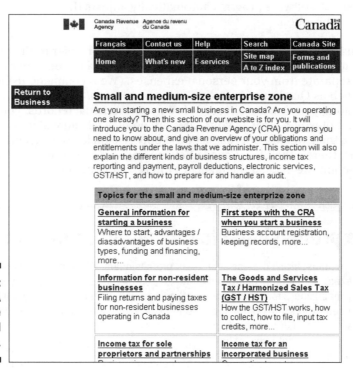

Figure 16-1:
The CRA home page for small businesses.

Supporting information

Aside from needing to know how your business is going (which is really important), the main reason to keep clear and concise records is because the Canada Revenue Agency may come knocking one day. You never know when tax auditors will choose *your* number and want to examine *your* records. In the following list, we highlight some of the important pieces of *supporting information* (things that support your expenses on your end-of-year tax return):

- **A daily calendar:** This is where a Palm handheld can be invaluable. Every time you leave your house or office on a business-related task, make note of it in your Palm. Keep as much minutia as you can stand. Your Palm Desktop can print a monthly calendar. At the end of the year, staple the pages together and include them in your files with your sub-stantiating information.

- **Business cards:** It may sound like we're stretching things a bit, but if you use your car to look at some merchandise, pick up a business card from the vendor. If you're out of town and have a meeting with someone, take a card. Having these business cards can help substantiate your deductible comings and goings.

- **Credit card statements:** You're already collecting credit card receipts (although ours frequently seem to disappear to the same place as all those missing socks). If you have your statements, you have monthly proof of expenses. When you get your statement each month, post it into your bookkeeping program and itemize each and every charge, detailing where you spent the money and what for. (QuickBooks has a split feature that accommodates all your categories.) File these statements with your tax return at the end of the year in your year-end envelope (shoe box?).

- **Merchandise invoices:** Saving all merchandise invoices is as important as saving all your receipts. If you want to prove that you paid $400 and not the $299 retail price for that PlayStation 2 that you sold on eBay for $500, you'd *better* have an invoice of some kind. The same idea applies to most collectibles, in which case a retail price can't be fixed. Save all invoices!

- **Outside contractor invoices:** If you use outside contractors — even if you pay the college kid next door to go to the post office and bank for you — ask them for an invoice to document exactly what service you paid for and how much you paid. This is supporting information that will save your bacon, if you ever need it saved.

- **Receipts:** Dear reader, heed this advice: Save every receipt that you get. If you're out of town on a buying trip and have coffee at the airport, save that receipt — it's a deduction from your profits. Everything related to your business may be deductible, so you must save airport parking receipts, taxi receipts, receipts for a pen that you picked up on your way to a meeting, *everything.* If you don't have a receipt, you can't prove the write-off.

We know that all this stuff will pile up, but that's when you go to the store and buy some plastic file storage containers to organize it all. To check for new information and the lowdown on what you can and can't do, ask a chartered accountant. Also visit the Canada Revenue Agency's Tax Information for Business site, shown in Figure 16-2, at

`www.cra-arc.gc.ca/tax/business/topics/keeprec-e.html`

Figure 16-2:
Get tax information from the horse's mouth here.

How long must you keep your records?

How long do you have to keep all this supporting information? We hate to tell you, but you'd best be saving it all for a long time. Marsha must have at least ten years of paperwork in old files and big plastic boxes in her garage. But you know, she's not too extreme; the period in which you can amend a return or in which the CRA can assess you to pay more tax is never less than three years from the date of filing — it can even be longer. As of our last visit to the Canada Revenue Agency's Web site, the information in Table 16-1 was valid.

Table 16-1	How Long to Keep Your Tax Records
Circumstance	*Keep Records This Long*
You owe additional tax	6 years
You file a fraudulent tax return	Indefinite
You don't bother to file a return	Indefinite
Dissolution of a corporation	2 years

Even though we got this information directly from the CRA Web site and literature (Publication RC4409(E), "Keeping Records"), it may change in the future. You can download a PDF copy of the booklet by going to the following address:

```
www.cra-arc.gc.ca/E/pub/tg/rc4409/README.html
```

If Adobe Acrobat Reader isn't installed on your computer, you can also view it as a Web page (HTML). It doesn't hurt to store your information for as long as you can stand it and stay on top of any changes the Canada Revenue Agency may implement.

Bookkeeping Software

Keeping track of your auctions is hard without software, but keeping track of the money you make without the help of software program is even harder (and more time-consuming). If using software to automate your auctions makes sense, so does using software to automate your bookkeeping. You can afford to make a mistake here and there in your own office, and no one will ever know. But if you make a mistake in the books, your partner (the CRA) will notice — and be quite miffed. They may even charge you a penalty or two so that you'll remember not to make those mistakes again.

The Canada Revenue Agency's penalties aren't small, either. In addition to penalties, the CRA can prosecute. Those found guilty can be subject to imprisonment and/or a minimum $1,000 fine. That can be quite an expensive lesson.

When Marsha started her business, she used accounting ledger pads (which had just replaced the chisel and stone format). She soon found that she had way too many ledgers to keep track of and cross-reference. A calculator was useful, based on the assumption that she typed the correct figures to start with.

TIP

Spreadsheet software can be a boon when you're just starting out. A program such as Microsoft Works (which comes free on many new computers) or Excel is an excellent way to begin posting the financial details of your business. The program can be set up to calculate your expenses, profits, and (we hope not too many) losses. Microsoft Works comes with several free financial worksheet templates that you can easily adapt for an eBay small business. Also, you can find current Excel templates to get you started at `office.microsoft.com` — there's no need to spend any extra money on templates when you're first starting!

With official bookkeeping software, reconciling a chequebook is a breeze. You merely click off the deposits and withdrawals (cheques) when the statement comes in. If you made a mistake when originally inputting the data, the software (comparing your balance and your bank's balance) lets you know that you made an error. This kind of efficiency would have put Bob Cratchit out of a job!

We have researched various Web sites to find out which software has sold the best and is easiest to use. We've also had many discussions with chartered accountants and bookkeepers. The software that these professionals most recommend for business is Intuit's QuickBooks. (Thank goodness that's the one we use.) QuickBooks is considered the best, which is why we devote so much of this chapter to it. Some people begin with Quicken and later move to QuickBooks when their business gets big or incorporates. Our theory? Start with the best. It's not that much more expensive — on eBay, we've seen the new, sealed, Canadian version of QuickBooks Pro 2006 software selling for as low as $120 USD — and it will see you directly to the big time. It's important to shop for the Canadian version of the software as it will allow you to carry on your business in both Canadian and U.S. dollars. It's also set up to reflect Canadian taxation and tax reporting.

QuickBooks: Making Bookkeeping Uncomplicated

QuickBooks offers several versions, from basic to premier solutions tailored to different types of businesses. QuickBooks Basic and QuickBooks Pro have a few significant differences. QuickBooks Pro adds job costing and expensing features and the ability to design your own forms to what is offered in the basic version. It also includes payroll functions and allows for multiple, simultaneous users. QuickBooks Basic does a darn good job too, so check out the comparison at `www.intuit.ca/store/en/quickbooks/compare_overview.jsp?catId=1` and see which version is best for you. We both use — and highly recommend — QuickBooks Pro, so that's the version we describe in the rest of this section.

Stephen L. Nelson wrote *QuickBooks "X" All-in-One Desk Reference For Dummies* (published by Wiley). His book is amazingly easy to understand. We promise that neither Steve nor our publisher gave us a nickel for recommending his book. (Heck, we've even had to pay for our copies.) We recommend *QuickBooks "X" All-in-One Desk Reference For Dummies* simply because it answers — in plain English — just about any question you'll have about using the program for your bookkeeping needs. Spend the money and buy it. (Any money spent on increasing your knowledge is money well spent — and may be a tax write-off!)

We update our QuickBooks software yearly, and every year it takes less time to perform our bookkeeping tasks because of product improvements. If you find that you don't have time to input your bookkeeping data, you may have to hire a bookkeeper. The bonus is that professional bookkeepers probably already know QuickBooks, and the best part is that they can print daily reports for you that keep you apprised of your business's condition. Also, at the end of each year, QuickBooks will supply you with all the official reports your tax professional or chartered accountant will need to do your taxes. (Yes, you really do need a tax pro or a chartered accountant; refer to the "Hiring a professional to do your year-end taxes" sidebar earlier in this chapter.) You can even send your professional a backup on a CD-ROM. See how simple bookkeeping can be?

QuickBooks Pro

When you first fire up QuickBooks Pro, you must answer a few questions to set up your account. Among the few things you need to have ready before you even begin to mess with the software are the following starting figures:

- **Cash balance:** This may be the amount in your chequing account (no personal money, please!) or the amount of money deposited from your eBay profits. Put these profits into a separate chequing account to use for your business.

- **Accounts receivable balance:** Does anyone owe you money for some auctions? Outstanding payments make up this total.

- **Account liability balance:** Do you owe some money? Are you being invoiced for some merchandise that you haven't paid for? Total it and enter it when QuickBooks asks you.

If you're starting your business in the middle of the year, gather any previous profits and expenses that you want to include because you'll have to input this information for a complete annual set of diligently recorded books. We can guarantee that this is going to take a while. But after you've gathered together your finances, even if it takes a little sweat to set it up initially, you'll be thanking us for insisting you get organized. It just makes everything work more smoothly in the long run.

QuickBooks integrates with PayPal

PayPal can provide your payment history in QuickBooks format. They even offer a settlement and reconciliation system download that breaks up your PayPal transactions into debits and credits — a handy feature! One warning, though: These are only financial transactions. When you use QuickBooks to its fullest, you will have your inventory in the program. When you purchase merchandise to sell, QuickBooks sets up the inventory — and deducts from it each time you input an invoice or a sales receipt. This way, your inventory receipts follow GAAP. In Marsha's book *eBay Timesaving Techniques For Dummies* (Wiley), she shows you the procedures for posting your weekly (or daily) sales in QuickBooks by using sales receipts.

QuickBooks EasyStep Interview

After you've organized your finances, you can proceed with the QuickBooks EasyStep Interview, which is shown in Figure 16-3. The EasyStep interview is designed to increase the comfort level for those with accounting-phobia and those using a bookkeeping program for the first time. If you mess things up, you can always use the back arrow and change what you've input. If you need help, simply click the Help button and the program will answer many of your questions. Hey, if worse comes to worst, you can always delete the file from the QuickBooks directory and start over.

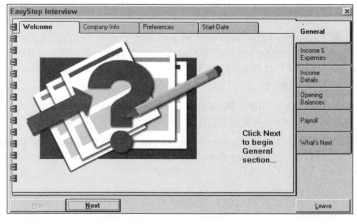

Figure 16-3: The QuickBooks Pro EasyStep Interview start page.

For the whirlwind tour through the QuickBooks EasyStep Interview, just follow these steps (which are only a general guideline):

1. **Start QuickBooks, then choose the Create a New Company option.**

    You're now at the EasyStep interview.

2. **On the first page of the interactive portion of the interview, type your company name (this becomes the filename in your computer) and the legal name of your company.**

    If you've registered a corporation (refer to Chapter 15), the fictitious name you've chosen is the legal name of your company.

3. **Continue to follow the program's prompts, answering other questions about your business, such as the address and the type of tax form you use.**

4. **When QuickBooks asks what type of business you want to use, choose Retail: General.**

    If you have another business than just your eBay sales (perhaps consulting or teaching others) you may want to just accept the QuickBooks with No Business option and build your chart of accounts from the one they give you — that's what we've done.

    QuickBooks doesn't offer an online sales business choice, so Retail: General is the closest to what you need (see Figure 16-4). With the chart of accounts that we feature in the following section, you can make the appropriate changes to your accounts to adapt to your eBay business.

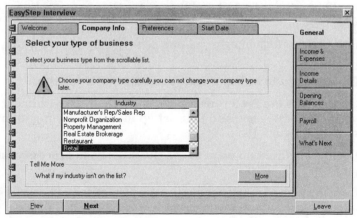

Figure 16-4:
Selecting
your com-
pany type.

5. **When QuickBooks asks whether you want to use its chosen chart of accounts, choose Yes.**

See Figure 16-5. You can always change the accounts later. If you want to spend the time, you can also input your entire custom chart of accounts manually (but we *really, really* don't recommend it).

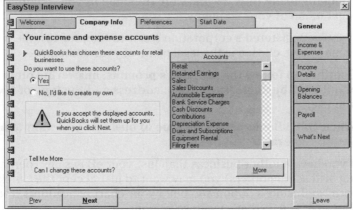

Figure 16-5:
Accepting
the
QuickBooks
chart of
accounts.

6. **Answer some more general questions, which we're sure you can handle with the aid of the incredibly intuitive QuickBooks Help area.**

7. **When the Preferences pages appear, we recommend that you select the "Enter the bills first and then enter the payments later" option.**

That way, if you input your bills as they come in, you can get an exact idea of how much money you owe at any time by just starting the program.

8. **Click the box to indicate that you collect sales taxes.**

9. **On the sales tax Preferences page, indicate the government for which you collect sales tax, and then set up the tax collecting information, as shown in Figure 16-6.**

10. **Decide whether you want to use QuickBooks to process your payroll.**

Even if you're the only employee, using QuickBooks's payroll information makes things much easier when it comes to filling out your payroll deposits. QuickBooks automatically fills in forms for your tax reporting and prints the appropriate form ready for your signature and mailing.

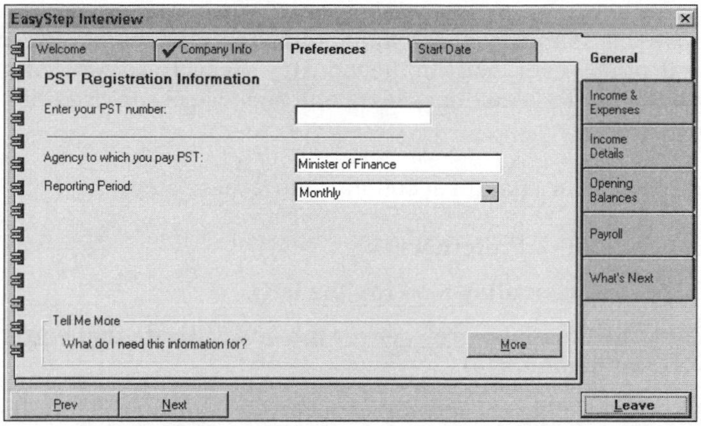

Figure 16-6:
Inputting
your
sales tax
information.

11. **Answer a few more questions including whether you want to use the cash basis or accrual basis of accounting.**

The *accrual* basis posts sales the minute you write an invoice or post a sales receipt, and posts your expenses as soon as you post the bills into the computer. Accrual basis accounting gives you a clearer picture of where your company is financially than cash basis accounting does. The *cash* basis is when you record bills by writing cheques — expenses are posted only when the cheques are written. This way of doing business may be simpler, but the only way you'll know how much money you owe is by looking at the pile of bills on your desk.

If you're new to bookkeeping, you may want to go through the Easystep Interview step-by-step with a tutor at your side. For more details, remember to check out *QuickBooks "X" All-in-One Desk Reference For Dummies* (Wiley) — this book can teach you almost everything you need to know about QuickBooks.

12. **If you're comfortable, just click Leave and input the balance of your required information directly into the program without using the interview.**

QuickBooks chart of accounts

After you've finished the EasyStep Interview and have successfully set yourself up in QuickBooks, the program presents a *chart of accounts*. Think of the chart of accounts as an organization system, such as file folders. It keeps all related data in the proper area. When you write a cheque to pay a bill, it deducts the amount from your chequing account, reduces your accounts payable, and perhaps increases your asset or expense accounts.

You have a choice of giving each account a number. These numbers, a kind of bookkeeping shorthand, are standardized throughout bookkeeping; believe it or not, everybody in the industry seems to know what number goes with what item. To keep things less confusing, we like to use titles as well as numbers.

To customize your chart of accounts, follow these steps:

1. **Choose Edit → Preferences.**

2. **Click the Accounting icon (on the left).**

3. **Click the Company preferences tab and indicate that you'd like to use account numbers.**

   An editable chart of accounts appears, as shown in Figure 16-7. Because QuickBooks doesn't assign account numbers as a default, you'll need to edit the chart to create them.

Figure 16-7:
Your chart of accounts now has numbers generated by QuickBooks.

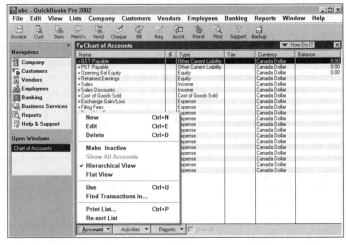

4. **Go through your QuickBooks chart of accounts and add any missing categories.**

   You may not need all these categories, and you can always add more later. In Table 16-2, we show you a chart of accounts that an accountant wrote for an eBay business. To get an idea of how you can customize the chart of accounts, also look at Figure 16-8, which shows you the chart of accounts from Marsha's business.

Table 16-2		eBay Business Chart of Accounts
Account Number	*Account Name*	*What It Represents*
1001	Chequing	All revenue deposited here and all cheques drawn upon this account
1002	Money market account	Company savings account
1100 credit	Accounts receivable	For customers to whom you extend
1201	Merchandise inventory	Charge to cost of sales as used, or take periodic inventories and adjust at that time
1202	Shipping supplies	Boxes, tape, labels, and so forth; charge these to cost as used, or take inventory at the end of the period and adjust to cost of sales
1401	Office furniture & equipment	Desk, computer, telephone
1402	Shipping equipment	Scales, tape dispensers
1403 pany	Vehicles	Your vehicle, if it's owned by the com-
1501	Accumulated depreciation	For your accountant's use
1601	Deposits	Security deposits on leases
2001	Accounts payable	Amounts owed for the stuff you sell, or charged expenses
2100	Payroll liabilities	Taxes deducted from employees's cheques and taxes paid by company on employee earnings
2200	Sales tax payable	Main category for sales tax collected at time of sale and owed to governments
2201	Provincial sales tax payable	Provincial Sales Tax
2202	Goods & services tax payable	GST Payable
2501	Equipment loans	Money borrowed to buy a computer or other equipment

(continued)

Table 16-2 *(continued)*

Account Number	Account Name	What It Represents
2502	Auto loans	When you get that hot new van for visiting your consignment clients
3000	Owner's capital	Your opening balance
3902	Owner's draw	Your withdrawals for the current year
4001	Merchandise sales	Revenue from sales of your products
4002	Shipping and handling	Paid by the customer
4009	Returns	Total dollar amount of returned merchandise
4101	Interest income	From your investments
4201	Other income	Income not otherwise classified
5001	Merchandise purchases	All the merchandise you buy for eBay; you'll probably use subaccounts for individual items
5002	Freight in	Freight and shipping charges you pay for your inventory, not for shipments to customers
5003	Shipping	Shipping to your customers: Canada Post, FedEx, UPS, and so on
5004	Shipping supplies	Boxes, labels, tape, bubble pack
6110	Automobile expense	When you use your car for work
6111	Gas and oil	Filling up the tank!
6112	Repairs	When your business owns the car
6120	Bank service charges	Monthly service charges, NSF charges, and so forth
6140	Contributions	Charity
6142	Data services	Do you have an outside firm processing your payroll?

Account Number	Account Name	What It Represents
6143	Internet service provider	What you pay to your Internet provider
6144	Web site hosting fees	Fees paid to your hosting company
6150	Depreciation expense	For your accountant's use
6151	eBay fees	What you pay eBay every month to stay in business based on your sales
6152	Discounts	Fees you're charged for using eBay and accepting credit card payments; deducted from your revenue and reported to you on your eBay statement
6153	Other auction site fees	You may want to set up subcategories for each site where you do business, such as Yahoo! or Amazon
6156	PayPal fees	Processing fees paid to PayPal
6158	Credit card merchant account fees	If you have a separate merchant account, post those fees here
6160	Dues	If you join an organization that charges membership fees (relating to your business)
6161	Magazines and periodicals	Books and magazines that help you run and expand your business
6170	Equipment rental	Postage meter, occasional van
6180	Insurance	Policies that cover your merchandise or your office
6185	Liability insurance	Insurance that covers you if someone slips and falls at your place of business (can also be put under Insurance)
6190	Disability insurance	Insurance that will pay you if you become temporarily or permanently disabled and can't perform your work
6191	Health insurance	You may be required to contribute for yourself or employees

(continued)

Table 16-2 *(continued)*

Account Number	Account Name	What It Represents
6200	Interest expense	Credit interest and interest on loans
6220	Loan interest	When you borrow from the bank
6230	Licenses and permits	Business licenses
6240	Miscellaneous	Whatever doesn't go anyplace else
6250	Postage and delivery	Stamps used in your regular business
6260	Printing	Your business cards, correspondence stationery, and so on
6265	Filing fees	Fees paid to file legal documents
6270	Professional fees	Fees paid to consultants
6280	Legal fees	If you have to pay a lawyer
6650	Accounting and bookkeeping	Bookkeeper, chartered accountant or tax professional
6290	Rent	Office, warehouse, and so on
6300	Repairs	Can be the major category for the following subcategories
6310	Building repairs	Repairs to the building where you operate your business
6320	Computer repairs	What you pay the person who sets up your wireless network
6330	Equipment repairs	When the copier or phone needs fixing
6340	Telephone	Regular telephone, FAX lines
6350	Travel and entertainment	Business-related travel, business meals
6360	Entertainment	When you take eBay's CEO out to dinner to benefit your eBay business
6370	Meals	Meals while travelling for your business
6390	Utilities	Major heading for the following subcategories

Account Number	Account Name	What It Represents
6391	Electricity and gas	Electricity and gas
6392	Water	Water
6560	Payroll expenses	Wages paid to others
6770	Supplies	Office supplies
6772	Computer	Computer and supplies
6780	Marketing	Advertising or promotional items you purchase to give away
6790	Office	Miscellaneous office expenses, such as bottled water delivery
6820	Taxes	Major category for the following subcategories
6830	Federal	Federal taxes
6850	Property	Property taxes
6860	Provincial	Provincial taxes

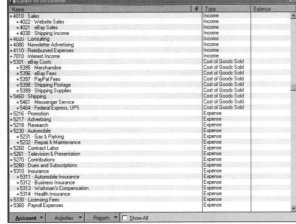

Figure 16-8: The chart of accounts from Marsha's eBay business.

Chapter 17

Building an eBay Back Office

*T*he more items you sell, the more confusing things can get. As you build your eBay business, the little side table you use for storing eBay merchandise is no longer going to be practical. You must think industrial. Even part-time sellers can benefit from adding a few professional touches to their business areas.

In this chapter, we emphasize the importance of setting up and organizing your back office. We cover everything from stacking your stock to keeping inventory to finding indispensable packing materials and buying online postage. Organization will be your byword. Dive right in. The sooner you read this chapter, the sooner you can build your eBay back office and get down to business.

The Warehouse: Organizing Your Space

Whether you plan to sell large items or small items, you need space for storing them. As you make savvy purchases, maintaining an item's mint condition will be one of your greatest challenges. Organized storage in itself is an art, so in this section, we cover the details of what you'll need to safeguard your precious stock.

Shelving your profits

Before you stock the shelves, it helps to have some! You also need a place to put the shelves: your garage, a spare room, or somewhere else. You have a choice between two basic kinds of shelves:

- **Plastic:** If you're just starting out, you can always go to the local closet and linen supply store to buy inexpensive plastic shelves. They're light and cheap — but they'll buckle in time.

- **Steel:** If you want to do it right the first time, buy steel shelving. The most versatile steel shelving is the wire kind (versus solid-steel shelves), which is lighter and allows air to circulate around your items. Steel wire shelving assembles easily; you can probably put it together without help. They often come with levelling feet and 4-inch (10-centimetre) casters, so if you need to move a shelf unit, you can. Installing the casters is up to you. You can combine steel wire shelving units to create a full wall of shelves. Each shelf safely holds as much as 600 pounds (about 272 kilograms) of merchandise.

  Search eBay to find sellers offering this kind of industrial shelving. The main problem with ordering this product online is that the shipping usually costs more than the item itself.

To save you time, dear reader, we researched the subject and found some readily available, reasonably priced shelves. Just go to Sam's Club or Costco and look for Seville Classics four-shelf commercial shelving, sold in 36- and 48-inch-wide (96- and 122-centimetre-wide) units. Each shelf will hold up to 500 pounds (about 227 kilograms). These shelves are also available on the Costco Web site, but you have to pay for shipping.

Box 'em or bag 'em?

Packing your items for storage can be a challenge. As long as you're picking up your shelving (see the preceding section), you can pick up some plastic bags in sandwich, litre, and larger sizes. The sandwich baggies are perfect for storing smaller items. When items are stored in plastic, they can't pick up any smells or become musty before you sell them. The plastic also protects the items from rubbing against each other and causing possible damage. If you package them one item to a bag, you can then just lift one off the shelf and put it directly into a shipping box when the auction is over.

Your bags of items will have to go into boxes for storage on the shelves. Clear plastic storage boxes, the kind you often find at superstores, are great for bulky items. They're usually 26 inches (66 centimetres) long, so before you buy these big plastic containers, be sure that they'll fit on your shelving comfortably and that you'll have easy access to your items. Using cardboard office-type file storage boxes from an office supply store is another option. These cardboard boxes are $10 \times 12 \times 16$ inches (about $25 \times 30 \times 41$ centimetres), which is a nice size for storing medium-size products. They are usually fairly cheap and amongst the most economical choices. The downside is that you can't see through cardboard boxes, so if your label falls off, you have to take the box off the shelf and open it to check its contents. Smaller see-through plastic boxes with various compartments, such as the kind home improvement stores carry for storing tools, work great for storing very small items.

When using large plastic bins, it's always a good idea to tape a pad of Post-it notes on the end of the box so you can quickly identify its contents. You *can* use regular sticky labels, but changing them will leave large amounts of paper residue over time, and your storage will look sloppy and icky.

Inventory: Keeping Track of What You Have and Where You Keep It

Savvy eBay sellers have different methods of handling inventory. They use everything from spiral-bound notebooks to sophisticated software programs. Although computerized inventory tracking can simplify this task, starting with a plain ol' handwritten ledger is fine, too. Choose whichever works best for you, but keep in mind that as your eBay business grows, a software program that tracks inventory for you may become necessary.

Planning: The key to good organization

When it became time for Marsha to put her eBay merchandise in order, she was busy with her regular business, so she hired people to organize her eBay area. This decision turned out to be one massive mistake. They organized everything and put all her items in boxes — but didn't label the boxes to indicate what was stored in each. She still hasn't recovered and doesn't know where a bunch of her stuff is!

A bit of advice: Think things out and plan where you'll put everything. Organize your items by theme, type, or size. If you organize before planning, you might end up with organized disorganization.

Most of these systems wouldn't work for a company with a warehouse full of stock but will work nicely in an eBay sales environment. Many sellers tape sheets of paper to their boxes to identify them by number, and use that as a reference to a simple Excel spreadsheet for selling purposes. Excel spreadsheets are perfect for keeping track of your auctions as well, but if you're using a management service or software, you don't need both for physical inventory. After you're running a full-time business, however, you have to keep the taxman happy with a dollars-and-cents accounting of your inventory, so keep your inventory records in a standardized program such as QuickBooks (discussed in Chapter 16). In Chapter 8, we detail a variety of auction management software programs and Web sites, many of which include physical inventory tracking features.

You may also want to use Excel spreadsheets for your downloaded PayPal statements; use it to hold information waiting to be transferred to your book-keeping program.

The Shipping Department: Packin' It Up

If you've read *eBay For Dummies,* you know all about the various ways to pack your items. We hope you've become an expert! In this section, we review some of the things you must have for a complete, smooth-running shipping department, such as cleaning supplies and packing materials. The *handling fee* portion of your shipping charges pays for these kinds of items. Don't run low on them, and pay attention to how you store them. They must be kept in a clean environment.

Removing musty odours from apparel items

Clothing can often pick up odors that you just don't notice. Marsha recently bought a designer dress on eBay from a seller who had the typical disclaimer in her description: "No stains, holes, repairs, or odors. Comes from a smoke-free, pet-free home." Unfortunately, the minute she opened the box I could smell the musty odor of an item that had been stored for a long time.

To prevent that icky, storage odor, keep a package of Dryel Fabric Care System around. This is a safe, do-it-yourself dry cleaning product. Just toss your better eBay clothing items in the patented Dryel bag with the special sheet and toss it in the dryer as per the instructions on the box. Your garment will come out smelling clean — and will be wrinkle-free. For more information, visit their Web site at www.dryel.com.

Packaging clean up

Be sure the items you send out are in tip-top shape. Here are a few everyday chemicals that can gild the lily:

- **WD-40:** The decades-old lubricant works very well at getting price stickers off plastic and glass without damaging the product. The plastic on a toy box may begin to look nasty, even when stored in a clean environment. A quick wipe with a paper towel containing a dash of WD-40 will make it shine like new. It also works incredibly well for untangling jewelry chains and shining up metallic objects.

- **Goo Gone:** Goo Gone (if you can find it) works miracles in cleaning up gooey sticker residue from nonporous items.

- **un-du:** Another hard-to-find product in Canada, this amazing liquid easily removes stickers from cardboard, plastic, fabrics and more without causing damage. It comes packaged with a patented mini-scraper top that can be used in any of your sticker-cleaning projects. If you can't find un-du, check out Marsha's Web site (www.coolebaytools.com) for places to purchase it. You can also use lighter fluid (which is, of course, considerably more dangerous and may damage your item).

Packing materials

So that you can always be sure your items will arrive at their destinations in one piece, you'll want to keep the following on hand at all times:

- **Bubble pack:** A clean, puffy product that comes in rolls, bubble pack is available in several sizes. Depending on your product, you may have to carry two sizes of bubble pack to properly protect the goods. Bubble pack can be expensive, but check out vendors on eBay; you'll find quite a lot of them (and possibly a deal). Another option is to call around to local shipping supply companies. You may have to buy larger quantities but the savings will often be worth it. Buying in larger quantities also poses storage problems so be prepared to devote some warehouse space to your packing materials. See Figure 17-1 for a sample listing on eBay.

- **Styrofoam packing peanuts:** Why they call them peanuts is anyone's guess — we suppose somebody thought they looked like peanuts. Nonetheless, Styrofoam peanuts protect just about everything you ship. Storing them is the tricky part. One of the most ingenious storage solutions we've seen is putting the peanuts into large 35 × 50-inch (roughly 90 × 130-centimetre) plastic trash bags and then hanging these bags on cup hooks (available at the hardware store) around the walls in a garage. When packing with peanuts, be sure that you place the item carefully and use enough peanuts to fill the box *completely*; leaving any airspace defeats the point of using the peanuts in the first place.

✔ **Plastic bags:** Buy plastic bags in bulk to save money. Make sure you buy various sizes and use them for both shipping and storing. Even large kitchen or trash bags are good for wrapping up posters and large items; the plastic protects the item from inclement weather by water-proofing it.

✔ **2- or 3-inch shipping tape:** You'll need clear tape for finishing up packages before shipping them out. You'll also need the clear tape to place over address labels to protect them from scrapes and rain. Both of us have received packages with address labels soaked with rain and barely legible. Labels printed on inkjet printers are especially susceptible to ink running when wet. Don't risk a lost package for want of a few inches of tape.

✔ **Bubble envelopes:** If you send items that fit nicely into bubble pack-lined envelopes, use them (see Figure 17-2). This type of envelope — with paper on the outside and bubble pack on the inside — is perfect for mailing small items or clothing when shipping by mail. The envelopes are available in quantity (an economical choice) and don't take up much storage space. For a real professional look and a higher degree of protection, bubble envelopes are now available with a poly exterior that resists water and tearing. Of course, they are also substantially more expensive. Table 17-1 shows you the industry-standard sizes of bubble envelopes and some suggested uses.

Figure 17-1: Bubble pack in its pure form.

BUBBLE PACKAGING

Case of 250 CD (7-1/4" x 8")
SELF SEALING BUBBLE MAILERS
(Internal Dimensions 7" x 7-1/4")

Figure 17-2:
Bubble
pack-lined
envelopes
for sale on
eBay.

Table 17-1		Standard Bubble-Padded Mailer Sizes
Size	*Measurements*	*Suggested Items*
#000	4" x 8" (10.6 x 2.32 cm)	Collector trading cards, jewellery, computer diskettes, coins
#00	5" x 10" (12.7 x 25.4 cm)	Postcards, paper ephemera
#0	6" x 10" (15.24 x 25.4 cm)	Doll clothes, CDs, DVDs, Xbox or PS2 games
#1	7¼" x 12" (18.42 x 30.48 cm)	Cardboard sleeve VHS tapes, jewel-cased CDs and DVDs
#2	8½" x 12" (21.59 x 30.48 cm)	Clamshell VHS tapes, books
#3	8½" x 14½" (21.59 x 30.48 cm)	Toys, clothing, stuffed animals
#4	9½" x 14½" (24.13 x 36.83 cm)	Small books, trade paperbacks
#5	10½" x 16" (26.67 x 40.64 cm)	Hardcover books, dolls
#6	12½" x 19" (31.75 x 48.26 cm)	Clothing, soft boxed items
#7	14¼" x 20" (36.20 x 50.8 cm)	Much larger packaged items, framed items and plaques

Packaging — the heart of the matter

Depending on the size of the item you sell, you can purchase boxes in bulk at reliable sources. Because you have a resale number (see Chapter 15), you can look in your local yellow pages for wholesale boxes or corrugated cartons to buy. (You still have to pay tax, but the resale number identifies you as a business and can often get you a lower price.) Try to purchase from a manufacturer that specializes in B2B (business to business) sales. Some box companies specialize in selling to the occasional box user. Knowing the size that you need enables you to buy in quantity. Some wholesalers specialize in buying up quantities of boxes from companies that no longer have a requirement for them. These can often be purchased in larger lots at lower than normal prices, but the boxes may be pre-printed with a brand or product name. Strategic placement of your shipping label may allow you to use these and still maintain a professional appearance.

Canada Post also offers free 16 x 12-inch (40.64 x 30.48 cm) poly envelopes that are perfect for shipping many soft goods. You'll need to add some additional padding as these are a very basic poly envelope with no cushioning protection, although they have a very professional appearance that makes them well worth the trouble. The envelopes feature a large eBay.ca logo and can be ordered online from the Canada Post On-line Business Centre (look for "eBay Pack # 533086682"); you can order a maximum of fifty at a time. Visit `www.canadapost.ca/obc` to place your order (see Figure 17-3). You'll need to create an account with Canada Post, which will only take a few moments.

Figure 17-3:
Order shipping supplies from Canada Post.

The Mail Room: Sendin' It Out

Canada Post now allows you a couple of options to purchase most of your postage requirements online — and at a savings. Targeted at the SOHO (small office/home office) market, these options allow you to avoid the lineups, letting you secure your postage and print sticker labels right from your PC. In this section, we give you the lowdown on using Canada Post's Electronic Shipping Tools, how to buy postage, and how to ship directly through PayPal.

Printing labels on your printer is convenient until you start sending out a dozen packages at a time — then cutting the paper and taping the labels gets a bit too time-consuming. We highly recommend you do yourself a favour and get a label printer. Yes, they can be expensive, but you can find some great deals on eBay. Marsha bought her heavy-duty, professional Eltron Zebra 2844 thermal label printer on eBay for one-fourth the retail price. (Search eBay for *Zebra 2844*). It has saved her countless hours. Dymo also makes a very good label printer for beginners that is readily found on eBay or at local office supply outlets.

Canada Post's Electronic Shipping Tools

Canada Post has made a serious effort to encourage shippers to use their online tools, hoping to reduce some of the lineups at their Retail Postal Outlets (RPOs). Aside from the convenience of printing postage from your home or office computer, Canada Post also offers a financial incentive with savings of up to 8 percent when you use the Electronic Shipping Tools (3 percent on selected shipping services and an additional 5 percent if you join the VentureOne' Preferred Small Business Client program).

Canada Post package pickup

Yes, they do provide this service, but for a price! If you print postage with Canada Post's Electronic Shipping Tools, you can arrange for the post office to make regularly scheduled pickups of your packages. Flat rates that are charged for this service exist, but Canada Post appears to frequently negotiate better deals for companies that ship larger quantities of packages on a daily basis. Your best bet is to call (toll free) 1-888-550-6333 and ask to speak to an account representative in your area.

To join the VentureOne' program with Canada Post, visit

```
https://obc.canadapost.ca/orc/init.do?viewType=0&language
              =EN&campaignSource=web
```

Once you have joined VentureOne', you have to decide if you want to use either the online version or the downloaded software version of the Electronic Shipping Tools. The downloaded option allows you to quickly process postage for many packages with only an accumulated single billing against your credit card. If you choose to use the online version, your credit card is billed an independent transaction for each package (no batch file transmit feature exists). This could lead to slow-downs during your busier periods.

PayPal shipping services

PayPal continues to add great features for sellers. Now you can not only buy postage through PayPal but also use it to print labels on your own printer. Or, if you ship lots of items and use a different service for printing your shipping data (for example, one of the other services mentioned in this chapter), PayPal allows you to input your tracking information on its site. Just click the Details link for the transaction and then click the Add button that appears, as shown in Figure 17-4. Input the tracking or delivery confirmation information from Canada Post, UPS, FedEx, or another shipping company, and PayPal sends an e-mail to your buyer with that information.

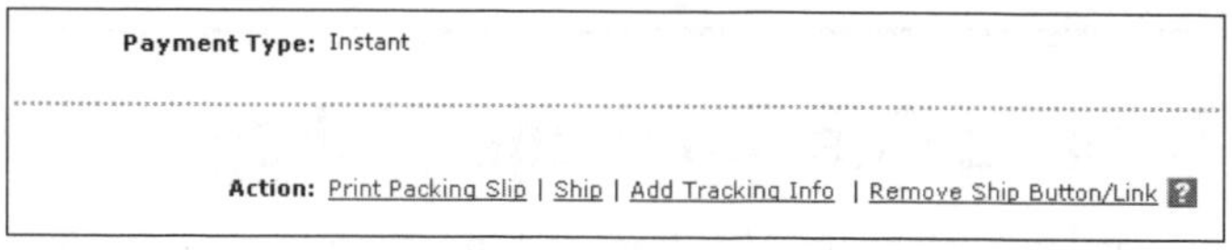

Figure 17-4:
Click the
Add button
in the pay-
ment record
to input
tracking
information
and gen-
erate an
e-mail to
your buyer.

Payment Type: Instant

Action: Print Packing Slip | Ship | Add Tracking Info | Remove Ship Button/Link ❓

The information you added appears in both the record of your PayPal transaction and the buyer's record in their account, as shown in Figure 17-5. (You can check the information by clicking the Details link again.)

Tracking Number: cx201777506CA
Carrier: Canada Post
Order Status: Shipped (Sep. 11, 2006)

Action: Print Packing Slip | Edit Tracking Info [?]

PayPal shipping services work great when you're just starting out in your eBay business but once you get rolling, you may want to switch over to using online shipping services provided by Canada Post or other companies. When you process your Canada Post postage and shipping with PayPal, the shipping amount is deducted from your PayPal (sales revenue) balance. For this reason, you may want to maintain a Canadian dollar balance to pay for your postage and to avoid paying excessive exchange rates. This is an important issue.

If you're starting a business in earnest, you need to keep track of your online and other business expenses separately (see Chapter 16). Allowing PayPal to deduct your shipping costs from either your incoming revenue or a Canadian balance can create a bookkeeping nightmare. You need to have exact figures for expense and income — and it really helps keep confusion to a minimum when your deposits (transfers from your PayPal account to your bank) match your sales receipts. If you want to ship through PayPal, be sure you transfer the amount of your sales from PayPal to your chequing account *before* you process your shipping. That way, your shipping can be charged to your business credit card for easier tracking.

To purchase postage and print your label for a specific purchase, click the Ship button next to the payment record in your PayPal account history overview, as shown in Figure 17-6. You'll be taken through a step-by-step process to pay for your shipping and print the appropriate label with your printer.

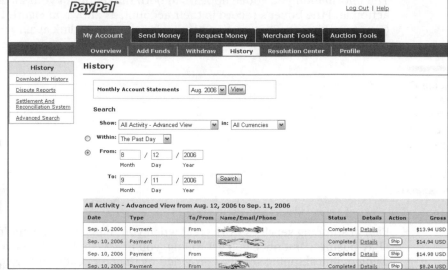

Figure 17-6:
Click the
Ship button
to ship your
item through
Canada
Post.

Because Staples delivers any order more than $50 CAD for free the next day, it's a great place to get paper and labels. Better buys on scales, though, can be found on eBay, especially if you search *postage scale*. Marsha uses a super-small, 13-pound (5.9-kilogram)-maximum scale manufactured by Escali that she bought on eBay for only $29.95 USD, complete with a five-year warranty.

Part V
The Part of Tens

The 5th Wave   By Rich Tennant

"You've opened an insect-clothing shop on eBay?
Neat! Where do you get buttons that small?"

In this part . . .

Not everyone is a shooting star at eBay, but it's a good goal to reach for. For your inspiration, we've included profiles on some interesting people from all walks of life who've turned eBay into a profitable enterprise — some working only part-time. These are not people in big companies. Instead, they're people like us, working hard to expand their business on eBay. In the second chapter, we provide information on moving merchandise that you think you might never sell.

Chapter 18

Ten Successful (and Happy) eBay Sellers and Their Stories

In This Chapter

▶ People who make their living selling on eBay . . .

▶ . . . and love it!

*W*e always enjoy hearing stories about how much people like eBay. We enjoy it even more when we hear that they're doing something that they get pleasure from while earning a good living. One of the best parts of teaching others about eBay or attending eBay Live is talking to the hundreds of sellers who attend. We get opportunities to bounce ideas around with them and find out about the creative ways they spend their time on eBay.

We thought you might like to know more about some of the people on eBay, too, so we interviewed them; it was so much fun getting to know about each one. They have different backgrounds and lifestyles, but they all have one thing in common: eBay!

In favour of highlighting some regular folks on eBay, we dispensed with the customary writer thing (you know, finding the largest PowerSellers on eBay to interview). No one's a success overnight, and the people we discuss in this chapter certainly have been plugging away at eBay, increasing their businesses and becoming successful. We especially wanted to feature sellers that were far from the center of the known universe to show that anyone can sell and be successful on eBay — you only need access to the Web and a local mailing point. Here are their stories — and their advice.

cdBasement

Member since January 2000; Feedback: 20,567; Positive Feedback: 99.8%

Allan Grusie of Cambridge, Ontario has created one of Canada's largest eBay compact disc sales operations from an interest in collecting. A self-proclaimed late starter, Allan initially viewed eBay as an opportunity to feed his passion for records and CDs. With a connection he developed from his collecting, he was given an opportunity to purchase several hundred CDs from a wholesaler on an all-or-nothing basis. He took the plunge and made that first lot purchase but realized that he needed a more appropriate selling name. (In those days, eBay allowed you to register as your e-mail address, which Allan did not find at all suitable to his selling effort.) With a bit of research and much thought, he arrived at the name "cdBasement" and began his eBay selling career. In just a few weeks, he had sold 75 percent of his initial purchase of CDs — at many times the cost of what he had paid for them. The remaining 25 percent he traded with another seller on a five-for-one basis to turn dead stock into more selling opportunities.

Allan considers his most important lesson learned to be "stick with what you know." In his view, finding an area of expertise and never deviating from selling in that area is critical. Allan learned his lesson from an attempt to branch out into DVDs and books. He found that, unless those forms of media were music-related, he generally lost his shirt.

Allan also found that plenty of wholesalers are willing to sell bulk lots of items, which are worthless for the most part. He has adopted a philosophy to "Buy from wholesalers at a fair price, low enough to make a profit, but high enough that the old adage 'too good to be true' still applies."

Along the way, Allan claims to have encountered his fair share of non-paying buyers, but also, and more importantly, thousands of repeat customers. Another part of his selling philosophy dictates the golden rule — always treat customers as you want to be treated. Allan started out as a buyer (he still buys a dozen or more items a month), so he remembers his buying experiences and allows them to guide his customer service efforts. Allan assures us that he has seen some dandy examples of both exceptional and horrible customer service over his years on eBay.

One of Allan's major concerns when starting out was inventory sourcing, but he no longer considers it an issue. He has found that establishing and building relationships with his suppliers is a critical "offline" part of his business. Building a mutually high level of trust with his suppliers has actually led to some of those suppliers referring Allan to their sources for items they don't normally stock. Allan says, "Regular contact is essential with potential suppliers and, in a weird sort of way, you will actually put on your 'sales hat' to work out the best terms possible. The relationship you have established with the supplier in the past will nearly always play in your favour to establish these terms. I've had instances where product sources have told me that, although they give me a better deal than a competitor, they'd rather do business with me."

Allan's advice? Never, ever insult your suppliers with ridiculous offers. Make your decision quickly based on the information you have — yes or no — so they can move on to the next buyer. Also, always pay them in full and right away, if possible.

Almost seven years after starting to use eBay, Allan has more than 20,000 positive feedback comments and tries to keep a minimum of 1,000 listings going at any time. These listings are split between his auctions and his eBay store, because he views the formats as equally important. "The auction format listings really do drive business to my eBay store, and I would encourage any new seller to consider using both formats," he says. Allan still operates as a one-man show, but knows that he may have to consider changing that soon. In summary, he says, "eBay is a lot of work, but the rewards can be terrific."

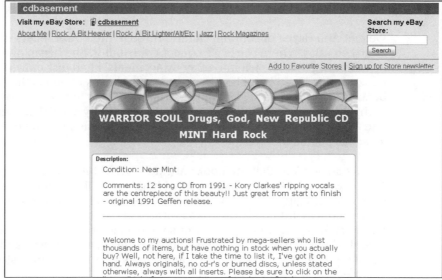

Figure 18-1:
A
cdBasement
auction.

TIP

More advice from Allan

Allan had so many great tips for new eBay sellers that we had trouble mentioning just a few. His most important advice for new sellers has to do with the record-keeping aspects of your eBay business. Allan suggests that once you decide your eBay use is no longer a hobby but a business, document everything. Some of his tips are as follows:

✔ "Keep track of profit and loss by product and item or product and supplier, or all three — I know it sounds like a lot of work, but a quick spreadsheet (or even a sheet of paper) can help you track how you are doing and determine whether you need to adjust pricing or your rates for shipping and handling."

✔ "Keep a separate bank account for your eBay business — this makes it so much easier for everyone, including the tax guys, to legitimize your business."

✔ "Know what your competition is doing. Is their shipping and handling cheaper? Are their start prices higher or lower? Keep your research efforts current."

Zarzuella

Member since October 1999; Feedback 3,657; Positive Feedback 99.9%

We met Ann Hayes of London, Ontario through the PowerSellers discussion board on eBay, where she is a frequent contributor. She began our interview by admitting that she fell into eBay by accident: "I had just moved into a new house and realized that I had brought several boxes of books that had not been unpacked since my last move." The books she had were about horses, Irish Wolfhounds, and other sighthounds — all fairly specialized and hard to find. "I had a notion that they were probably valuable but did not have a large local market for their resale."

Then it struck Ann that the books might be perfect for the eBay marketplace. "On eBay my books were exposed to a huge international market and sold very well, bringing prices I would never have seen if I'd sold them to the local second-hand bookstore. I was thrilled and hooked at the same time!" She started selling other books, but soon decided to work within the niche that she knew fairly well — animal books. "I sell used and new, and have expanded my eBay business to include an eBay store (the eBay store format is perfect for booksellers!)"

Ann finds that benefits exist to selling on the eBay.com site as opposed to eBay.ca: "More than 85 percent of my books are sold to a U.S. clientele; selling on the U.S. site just makes it easier for them to find me."

Ann tries to make all of her transactions as painless for her customers as possible, which requires that she maintain open communication with them at every step of the sale process. "One of the biggest mistakes an eBay seller can make is to not communicate well," she says. She suggests that you put yourself in a buyer's shoes. "If you were to buy an item online and pay immediately through PayPal, you would really want to hear from the seller — both that your payment had been received and that (or when) your purchase is shipped. Too many sellers think they are too busy to maintain that level of communication — but usually not for long," she says. Ann also makes sure that she mentions her online Web store at www.zarzuellabooks.com in all of her e-mail correspondence.

Ann has found that the eBay site has changed dramatically over the past few years: "I don't always agree with all of the changes, some of which have negatively impacted my business, but it is their game, and it's still the best game around — no other online auction site draws as much traffic." Ann considers the changes that eBay has made — good or bad — as an opportunity for her to re-evaluate her business plan and stay on her toes. In the end, she considers that to be a good thing.

Figure 18-2:
The Zarzuella eBay store home page.

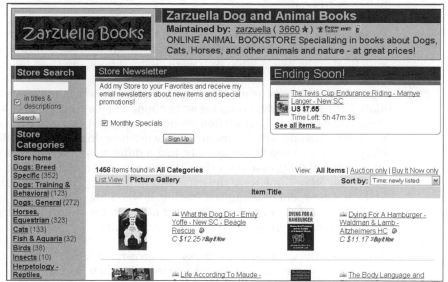

Ann believes that some of the best resources on eBay are the various discussion boards. "I have learned so much from other sellers," she says. "In my experience, the member community is actually much more helpful than eBay itself, which tends to reply to questions with canned responses — often without even addressing the question asked."

Muminlaw

Member since August 1999; Feedback 1099; Positive Feedback 100%

John and Glenda Cheramy started their business long before eBay — or even personal computers. They began their mail-order business of selling collectable world coins and tokens by advertising in coin collecting magazines. (Tokens are coin-sized, die-stamped pieces, usually made of brass, copper, aluminum, or, more recently, plastic. They are issued by individual merchants and can be traded back to those merchants in exchange for products. For example, a local dairy may issue tokens "good for 1 quart of milk.") They soon developed their own database of customers and began sending out fixed-price lists of items they had for sale by direct mail. Their first sales list was typed on an electric typewriter and then sent to a printer to have several hundred copies made. Then, they would collate, staple, fold, and stuff the lists into envelopes and address them before applying postage so they would be ready to send.

When personal computers came along, the job of maintaining their client database became a lot less work. The introduction of the Internet, e-mail, and, finally, the World Wide Web were all great boons to their business.

According to Glenda, when eBay came along, she and John were a little intimidated at first: "We signed up for an account and just watched for awhile, then tried some bidding. That's when we discovered that many of the same people we'd been trading with for many years were now doing the same thing on eBay — the same basic community, just a different venue!" At that point it was a natural progression for the Cheramys to begin offering their coins and tokens on eBay. Gone were the expenses for printing, envelopes, and postage, and the time spent stapling and folding. It was a big plus for their business to finally have access to millions (instead of just a few hundred) collectors — in Glenda's words, selling on eBay was a "no-brainer!"

Since then, the Cheramys' business has grown to include another field of collectibles — antique and vintage postcards. They were already collecting early postcards depicting the area where they grew up; recently, they have begun offering postcards they have acquired but don't collect (for example, from geographic regions they are not interested in) and postcards of which they have duplicates. In no time, it seems, the Cheramys have reached a volume of sales that has brought them PowerSeller status.

The Cheramys' business has grown to the point where they have now added a part-time partner under another eBay ID (also now a PowerSeller). Also, they have slowed down business in the auction format under their original ID in favour of opening an eBay store. In this new endeavour, they gratefully accepted the assistance of a very patient eBay employee who spent several hours on the phone walking them through the steps required to give their virtual store a professional appearance. What impressed John and Glenda most was that all of this was on eBay's expense — "They phoned us!"

John and Glenda have reconnected with a lot of old friends through eBay and made even more new ones, most of whom they'll never meet face-to-face. But they all share a common interest as users of eBay — a global community in the truest sense of the word!

Figure 18-3:
An eBay listing from eclectic seller Muminlaw.

Both John and Glenda agree — eBay offers a great opportunity for those who have retired or semi-retired from the nine-to-five work world. They are now both at retirement age and enjoy the idea of, on eBay, earning enough to supplement their pensions, plus a little extra to help them enjoy their newest passion — golf! Glenda admits, "We're far from good at it, but we do enjoy the excuse for fresh air and exercise." This, in their view, is one of the beauties and strengths of eBay — you can work your own hours. Work at it just enough to provide for a few extras, or hard enough to earn a comfortable living — every individual can determine their own path.

Nightlight 1960

Member since November 2002; Feedback 1,984; Positive Feedback 99.9%

Pamela Denis-Iles is such an eBay fan that she even announces it on her car's license plate: she is "MS EBAY."

It began innocently enough four years ago when her husband decided to hunt down and eventually purchase what was, according to Pam, a "torqued-out-bindle-rotor-electrical-gizmo." She wasn't too excited at the time — she couldn't wear it, it didn't do anything she was interested in, and it wasn't a nice colour or sleekly designed. The only thing that really caught Pam's attention was the thousands of dollars her husband saved buying it on eBay instead of at a local retail outlet. From there it was just a matter of time before Pam was on eBay herself, where she noticed the "Clothing, Shoes, and Accessories" category and found an abundance of well-priced items — in her size! Before long, she had packages arriving from all over the world.

Pam had just recently moved to White City, Saskatchewan from Saskatoon after getting married and leaving her well-paying civil service job after nine-teen years. Now unemployed and a little uncertain of the future, she decided to begin to sell her professional wardrobe on eBay. Soon she had repeat customers asking when her next listings would begin. She was hooked and began to actively look for sources of supply.

Now, four years later, Pam is the owner/operator of Nightlight's Niche, an eBay featured store, and has more than 5,000 successful transactions behind her. In addition, she is a PowerSeller, a Trading Assistant and a top-ranking contributor to eBay's Reviews and Guides. She also contributes to eBay's *Voices of the Community* program, a select group of Canadian buyers and sellers who gather at eBay Canada's head office to brainstorm for positive change to the site. She has also now added the role of an Education Specialist trained by eBay to her resumé, acknowledging her desire and passion to teach others what she has frequently had to learn on her own.

Ask Pam what lies ahead and she responds, "My future holds the promise of continued eBay sales with a focus on training geared toward new eBay buyers and sellers. I plan to teach eBay wherever and whenever I'm able, ensuring that learning is fun, informative, and supportive." Pam adds that she considers her eBay experiences to play a major role in what she believes is "the best time of my life!"

Pam is a strong believer in networking. Says Pam, "Today I love to share my experience, strength, humour and hope with friends, family, acquaintances and complete strangers. Everyone seems to love to talk eBay! In general, I find people are natural extraordinary networkers, which is a tremendous advantage when eBaying."

Figure 18-4:
A trip inside
Nightlight's
Niche, an
eBay store.

Beansantiques

Member since August 2001, Feedback 7,707; Positive Feedback 100%

Sheri and Ron Walker make no bones about it — they are avid eBayers and love to share their story.

Together, they started a small antique and collectible business ten years ago in Victoria, British Columbia. At that time they opened a retail store named Beans Antiques and enjoyed some reasonable success. Some friends suggested that they try to sell off their inventory on eBay but, fearing they did not have the computer skills, they were reluctant to try.

With a little more urging from their friends, they relented and listed a few small things through another seller. According to Ron, "The results shocked us, and we immediately caught the eBay bug!" In their minds, that was the day that they decided to close their retail store and their online selling careers began. It took another six months to physically close down the brick and mortar store, but they were off and running.

Their first order of business, in August of 2001, was to go out and purchase three computers to launch their eBay selling career. That first day was not without its difficulties; it took a frantic phone call to the computer salesman for instructions on how to actually turn the computers on before things got under way. Sheri admits that they got off to a somewhat shaky start!

Initially, they hoped they could manage to list ten items a week; in their minds, this was as close to rocket science as they would ever get. Within that first month, they discovered what many others have also learned — that eBay is a great equalizer. People with few computer skills and those that are very talented with HTML are on a level playing field. They found the site to be very user-friendly and that they could actually manage quite well with just a little patience. Very soon, Sheri and Ron were listing more than twenty items a day out of one-third of their closed retail store.

It was also around this time that they started to look at real estate on eBay. The thought had occurred to both Sheri and Ron that they could run their new online business from anywhere in the country. This was when they "discovered" Nova Scotia. There, they could actually own their own home and store instead of renting a condo and a store. They started to sell off the contents of their closed store and, six months later, they were off in their cube van to a new life at the other end of the country!

Not long after, Sheri and Ron bought their new home and future retail store in Wilmot, Nova Scotia. This is where Ron picks up the story: "Our first order of business was to start our eBay StoreFront back up. This electronic store has now grown to over 2,000 items, and we have future plans to increase it to 5,000 items. We also run a number of auctions every week to keep the traffic up."

During their short time on eBay, they have sold well over 30,000 items and now have a feedback rating of over 8,000 — and it's still 100 percent positive. Sheri and Ron have now also opened a second eBay store and selling ID under the name "painlesstransactions." Both agree that they have "met" some of the nicest people through eBay, and from every corner of the world. They still include their phone number in each listing and, because of that, they have had people call them from across the globe. Over the phone, Sheri and Ron have even helped people to sign up on eBay and bid on items (mostly from other sellers); also, they have answered questions that they would not even think to ask.

Although their business is still just a husband-and-wife operation, both Sheri and Ron agree that the flexibility of selling on eBay fits well around the rigid hours of their retail store. eBay has afforded them the opportunity to live in a very small community but still have the financial benefits of selling to a customer base of millions. Selling on eBay has given them the opportunity to own their home, open a new and improved brick and mortar retail store in a location that they own, and live a lifestyle that they could have only dreamed about. Ron sums it all up by saying, "We are just one of the many success stories that eBay has created and, believe me, if we can do it — anyone can."

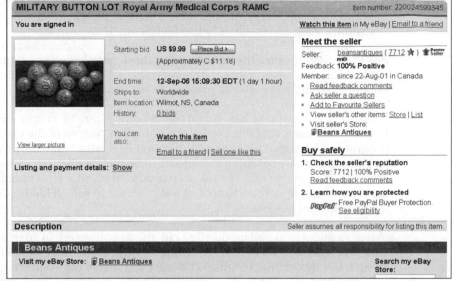

Figure 18-5:
One of
Beansantiq
ues antique
auctions —
without a
reserve!

Flying_Pat

Member since November 2001; Feedback 3,452; Positive Feedback: 100%

Sylvain Carrier is both young and smart and he is not at all shy about saying so. At 23, he still refers to difficulties he had with his teachers — and authority in general — like they were yesterday. He was a very capable student but too stubborn to get along with some of the authority figures at his school. As a result, he never did achieve a high degree of academic success. "I was actually more interested in video gaming, like most kids in my generation. As a French Canadian living in a small town in Quebec, I actually learned most of the English I know through them. I also developed my sense of logic and learned how to strategically solve problems by playing different kinds of strategy games."

That's how Sylvain would like to think of eBay — as one giant strategy game. "When I found out about eBay, I set about to make it my game; solving daily problems for my customers, establishing my selling strategies, and building and streamlining my system." Sylvain is now justifiably proud that he has been able to trade up his somewhat useless game scores for substantial paycheques.

Sylvain started selling on eBay in November of 2001, and soon he was selling full-time for a car parts manufacturer. "I started selling under the store name Distributor King and eventually used it to launch my own internet sales company in May of 2004 — SC Internet Solutions (`www.scinternetsolutions.com`)." He also stresses the value of using third-party listing solutions providers such as ChannelAdvisor (`www.channeladvisor.com`) to free up much of his time and make it easier to manage all his listings.

Sylvain's eBay business has grown to the point where he is now a Platinum PowerSeller and a valuable part of the Canadian "Voices of the Community" program: "I have also become an Education Specialist trained by eBay in the last year and enjoy teaching the 'Basics of Selling on eBay.' It allows me to share my knowledge and spread my passion." He also adds Trading Assistant services to his eBay repertoire and will contract to sell all kinds of items for individuals and businesses.

Sylvain's success at selling on eBay did not go unnoticed. In June of 2005, he was asked to join PESA (The Professional eBay Sellers Alliance), a large non-profit trade association comprised of the most highly regarded merchants from all categories on eBay. "I am very proud to be a member of this group, as they have developed a very fruitful relation with eBay through the years," he says. "It is also very interesting to brainstorm with other high-performance sellers and exchange ideas with some of the brightest minds in e-commerce today."

Sylvain works hard to keep his eBay business growing, and he definitely feels the business is worth all the time and effort he puts into it: "Each new day brings with it new challenges and opportunities. The future of e-commerce is bright, and I certainly plan to be a part of it."

Figure 18-6:
A Distributor King auction.

Sylvain's tips on e-commerce are simple but sound: "My advice to new eBay business owners is to be fair, honest, and to always do your best to please your customers. With its feedback system, eBay is a marketplace where the trust you earn really pays off by giving you a good reputation and sometimes the edge you need over your competitors."

Whoscloset

Member since August 2003; Feedback: 1,952; Positive Feedback 99.9%

Monique Egerton did not begin her career hoping to be a success on eBay. Back in the late '90s, thanks to a business degree, she considered herself lucky be on the fast track to the executive ranks at Canada's largest retailer. Her career was put on hold when she had her children, after which working long days and weekends no longer held such great appeal. After only a few years as a full-time mother, she explains, "My husband quickly became concerned with the amount of time and money I spent decorating our home. I would watch all of the decorating shows and loved so many different styles that I could not incorporate them all." It seemed that whenever she had a spare moment, she would begin envisioning some newly redecorated room or another! After re-doing their family room three times in one year, she realized (with more than a little nudge from her husband) that she needed to put her excess energy and decorating talents to a more productive and economical use.

Like many others, Monique began on eBay as a buyer and got a thrill from hunting for rare, inexpensive items for her home decorating projects. In order to continue on her home improvement spree, she began to sell things from around the house that she no longer needed — baby items, old collectables, and other items being replaced.

She had promised herself that she would get back into the corporate ranks when her children began school but was not looking forward to it. She loved working but wanted to be the one to pick her children up after school each day. It was then that Monique decided to try starting her own eBay business. With a very modest initial investment of $1,000, her eBay store "Who's Closet" was born. A business license provided access to the wholesale market and an inexpensive digital camera (purchased on eBay, of course!) was all she needed. At the time, Monique confesses, she knew very little about what she was getting into but realizes now that eBay selling is very much a learn-as-you-go business.

With the guidance and inspiration of many helpful sellers on the eBay discussion boards, Monique has learned a great deal about branding, Web-page design, search engine optimization, e-mail marketing, and more. Her business has grown into a very successful and profitable venture, but one that she is still able to operate largely on her own. Says Monique, "One of the things I like most about selling on eBay is the total diversity of my day. I handle the photography, product sourcing, marketing, research, Web page development, shipping, accounting and more. And each day I have the opportunity to learn something new." eBay selling provides Monique with the income that she needs while still allowing her to spend the time she wants with her family.

Monique's best eBay advice? "Don't follow the crowd. Spend some time in the beginning to research the marketplace. Find a unique product to sell that sets you apart from other eBay sellers and allows you a large enough profit margin to weather the site's inevitable fee increases. And smile — you're your own boss now!"

Figure 18-7:
A look at the well laid out and imaginative Who's Closet eBay store.

PurpleFerret999

Member since April 2003; Feedback: 903; Positive Feedback: 99.9%

Marian Munro was a reluctant eBayer at first: "Initially, I logged onto the eBay site looking for a sextant to give as a Christmas present. I was overwhelmed by the number, variety, and locations of available instruments." It was to be another year before she started surfing the site to really see what all the buzz was about.

"For the first year, I really did nothing but search the site and read the Community Boards," she admits. "I had not even signed on for Internet banking, never mind shopping for fun or profit online." In early 2003, Marian finally made her move and registered. Over the next three months, she was busy shopping on eBay to add small lots of used postage stamps to her collection.

During that summer, Marian realized that she might also be interested in selling on the eBay site. From reading the threads on the eBay discussion boards, she learned of the importance of positive feedback. After receiving 30 positive feedback comments, she registered her credit card and began her selling career slowly — she only listed about three or four items a week at first. A month later she added PayPal as a payment option and saw her sales quadruple almost immediately. Before the close of 2003, she had set up her eBay store — Purple Ferret Post Cards and Paper — with upwards of 400 items offered at any one time.

Marian came about her user ID, "Purpleferret999," by following eBay's advice. When she got stuck trying to pick a catchy name that was not already in use, she decided to follow eBay's suggestion to use a combination of her favourite pet, favourite colour, and favourite numbers. It has taken three years, but Purpleferret999 and Purple Ferret Post Cards and Paper are now widely known dealers of fine paper collectables such as post cards, calendars and even original art. "I also ensure I include top-notch personal service," adds Marian.

Marian has not lost sight of her beginnings on the Community Boards. She is one of many eBay users that freely give of their time, knowledge, and experience to lend a helping hand to panicked and frustrated newbies. "Many helped me and still do," insists Marian. She frequents the Canada Town Square and the newer Crafts and Hobbies boards in an effort to return something to the community. When eBay Canada sought volunteers for their On The Road program, she jumped at the chance to spend three days with company staff when they came to Nova Scotia. Shortly thereafter, she was invited to participate as part of the "Voices of the Community" program. And when Power-U needed volunteers to beta-test the Canadian content and site for their Education Specialist program, Marian's hand was one of the first held high. She still offers personal classes to individuals and groups through her Web site, found at www.thepurpleferret.com.

Marian's never-ending support of the eBay community was recognized in June 2006 at eBay Live in Las Vegas when the company presenting her one of the highest awards given to members — the Community Hall of Fame Award. She was the first and only Canadian to be nominated. She says, "I was proud to accept my crystal plaque and certificate from Bill Cobb, President of eBay North America; Meg Whitman, CEO of eBay Inc.; and Griff, the Dean of eBay University and host of eBay Radio while wearing my eBay.ca hat!" She found it to be a truly exhilarating experience, especially because another part of the award was a donation in her name from the eBay Foundation to a charity of her choice. She selected the Louisiana SPCA to receive that donation to assist in rebuilding after Hurricane Katrina.

Marian freely tells everyone she meets that her eBay career excites her with its possibilities. "Even with the steep learning curve I experienced, it has been nothing but fun, fun, fun!"

SOLID BRASS FAN, Decorative, Winged Dragon, Phoenix	Item number: 130025299234

You are signed in — Watch this item in My eBay | Email to a friend

Meet the seller

Starting bid **US $9.69** [Place Bid >]
(Approximately C $10.84)

Seller: purpleferret999 (906 ⭐) me
Feedback: **99.9% Positive**
Member: since 05-Apr-03 in Canada
- Read feedback comments
- Ask seller a question
- Add to Favourite Sellers
- View seller's other items: Store | List
- Visit seller's Store:
  📇 **Purple Ferret Post Cards and Paper**

End time: **15-Sep-06 22:00:00 EDT**
(4 days 8 hours)
Shipping costs: **US $1.50** (discount available)
Standard Flat Rate Shipping Service
(more services)
Ships to: Worldwide
Item location: fog-bound coast of NS, Canada
History: 0 bids

You can also: **Watch this item**
Email to a friend | Sell one like this

Buy safely

1. **Check the seller's reputation**
   Score: 906 | 99.9% Positive
   Read feedback comments

2. **Learn how you are protected**
   PayPal Free PayPal Buyer Protection.
   See eligibility

Listing and payment details: Show

Description — Seller assumes all responsibility for listing this item.

Purple Ferret Post Cards and Paper > Other Vintage Items > Vintage Accessories

Purple Ferret Post Cards and Paper

Purple Ferret Post Cards and Paper

Visit my eBay Store: 📇 Purple Ferret Post Cards and Paper
Artist-signed cards | US views | Paintings-Acrylic | RPPCs | Philatelic

Figure 18-8:
A PurpleFerret 999 auction.

Marian says, "If I could give one piece of advice for buyers or sellers, it would be to continually keep communication going. Internet trade, including eBay, demands a level of trust between strangers, unrivalled by brick and mortar shopping. One of the easiest ways to instill confidence is by a friendly tone and prompt contact." She adds, "But if I had the luxury of offering a second piece of advice, it would be for sellers only — know what you sell, and sell what you know."

Marsu450

Member since March 2001; Feedback: 3,975; Positive Feedback: 100%

Frederic Flower has always had a plan. He credits his eBay success as a seller to his ability to develop his plan and then stick to it: "Caroline (his wife and business partner) and I started our first brick and mortar retail store in Montreal more than 11 years ago. We knew that we were offering a unique product." Their business specializes in comic or cartoon figurines that they import from Europe and then resell.

Five years ago, Frederic and Caroline's business had grown to incorporate eight employees spread between two brick and mortar retail outlets in the Montreal area. That was when Frederic started investigating eBay as a natural extension of the business. "When the idea first occurred to us to sell on eBay, we knew that we would be offering items that were going to make us stand out in the crowd," he says. "We saw eBay as a way to showcase our products to a much larger audience of potential customers. We had an idea that our product line would attract collectors from all over the world if we could get the right exposure." Those five years have proved him right. "*Il Etait une Fois . . .*" (meaning "Once upon a time . . .") is the name of their eBay store.

Today Frederic spends much of his time devoted to the eBay part of the business while Caroline concentrates on the retail side. "We feel we pioneered the sale of our category of products on eBay and we credit our uniqueness to our on-line business success. Although we started strictly with European imports, we are expanding rapidly into licensed lines that we import from the U.S." Looking ahead, Frederic feels that, provided they can resist the temptation to become a "me too!" seller (selling something that everyone else does), the future of their company on eBay remains very bright. Frederic reminds us that repeat customers are a very significant part of his eBay business: "Offering new products that catch the discriminating eye of our customers will always be a high priority for us."

Looking forward, Frederic sees eBay as a major part of his continuing success in business. "We are always looking for ways to streamline and improve our customers' buying experience," he says. "It's what keeps our repeat customers coming back."

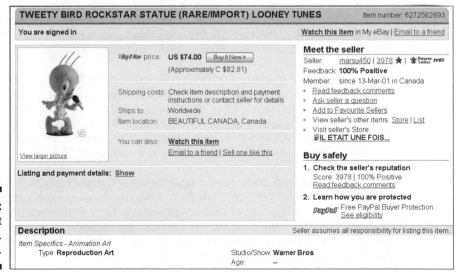

Figure 18-9:
An Il Etait une Fois . . . store listing.

Frederic shows no hesitation when asked to give advice to new eBay sellers: "Look to set yourself apart from the crowd on eBay. Your success will largely be determined by the degree to which you are capable of carving out your own niche in a huge marketplace." So true, Frederic, so true.

Bubblefast

Member since May 1999; Feedback: 18,935; Positive Feedback 100%

We chose to include this great eBay seller because it now actively sells throughout Canada from a location in Etobicoke, Ontario. Also, most eBay sellers will, at some time or another, be looking for a source of supply for shipping products.

Marsha first met the Bubblefast "family" when she needed to move her mother's things from Florida to California. When she got the price quote for rolls of cushioning from the moving company, it was so high she nearly fell over! She knew that she could find a better price on eBay — and she did. Bubblefast's prices were 50 percent lower than the moving company had quoted, and they shipped the wrap directly to her mom's house so that she could meet it there to wrap her mother's valuables.

The Bubblefast business began with Robin and her husband Alan. Their first transaction on eBay took place in early 1999, when Alan bought a Macintosh computer. When they were finally ready to start selling and had to choose a product, Alan figured that all eBay sellers would need shipping supplies. At first, they sold just one product: a 150-foot roll of ³⁄₁₆" (small size) bubble cushioning. Now, they sell more than 65 variations of eight or nine products: bubble cushioning, antistatic bubble, bubble bags, bubble-lined mailers, rolled shipping foam, boxes, sealing tape, and stretch film.

Alan passed away in 2001, after which Robin and her family carried on the business. On the bright side, Robin has remarried, and now the company (run by a combined family) has even more indentured employees. The Le Vine Family — Robin and her second husband, Mark; Jenny, 16; Steven, 11; Sara, 9; Michelle, 20; and Grandma Gloria — along with family friends Syble and Billy, work closely together, putting in a combined 70 to 80 hours a week.

Already a seller with many repeat customers and more than 35,000 positive feedback comments (repeat customers help build businesses!), they decided to branch out and go into consignment selling. They registered on eBay as Trading Assistants and now they're "up to their eyeballs in new business." The situation works out very well for them, because they're already in the shipping supply business. No package is a challenge!

Mark uses Turbo Lister for the Bubblefast auctions. Fashion mavens Jenny and Michelle scrutinize and help write descriptions for consignment listings of clothing. Jenny also posts feedback several times a week. Robin still handles order entry and answers the phone and e-mail. Grandma Gloria, her friend Syble, and elf Billy handle the packing and shipping. Bubblefast ships anywhere from 100 to 200 orders a day — their total shipping bill runs between $25,000 to $30,000 a month. The family has customers from around the world who buy from their auctions, eBay store and Web site — they've shipped to every state in the U.S. and internationally as far as Japan. When Marsha first interviewed them, their business had grossed $650,000 for a single year. While it has continued to grow since then, the profit margin for their product category is low, so they have to make up for it in volume. Visit them on the Web at www.bubblefast.com.

The lives of this family have been totally changed by eBay. Alan used to say of the family business he started: "Our family is together all the time now; we've learned to pull together for a common goal." This is still true today for the Le Vine family.

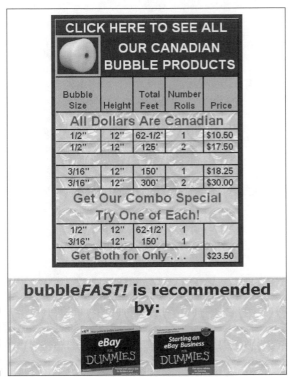

Figure 18-10: A Bubblefast store link.

CLICK HERE TO SEE ALL OUR CANADIAN BUBBLE PRODUCTS

Bubble Size	Height	Total Feet	Number Rolls	Price
All Dollars Are Canadian				
1/2"	12"	62-1/2'	1	$10.50
1/2"	12"	125'	2	$17.50
3/16"	12"	150'	1	$18.25
3/16"	12"	300'	2	$30.00
Get Our Combo Special				
Try One of Each!				
1/2"	12"	62-1/2'	1	
3/16"	12"	150'	1	
Get Both for Only . . .				$23.50

bubbleFAST! is recommended by:

eBay for DUMMIES

Starting an eBay Business for DUMMIES

The Le Vine family's tip for eBay sellers is this: "If you want to create a thriving eBay business and are willing to put the time and energy into it, the possibilities are endless. With a minimal investment of money, you have the potential to reach the world! Treat every customer like you want to be treated. After all this time, the customer is still always right."

Chapter 19

Ten Other Places to Move Merchandise

. . . .

In This Chapter

▶ Giving it away: Charitable donations

▶ Going to garage sales, swap meets, the local antique mall, and community events

▶ Unloading on other eBay sellers

▶ Going, going, gone: Turning over your goods to a live auctioneer

▶ Finding a place that specializes

▶ Placing a classified ad

▶ Selling it cheap: A last-ditch effort

. . . .

*W*hen a corner of your eBay storage area becomes a graveyard for unsold stuff (at some point it will — believe us), whatcha gonna do? Inevitably, you'll find yourself holding on to some merchandise that you feel may never scrape together a profit, and you'll become sick of looking at it. Whether thousands of those salad spinners that you bought to sell on eBay are suddenly appearing in multiple auctions or you jumped on the opportunity to buy a truckload (literally) of bargain-priced cat scratching posts, you have to make room for your stuff immediately or sell it fast.

Every business has a problem with excess inventory, so don't feel bad about yours. You can't expect to bat .300 every time you choose a product to sell. The key is getting rid of excess products while losing nothing on your investment. None of your merchandise is trash — we hope — so someone out there may want it and will pay *something* for it. If not, you can always give it away. In this chapter, we highlight the top ten ways to move that superfluous merchandise and still (hopefully) save your investment.

Donate to Charitable Organizations

Charitable donating is our personal favourite way to unload unwanted items. Not only are you doing something good for someone else, but your donation may be a 100 percent business write-off. Most communities have many private schools, churches, and synagogues. What these places all have in common is putting on fundraisers (auctions, raffles, tournaments, bingo) and welcoming donations. You have to give the best stuff to your schools or churches — especially if your item will be some sort of prize. Many charities often gratefully take boxes of miscellaneous stuff (think Salvation Army and Goodwill).

One idea is to put together little gift baskets for charity auctions. You might take a bunch of female-related, male-related, or kids' items and put them in a basket on a base of shredded Sunday comics. Keep a roll of clear cellophane on hand to wrap the entire thing. You can then top it off with a nice big bow. A gift basket is always an appreciated donation and, wrapped up this way, it always gets a higher price at bazaars or silent auctions.

Have a Garage Sale

Sell your items to other eBay sellers. Hee hee, only kidding (maybe not). Perhaps some of the stuff you have appeals to the locals (some of whom probably do sell on eBay). Garage sales draw big crowds when promoted properly, and you'll be surprised at the amount of stuff you'll unload. An especially good time to have a garage sale is throughout the fall — just in time for the holidays.

Because you've probably been to a bunch of garage sales but may not have held one in a long, long time, here are a few reminders:

- **Plan the sale at least three weeks in advance:** Decide on the weekend of your sale well beforehand and be sure to set a specific opening time. If you welcome *early birds* (people who like to show up at 6 or 7 a.m.), be sure to put that in your ad and flyers.

- **Invite neighbours to participate:** The more the merrier, right? Also, the bigger the sale, the more customers you're likely to entice. Everyone can drum up at least a few items for a garage sale.

- **Gather and price items to go in the sale:** After you set a date, immediately start putting things aside and pricing them with sticky tags. This way, you won't have to scramble the day before to find things.

- **Place a classified ad:** Call your local newspaper a week before the sale and ask the friendly classified department people when the best time is to run an ad. Take their advice — they know what they're talking about!

✓ **Make flyers to post around the neighbourhood:** Fire up your computer and make a flyer; include your address, a map, the date, and the starting time. Be sure to mention special items that you've thrown into the sale to bring 'em in — mentioning that many items are new also attracts customers. If two or three families are participating in the sale, mention that, too. If you have small, throwaway types of items, include the line "Prices start at 25 cents." Hang the flyer in conspicuous places around your neighbourhood.

✓ **Post large signs on nearby corners:** The day before the sale, put up *large* posters advertising the sale. (You can pick up 56×71 centimetre poster board from any art or office supply store.) When you make the posters, use thick, black shipping markers on a light board. Use few words, including only the basic details. For example, "Garage Sale June 22–24, 8 a.m., Tons of Stuff, 1234 Extra Cash Blvd" will suffice. Also make a sign to hang at the sale location that reads something like: "Sale Continues Tomorrow, New Items will be Added!"

✓ **Clean up any dusty or dirty items:** If you want someone to buy it, you have to make it look good.

✓ **Gather supplies:** Get lots of change; make sure you have plenty of tens and fives, a ton of loonies and toonies, and several rolls of smaller coins. Get a calculator for each person who will be taking money. Set aside a container to use as the cash box. Collect all the supermarket shopping bags that you can for those with multiple purchases.

✓ **Hang helium balloons to draw attention to your signs:** The day of the sale, go to the busiest intersection near your sale and tie some helium balloons to your sign — that's sure to attract attention. Do the same thing at the street corner near your sale and also at the curb of the sale.

✓ **Display everything in an orderly fashion:** Pull out your old card tables and arrange items so that people can easily see what's there; a literal pile of junk will turn them off. Hang clothes on a temporary rack (or use a clothesline on the day of the sale).

✓ **Get ready to negotiate:** Talk to people when they approach and *make that sale!*

Rent a Table at the Local Flea Market

Local *flea markets* (regularly scheduled events where you can rent space for a token fee and sell your wares) can be a great place to meet other eBay sellers. But whatever you do, don't mention that you sell on eBay. Let the customers think that you're a rube and that they can get the best of you. Offer great deals; give 'em a discount if they buy a ton of stuff. Just like with a garage sale (refer to the preceding section), you can move lots of merchandise here.

Don't forget to try to unload your goods to other sellers; perhaps they can do with a little extra inventory. Check the classifieds of local newspapers for flea markets; you will most likely be able to find ads listing these types of sales which occur once a month in some towns.

Consign Merchandise to the Local Antique Mall

An *antique mall* is a retail store that's often run by several people who take your merchandise on consignment. You can probably find a few in your area. Your items are sold in the store (good for you), and the storeowners take a commission on each sale (good for them). They take your items, tag them with your own identifying tag, and display them for sale. Antique malls usually see an enormous amount of foot traffic, and this may be as close to having a retail store that you'll ever get.

Take a Booth at a Community Event

In many cities and towns, the local business community may hold special events: street fairs, Canada Day extravaganzas, pumpkin festivals, and other types too numerous to mention. As a vendor, you can rent a booth at such events to peddle your wares. For seasonal events, purchasing a bunch of holiday-related items to decorate your table for the festivities is a savvy marketing idea. Your excess eBay inventory will just be part of the display — and a big part of your sales. You might even consider donating a percentage of your sales to a local non-profit to help boost traffic.

If the event is in the evening, purchase a few hundred glow-in-the-dark bracelets on eBay (you can often get 100 for about $20). The kids love them and will drag their parents to your booth. Be creative and think of other ways to make your booth stand out. Support your community, have a barrel of fun, and make some money!

Resell to Sellers on eBay

Package up your items into related lots that will appeal to sellers who are looking for merchandise online. If you're overstocked with stuffed animals, put together a lot of a dozen. If you don't have a dozen of any one item, make packages of related items that will appeal to a certain type of seller.

Be sure to use the words *liquidation, wholesale,* or *resale* (or all three) in your title. A world of savvy sellers are out there looking for items to sell. Maybe another seller can move the items later or in a different venue.

Note that eBay has Wholesale subcategories for almost every sort of merchandise.

Visit a Local Auctioneer

Yes, when we tell you to visit a local auctioneer, we mean a real live auctioneer, one who holds live auctions at real auction houses that real people attend. Many people enjoy going to live auctions. (We recommend that you go occasionally to acquire unique items you can resell on eBay.) Shopping at auctions can be addictive (duh), and live auctions attract an elite group of knowledgeable buyers.

The basic idea is to bring your stuff to an auctioneer, who auctions off lots for you. Good auctioneers can get a crowd going, bidding far more than an item was expected to sell for. Do a Web search for local auction houses — you'll be amazed at how many are actually out there. Figure 19-1 shows an example of the search results returned.

Figure 19-1:
Sample search results for auctioneers.

Here are a few facts about real, live auctioneers and some pointers to keep in mind when looking for one:

- **Make sure that the auction house you choose is licensed to hold auctions in your province and is insured and bonded.** You don't want to leave your fine merchandise with someone who will pack up and disappear with your stuff before the auction.

- **Get the details before agreeing to the consignment.** Many auction houses give you at least 75 percent of the final hammer price. Before you consign your items, ask the auctioneer's representative about the details of the auction, such as

  - When will the auction be held?

  - How often are the auctions held?

  - Has the auctioneer sold items like yours before? If so, how much have they sold for in the past?

  - What is the "hammer fee" or auctioneer commission? And when will the auction house give you the proceeds?

  - Will there be a printed catalog for the sale, and will your piece be shown in it?

  Get the terms and conditions of the auction in writing and have the rep walk you through every point so that you thoroughly understand each.

- **Search the Internet.** Type **licensed auctions** and see what you come up with it can't hurt.

- **Contact local auctioneers.** If your items are of good quality, a local auction house may be interested in taking them on consignment.

Find Specialty Auction Sites

If you have some specialized items that just don't sell very well on eBay, you might look for a different venue. Although eBay is the best all-purpose selling site in the world, you may have an item that only a specialist in the field can appreciate.

For example, we've seen some fine works of art not sell on eBay. But don't fret, you'll find many other places online where you can sell these items. For example, we've searched Yahoo! for **art auctions**. Under the <u>Web Results</u> heading, we found more than 6 million Web sites that auction artwork. You might want to redefine your search with your telephone area code so that you find auction locations in your immediate area.

You may find an online auctioneer who specializes in the particular item you have for sale, something too esoteric for the eBay crowd. We've found some incredible bargains on elegant new sunglasses made by a company in Italy called Persol, a company world famous for crystal lenses and ultra-fine quality. The super-famous wear these sunglasses: Robert De Niro, Tom Cruise, Donald Trump, Sharon Stone, Mel Gibson, and Cindy Crawford. These sunglasses normally retail for between $150–$300 USD a pair, but you can sometimes find them on eBay for as low as $40 USD. Unless you're buying them dirt cheap, you're not making your profits on eBay. Maybe the crowd just doesn't know about them, but they sell well elsewhere.

Run a Classified Liquidation Ad

Sell your special items in the appropriate categories of the classifieds. Sell the rest of them in preassigned bulk lots for other sellers. When you write your ad, make your lots sound fantastic; give the reader a reason to call you. When they call, be excited about your merchandise. But be honest and tell them you're just selling the stuff to raise cash.

As an alternative to newspaper classifieds, consider placing an ad on Kijiji, a great site that is actually owned by eBay. Unlike the eBay site, Kijiji is for classified ads only — not auctions. Kijiji is expanding rapidly and is now available in many larger communities in Canada. They allow ads for anything legal and tasteful — and the best thing is that using it is FREE! Make sure you describe your items well and include a photo to ensure you get the best response. You can visit Kijiji at

```
www.kijiji.ca/
```

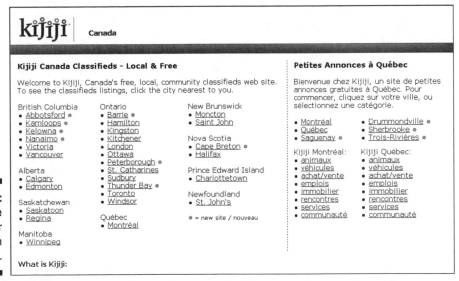

Figure 19-2:
The home page for Kijiji in Canada.

Sell Everything on eBay for a $0.99 Opening Bid . . .

. . . and take what you get.

Part VI
Appendixes

The 5th Wave By Rich Tennant

"How many times have I told you that you can't sell your brother on eBay?"

In this part . . .

Appendix A is our random glossary of words that may be new to you but will soon become part of your day-to-day vocabulary; refer to it often as you peruse other parts of the book. In Appendix B, we briefly discuss home networking: what it is, how to set one up, and how it can benefit you.

Appendix A

Glossary

● ●

About Me page: The free Web page given to every eBay user. An excellent promotional tool.

absentee bid: A bid that an auction house employee places on a lot (or lots) in your absence — the employee will bid up to a maximum amount that you designate. When you want to participate in a live auction but can't attend it physically, you can prearrange this service.

accounts payable: The amount your business owes to vendors, office supply stores, your credit card charges, and the like. This includes any money your business owes.

accounts receivable: The money people owe you, such as the cheques and money orders you're expecting in the mail and the money sitting in your PayPal account that you haven't transferred to your chequing account.

Announcements pages: eBay pages where you get all the latest eBay information. You need to check these pages periodically. If you follow the Announcements link at the bottom of any eBay page, you end up at the Community announcements page at www2.ebay.com/aw/marketing-ca.html. If you're wondering whether it's your computer's problem or an eBay problem when the search engine isn't working, check out the System Status Announcements Board at www2.ebay.com/aw/announce.html.

as is/where is: An item that comes with no warranty, implied or otherwise; speaking to the merchantability of the product.

bid increment: The amount that a bid must advance, based on the auction's high bid.

bid retraction: A cancelled auction bid. Retractions can occur only under extreme circumstances (such as when you type the wrong numerals).

bid shielding: An illegal process wherein two bidders work together to defraud a seller out of high bids by retracting a bid at the last minute and granting a confederate's low bid the win. Not as much of an issue anymore due to eBay's new bid retraction policy; *see also* bid retraction.

bonding: A surety bond can be issued by a third party (usually an insurance company) to guarantee a seller's performance in a transaction.

card not present: Credit card services use this term to describe transactions that typically happen over the Internet or by mail order. It means that the seller hasn't seen the actual card.

caveat emptor: Latin for *let the buyer beware.* If you see this posted anywhere, proceed cautiously — you're responsible for the outcome of any transaction in which you take part.

chargeback: When someone calls his or her credit card company and refuses to pay for a transaction. The credit card company will credit the card in question while making you pay back the amount.

consignment: When someone hands over their merchandise to you, which you then auction on eBay. Acting as a consignor allows you to make a small commission and lets the other person involved (the consignee) sell something without the hassle.

cookie: A small text file that may be left on your computer to personalize your experience on a particular Web site. When you sign on to eBay, a cookie is placed on your computer that keeps your user ID and password active for as long as you're on the site.

corporation: An independent entity set up to do business.

CA: Chartered Accountant. Someone who has been educated in accounting and has passed a certification test. CAs are at the top of the professional heap in the field of accounting.

CRA: Canada Revenue Agency. This federal department governs tax laws, international trade legislation, and the implementation of all social and economic programs administered through the tax system in Canada. All Canadian businesses and individuals must report regularly to the CRA.

DBA: Doing Business As. These letters appear next to the common name of a business entity, sole proprietorship, partnership, or corporation that conducts business under a fictitious name.

DOA: Dead On Arrival. The product you purchased doesn't work from the moment you open the package.

DUNS number: Data Universal Numbering System number. An identification number issued to businesses from a database maintained by the powerful Dun and Bradstreet. These nine-digit numbers are issued to allow your business to register with more than fifty global, trade, and industry-related associations, including the United Nations, the Canadian, U.S., and Australian federal governments, and the European Commission. More than 110 million businesses worldwide have registered to secure their number. You can get yours at no cost by calling Dun and Bradstreet at 1-800-463-6362 or by registering online at `https://dnbdirect.ca/selfdunsrequest.asp`.

EN: Employer Number. If you run your business as a partnership or a corporation, you need an EN number from the CRA. If you're a sole proprietor, your Social Insurance number is your EN because you file all of your business in your personal tax return.

entrepreneur: That's you! An entrepreneur is someone who takes the financial risk of starting a business. Even if you're buying and reselling garage sale items, you're considered an entrepreneur.

FOB: Free On Board or Freight On Board. When you begin purchasing large lots of merchandise to sell, you'll encounter this term. The FOB location is technically the place where the seller will deliver the goods. If the price you're quoted is FOB Montreal, you're responsible for all shipping costs to get the goods from Montreal to your home city.

FTP: File Transfer Protocol. The protocol used to transfer files from one server to another.

hammer fee: A fee that the auction house charges at a live auction. Be sure to read the information package *before* you bid on an item in a live auction. Hammer fees usually add 10–15 percent to the amount of your bid.

HTF: Hard To Find. An abbreviation that commonly appears in eBay auction titles to describe items that are, uh, hard to find.

invoice: A bill that outlines the items in a specific transaction; includes who the item is sold to and all costs involved.

ISBN: International Standard Book Number. Just like a car's VIN (Vehicle Identification Number) or the UPC (Universal Product Code) on a can of beans, the ISBN identifies a book by a universal number.

keystone: In the brick-and-mortar retailing world, a 100 percent markup. A product sells for keystone if it sells for twice the wholesale price. Products that you can sell at keystone are very nice to find.

live auctions: Auctions held online in real time. Check out `www.ebaylive auctions.com`.

mannequin. A representation of the human form made of wood, fiberglass, or plastic. Essential for modeling clothing for your eBay apparel sales.

MIB: Mint In Box. The item inside the box is mint, but the box looks like a sixteen-wheeler ran over it.

MIMB: Mint In Mint Box. Not only is the item in mint condition, but it's in a perfect box as well.

mint: An item in perfect condition is described as mint. This is truly a subjective opinion, usually based on individual standards.

MSRP: Manufacturer's Suggested Retail Price. A price that hardly anybody pays.

NARU: Not A Registered User. A user of eBay or other online community who has been suspended for any number of reasons.

OOP: Out Of Print. When a book or CD is being published, it usually has its own life span in the manufacturing process. When it is no longer being made, it's out of print, or OOP.

provenance: The story behind an item, including who owned it and where it came from. If you have an interesting provenance for one of your items, be sure to put it in the auction description because it adds considerable value to the item.

QuickBooks: A top-of-the-heap accounting program that helps you keep your records straight.

register: Similar to a chequebook account listing, QuickBooks keeps registers that go up and down depending on the amount of flow in an account balance.

ROI: Return On Investment. A figure expressed as a percentage that stands for your net profit after taxes and your own equity.

sniping: The act (or fine art) of bidding at the very last possible second of an auction.

sole proprietorship: A business that's owned by only one person where the profits and losses are recorded on that person's personal tax return.

split transaction: A transaction that you must assign to more than one category when doing the bookkeeping for your business. If you pay a credit card bill and a portion of the bill went to purchased merchandise, a portion to gas for business-related outings, and yet another portion to eBay fees, you must post each amount to its own category.

T1 or T2: An end-of-year form that you file with the CRA for tax purposes. The T1 is used by individuals or sole proprietorships and the T2 is used by corporations or partnerships.

tax deduction: An expenditure on your part that represents a normal and necessary expense for your business. Before you get carried away and assume that *every* penny you spend is a write-off (deduction), check with your tax professional to outline exactly what is and what isn't.

TOS: Terms Of Service. An agreement that outlines the rules and conditions of doing business with a company. eBay has a TOS agreement; check it out at `pages.ebay.ca/help/policies/user-agreement.html`.

wholesale: Products sold to retailers (that's you) at a price above the manufacturer's cost, allowing for a mark-up to retail. We hope you buy most of your merchandise at wholesale. Stores such as Costco or Sam's Club, while offering items for cheaper than some other retailers, sell items in bulk at prices marginally higher than wholesale. You must get a resale number from your province to buy at true wholesale.

Appendix B

The Hows and Whys of a Home Network

· ·

*W*hat is a network? A *network* is a way to connect computers so that they can communicate with each other — as if they were one giant computer with different terminals. The best part of having a network is that it enables various computers — as well as printers and other peripherals — to share a high-speed Internet connection. By setting up a computer network, one computer might run bookkeeping, another might run a graphics server, and others might be used as personal PCs for different users. From each net-worked computer, it's possible to access programs and files on all other networked computers.

Today's technologies allow you to perform this same miracle on a *home net-work*. At home, you can connect as many computers as you like and run your business from anywhere in your home — you can even hook up your laptop from the bedroom if you don't feel like getting out of bed.

Now for the *whys* of a home network. A network is a convenient way to run a business. All big companies use them, and they are a good idea for you, too. You can print your postage, for example, on one printer from any computer in your home or office. You can extend your DSL line or Internet cable con-nection so that you can use it anywhere in your home — as well as in your office.

In a network, you can set certain directories in each computer to be *shared*. That way, other computers on the network can access those directories. You can also password-protect certain files and directories to prevent others — your children or your employees — from accessing them.

We devote the rest of this appendix to a quick and dirty discussion of home networks installed on Windows-based PCs. We give you a lesson on what we know works for most people. (Hey, if it doesn't work, don't e-mail us — head back to the store and get your money back!)

At this point, we want to remind you that we are not techies (just like we're not lawyers or accountants). For more information on anything you'd like to ask about home networking, we defer to Kathy Ivens, author of *Home Networking For Dummies* (Wiley).

What we know about home networks, we've found out the hard way — from the school of hard knocks. A lot of research went into this appendix as well, so humour us and read on.

Variations of a Home Network

You have a choice of four types of home networks: Ethernet, powerline, home phoneline, and wireless. See Table B-1 for a quick rundown of some pros and cons of each.

Table B-1	Types of Networks Pros and Cons	
Type	**Pros**	**Cons**
Traditional Ethernet*	Fast, cheap, and easy setup	Computers and printers must be hardwired; cables run everywhere
Home phoneline	Fast; runs over your home phone lines	Old wiring or not enough phone jacks may be a hindrance
Powerline	Fast; your home is already prewired with outlets	Electrical interference may degrade the signal
Wireless network**	Fairly fast; wireless (no ugly cords to deal with)	Expensive; may not be reliable because of interference from home electrical devices

Connects computers with high-quality cable over a maximum of 100 metres of cabling.

**Several flavours of wireless are available. See "Hooking up with wireless" later in this chapter.*

Home phoneline networks are fading in popularity because people don't have enough phone jacks in their houses to make it an easy proposition.

Wireless networks are currently the hot ticket and highly touted by the geek gurus. However, wireless signals may experience interference because the network runs with the same 2.4 GHz technology as some home wireless telephones. Bill uses a wireless network exclusively and gets very good results. Marsha has a wireless network as a secondary network, and it works — kind of. Her primary network is a hybrid, combining Ethernet, home phoneline, and wireless.

With broadband over a powerline network, you get high-speed Internet directly through your home electrical system. Just plug in your powerline boxes (more on that later), and you're up and running!

All networks need the following two devices:

✔ **Router:** A router allows you to share a single Internet IP address among multiple computers. A router does exactly what its name implies; it routes signals and data to the different computers on your network. If you have one computer, the router can act as a firewall or even a network device leading to a print server (a gizmo that attaches to your router and allows you to print directly to a printer without having another computer on).

✔ **Modem:** You need a modem to establish an Internet connection. You can get one from your cable or phone company and plug it into an outlet with cable (just like your TV); alternatively, if you have DSL, you can plug it into a special phone jack. The modem connects to your router with an Ethernet cable.

If you have broadband, you don't need to have a main computer turned on to access your internet connection anywhere in the house. Alternatively, if you keep a printer turned on (and you have a print server), you can connect that to your router and print from your laptop in another room — right through the network.

Before touching your network card or opening your computer to install anything, touch a grounded metal object to free yourself of static electricity. Otherwise, a spark could go from your hand to the delicate components on the network card or another card, thereby rendering the card useless. Better yet, for safety, go to an electronics store and purchase a wrist grounding strap that has a cord with a gator clip, which you attach to a metal part of the computer before touching anything inside.

Powerline network

An ingenious invention, a powerline network uses your existing home powerlines to carry your network and your high-speed Internet connection. You access the network by plugging a powerline adapter from your computer into an electrical outlet on the wall. Powerline networks have been around for a while and are considered quite reliable.

Hooking up a powerline network is so easy that it's a bit disappointing — you'll wonder why the process isn't more complicated. Most installations work immediately, right out of the box. Figure B-1 shows you the basic setup. Computers in other rooms need only a powerline bridge adapter with an Ethernet cable to a network card.

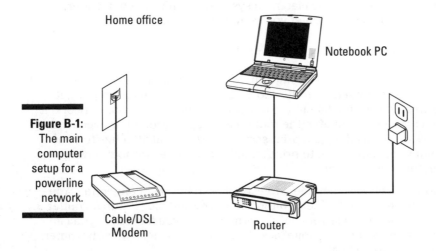

Home office

Notebook PC

Figure B-1:
The main
computer
setup for a
powerline
network.

Cable/DSL
Modem

Router

To set up a powerline network, you'll need the following (in addition to a router and modem):

- ✔ **An Ethernet card for each computer:** Many new computers already have an Ethernet card. If yours doesn't, you can buy inexpensive Ethernet cards for around $10.

- ✔ **Electrical outlets:** We bet you have more than one in each room of your house.

- ✔ **Powerline Ethernet bridge for each computer:** You plug an Ethernet cable from your computer into the powerline Ethernet bridge, and then plug Netgear's Ethernet bridge into a wall outlet. See Figure B-2.

Figure B-2:
Netgear's
Ethernet
bridge.

Hooking up the powerline network goes like this:

1. **Plug the cable line (or phoneline for DSL) into your modem to access your high-speed connection.**

2. **Connect one "in" Ethernet cable from your modem to a router.**

3. **Connect one "out" Ethernet cable from the router to a local computer.**

4. **Connect another "out" Ethernet cable to the powerline adapter.**

5. **Plug the powerline box into a convenient wall outlet.**

Home phoneline

According to the Home Phoneline Networking Alliance (HPNA) — the association that works with hardware companies to develop a single networking standard — tests indicate that phoneline network technology can be successfully installed and operational in 99 percent of today's homes. In real life, how your home is wired and the quality of those wires dictates that success.

Marsha claims that she can successfully hook up to her network from 90 percent of the phone jacks in her house. The telephone cabling within your walls contains four wires, and your telephone uses only a portion of two. There's plenty more room in the cable for your network. Figure B-3 shows you what the typical home phoneline setup looks like.

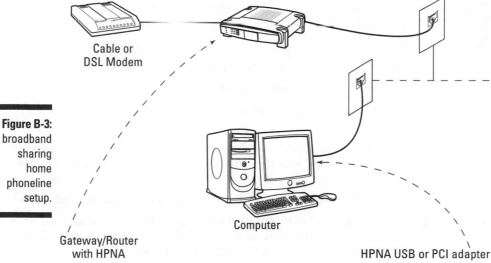

Cable or
DSL Modem

Figure B-3:
A broadband
sharing
home
phoneline
setup.

Gateway/Router
with HPNA

Computer

HPNA USB or PCI adapter

A phoneline network sends data at a speedy 10MB per second (the same speed as a regular Ethernet network). It can operate with computers or other equipment placed as far as 305 metres apart and will work in homes as large as 3,048 square metres. Best of all, you can simultaneously use the connected phoneline for your network and to talk without causing any interference to either.

Take a look at the jacks at the end of all your phone cords; if you see only two copper-coloured wires in the plastic jack, toss the cord. The ones that you need to carry your full load must have *four* wires visible in the clear plastic end of the jack.

To set up your network to carry files and your high-speed connection throughout the house, you need some extra hardware:

- **Bridge:** A device that connects your Ethernet (router connection) with your powerline network. You can get a device that combines the router and the bridge.

- **HPNA network adapter for each computer:** You need an adapter that enables your computer to become one with other computers on the network. These adapters are also available as a USB device, eliminating the need to install a card in your computer.

- **Phone jacks:** Kind of essential for plugging in the phone wire from the adapter.

To install a home phoneline network, just follow these steps (but be sure to follow your manufacturer's instructions if they vary from this information):

If you're installing a USB (universal serial bus) adapter, don't bother trying to open your computer. Just plug in the adapter to an available USB port and proceed to Step 5.

1. **Turn off your computer and disconnect its power cord.**

2. **Open the cover of your computer.**

3. **Install the network card in an available slot.**

   Touch the card only by the metal part on its outside edge. When installing the card, press firmly down on the top of the card with your thumb to properly seat the card in the slot. Fasten the card to the chassis by tightening the screw on the metal edge.

4. **Replace the cover on your PC and reconnect the power cord.**

5. **Connect one end of the (RJ-11) telephone cord that came with your network card to the port on the card labelled *To Wall*, then plug the other end into a convenient wall telephone jack.**

   If you have a telephone that needs to use that wall jack, connect the cord to the port labelled *To Phone;* your telephone will work through the network card.

6. **Power up your computer.**

   If you're lucky, your computer will see the new hardware and ask you to install the driver. If you're not lucky, check the instructions (as a last-ditch effort!) for troubleshooting tips.

7. **When asked, insert the CD or the disk that came with the card (containing those tricky drivers) and follow the on-screen instructions.**

   As you go through the instructions, decide on a name for each computer that you want to install on the network.

8. **Set up directories that you want shared on the network.**

   Go to My Computer, select the directories (denoted by folder icons) that you want to share, right-click, and then indicate that you want to share these directories with other computers on the network. Do the same with your local printers.

9. **Repeat Steps 1–8 on each computer.**

   As you add each computer, double-check that it can communicate with the other computers that you've already installed. Do this by trying to open a shared directory on a remote computer and printing a test page on a remote printer.

10. **If your network is not functioning properly after you complete all the recommended steps, call tech support as many times as necessary to get your network up and running.**

    When your network connection is off the ground and working flawlessly, it's time to add your broadband.

11. **To install the broadband connection, take the Ethernet cable from the modem and connect it to the back of your router. Then connect another Ethernet cable from the router to the phoneline network bridge.**

12. **Connect the phoneline that comes with your bridge from the bridge to a telephone wall jack.**

    Voila — you will now most likely be good to go with your Internet connection on all the computers in your network.

Your wall connectors each have an outlet for a telephone cord that you plug into your wall jack. (Marsha cheated in one room and connected two computers to one phone jack with a splitter that makes two jacks out of one.)

Hooking up with wireless

Wireless networking — also known as WiFi or, to the more technically inclined, IEEE 802.11 — is the hot, new technology for all kinds of networks. It's an impressive system when it works, with no cables or connectors to bog you down.

If you're worried about your next-door neighbour hacking into your computer through your wireless connection — stop worrying. Wireless networks are protected by their own brand of security called WEP (or Wired Equivalent Privacy). WEP encrypts your wireless transmissions and prevents others from getting into your network. Although super-hackers have cracked this security system, it's the best one available at this time.

To link your laptop or desktop to a wireless network with WEP encryption, you have to enter a key code from the wireless access point. Just enter it into your wireless card software on every computer that uses the network.

You may get confused when you see the different types of wireless available. Here's the lowdown on the variations:

- **802.11a:** This wireless format works really well — it's fast with good connectivity. This format is used when you have to connect a large group, such as at a convention center or in a dormitory. It delivers data at speeds as high as 54 Mbps (megabits per second). It runs at the 5 GHz band (hence its nickname WiFi5), so it doesn't have any competition for bandwidth with wireless phones or microwave ovens.

- **802.11b:** Marsha's laptop has a built-in 802.11b card, so she is able to connect to the popular HotSpots in Starbucks and at various airports. It's considered a little older now but still a very common type of wireless and is used on many platforms. It travels over the 2.4 GHz band. The 802.11b version is slower than the 802.11a version, transferring data at only 11 Mbps. It's a solid, low-cost solution when you have no more than thirty-two users per access point.

  The lower frequency of 2.4 GHz drains less power from laptops and other portable devices, so laptop batteries will last longer. Also, 2.4 GHz signals travel farther and can work through walls and floors more effectively than 5 GHz signals.

- **802.11g:** This is the newest flavour and is based on the 2.4 GHz band. Bill gets data speeds up to a possible 108 Mbps on his laptop, although 60 Mbps are more common, and it's backward compatible with 802.11b service.

Installing your wireless network isn't normally a gut-wrenching experience (although it can be, if the signal doesn't reach to where you want it). You hook up your computer (a laptop works best) to the wireless access point (the gizmo with the antenna that broadcasts your signal throughout your home or office) and then perform some setup tasks, such as choosing your channel and setting up your WEP code. (The wireless access point will come with its own instructions.)

After you complete the setup and turn on your wireless access point, you have a WiFi hotspot in your home or office. Typically, a hotspot provides coverage for about 30 metres in all directions, although walls and floors cut down on the range.

Here are some simplified steps to follow when configuring your network:

1. **Run a cable from your cable connection or a phone cord from your DSL line to your modem.**

2. **Connect one Ethernet cable from your modem to your router.**

3. **Connect one Ethernet cable to your wireless access point.**

Take a look at the network diagram from Netgear in Figure B-4 for more information.

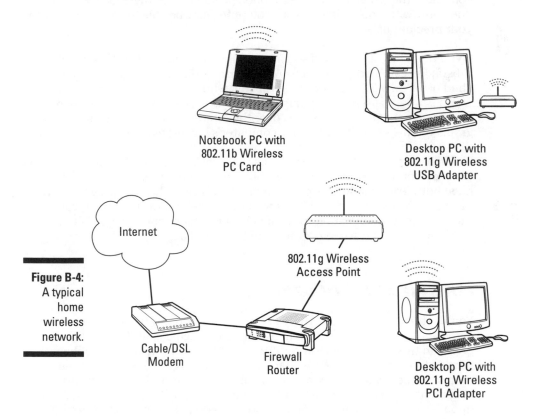

Figure B-4: A typical home wireless network.

Notebook PC with 802.11b Wireless PC Card

Desktop PC with 802.11g Wireless USB Adapter

802.11g Wireless Access Point

Internet

Cable/DSL Modem

Firewall Router

Desktop PC with 802.11g Wireless PCI Adapter

Internet Security and Your Home Network

A dial-up connection exposes your computer to the Internet only when you dial up and get connected. Most broadband Internet connections are always on, which means your computer is always exposed. Shield your computer with a strong firewall and an antivirus program.

Firewall software

When you're connected to the Internet, you're exposed not only to hackers, but also to threats such as *Trojan horses,* programs that can get into your computer when you innocently view an infected Web site. Once inside your computer, the Trojan horse, like ET, phones home. From there, an evil-deed-doer, now with a direct line to your computer, may be able to wreak havoc with your precious data.

If you're technically inclined — and even if you're not — visit the Web site for Gibson Research Corporation (`www.grc.com`). Gibson Research is the brainchild of an early PC pioneer, Steve Gibson, who's renowned as a genius in the world of codes and programming. Steve is *the* expert when it comes to exposing the vulnerabilities of systems over the Internet. A few free diagnostic programs on this site will check your computer's vulnerability to Internet threats.

ShieldsUp and LeakTest are programs that test your computer and terrify you with results that expose the vulnerability of your Internet connection. We have both learned about ZoneAlarm on Steve's site. This free program (the Pro version costs $39.95 USD) has won every major award in the industry as the most secure software firewall. If your main concern is safety, visit `www.zonelabs.com` for a free download of ZoneAlarm.

Antivirus software

You're still going to need antivirus software to protect you from the idiots who think it's fun to send destructive code through e-mail. The leading programs in this area are Norton AntiVirus and McAfee. One of the problems inherent in buying software is that you might be urged to load much more than you need onto your computer. If all you need is antivirus software, purchase only antivirus software. But don't delay — buy it now and be sure to update the antivirus files each week so that you're fully protected from the latest viruses.

Index

• *B* •

• F •

• N •

• P •

Notes

Notes

Notes

Notes

BUSINESS & PERSONAL FINANCE

0-470-83768-3

0-470-83418-8

Also available:

- Accounting For Canadians
  For Dummies
  0-470-83878-7
- Business Plans For Dummies
  0-7645-7652-6
- Canadian Small Business Kit
  For Dummies
  0-470-83818-3
- Investing For Canadians
  For Dummies
  0-470-83361-0
- Leadership For Dummies
  0-7645-5176-0

- Managing For Dummies
  0-7645-1771-6
- Marketing For Dummies
  0-7645-5600-2
- Money Management All-in-One Desk
  Reference For Canadians
  For Dummies
  0-470-83360-2
- Stock Investing For Canadians
  For Dummies
  0-470-83342-2

HOME & BUSINESS COMPUTER BASICS

0-471-75421-8

0-7645-8849-4

Also available:

- Blogging For Dummies
  0-471-77084-1
- Excel 2007 For Dummies
  0-470-03737-7
- Macs For Dummies
  0-7645-5656-8

- Office 2007 For Dummies
  0-470-00923-3
- Outlook 2007 For Dummies
  0-470-03830-6
- PCs For Dummies
  0-7645-8958-X
- Upgrading & Fixing PCs
  For Dummies
  0-7645-1665-5

Available wherever books are sold. For more information or to order direct: U.S. customers visit www.dummies.com or call 1-877-762-2974. U.K. customers visit www.wileyeurope.com or call 0800 243407. Canadian customers visit www.wiley.ca or call 1-800-567-4797.

FOOD, HOME, GARDEN, HOBBIES, MUSIC & PETS

0-7645-9904-6

0-7645-5232-5

Also available:

- Diabetes Cookbook For Dummies
  0-7645-5130-2
- Gardening For Canadians
  For Dummies
  1-894413-37-7
- Holiday Decorating For Dummies
  0-7645-2570-0
- Home Improvement All-in-One
  Desk Reference For Dummies
  0-7645-5680-0
- Knitting For Dummies
  0-7645-5395-X

- Piano For Dummies
  0-7645-5105-1
- Puppies For Dummies
  0-470-03717-2
- Scrapbooking For Dummies
  0-7645-7208-3
- Sudoku For Dummies
  0-470-01892-5
- Dog Training For Dummies
  0-7645-8418-9
- 30-Minute Meals For Dummies
  0-7645-2589-1

INTERNET & DIGITAL MEDIA

0-7645-9802-3

0-471-74739-4

Also available:

- CD & DVD Recording For Dummies
  0-7645-5956-7
- eBay For Dummies
  0-470-04529-9
- Electronics For Dummies
  0-7645-7660-7
- Fighting Spam For Dummies
  0-7645-5965-6
- Genealogy Online For Dummies
  0-7645-5964-8

- Google For Dummies
  0-7645-4420-9
- Home Recording For Musicians
  For Dummies
  0-7645-8884-2
- The Internet For Dummies
  0-7645-8996-2
- Podcasting For Dummies
  0-471-74898-6

SPORTS, FITNESS, PARENTING, RELIGION & SPIRITUALITY

0-471-76871-5   0-470-83945-7

Also available:
- The Bible For Dummies
  0-7645-5296-1
- Catholicism For Dummies
  0-7645-5391-7
- Coaching Hockey For Dummies
  0-0470-83685-7
- Curling For Dummies
  0-470-83828-0

- Fitness For Dummies
  0-7645-7851-0
- Pilates For Dummies
  0-7645-5397-6
- Teaching Kids to Read
  For Dummies
  0-7645-4043-2
- Weight Training For Dummies
  0-7645-76845-6

NETWORKING, SECURITY, PROGRAMMING & DATABASES

0-7645-3910-8   0-7645-5784-X

Also available:
- Ajax For Dummies
  0-471-78597-0
- Access 2003 All-in-One Desk
  Reference For Dummies
  0-7645-3988-4
- Beginning Programming
  For Dummies
  0-7645-4997-9
- C++ For Dummies
  0-7645-6852-3
- Firewalls For Dummies
  0-7645-4048-3

- Network Security For Dummies
  0-7645-1679-5
- Networking For Dummies
  0-7645-7583-X
- TCP/IP For Dummies
  0-7645-1760-0
- XML For Dummies
  0-7645-8845-1
- Wireless All-in-One Desk Reference
  For Dummies
  0-7645-7496-5

HEALTH & SELF-HELP

0-470-83370-X

0-470-83835-3

Also available:

Arthritis For Dummies
0-7645-7074-9

Asthma For Dummies
0-7645-4233-8

Breast Cancer For Dummies
0-7645-2482-8

Controlling Cholesterol For Dummies
0-7645-5440-9

Depression For Dummies
0-7645-3900-0

Fertility For Dummies 0-7645-2549-2

Fibromyalgia For Dummies
0-7645-5441-7

Improving Your Memory
For Dummies
0-7645-5435-2

Menopause For Dummies
0-7645-5458-1

Pregnancy For Dummies
0-7645-4483-7

Relationships For Dummies
0-7645-5384-4

Thyroid For Dummies
0-471-78755-8

EDUCATION, HISTORY & REFERENCE

0-470-83656-3

0-7645-2498-4

Also available:

Algebra For Dummies
0-7645-5325-9

British History For Dummies
0-7645-7021-8

English Grammar For Dummies
0-7645-5322-4

Forensics For Dummies
0-7645-5580-4

Freemasons For Dummies
0-7645-9796-5

Italian For Dummies
0-7645-5196-5

Latin For Dummies
0-7645-5431-x

Science Fair Projects For Dummies
0-7645-5460-3

Spanish For Dummies
0-7645-5194-9

U.S. History For Dummies
0-7645-5249-x